ASP.NET For Dummies®

Cheat Sheet

$4 CP

Common Server Control Properties for Label, TextBox, Button, and Others (See Chapters 8 and 10)

Property	What It Specifies	How You Set It
Text	The contents of the label	string
ForeColor, BackColor, BorderColor	Text color, background color, and border color of the control	Drawing.Color enumeration properties (Red, Green, Blue, and so on) or FromARGB function
BorderStyle	The look of the border surrounding the control	BorderStyle enumeration properties (Solid, Dashed, Dotted, Double, and so on)
Font.Bold, Font.Underline, Font.Italic	That you want to apply the associated style to the text	true or false. Default: false
Font.Name	The name of the typeface	string
Font.Size	Size of the text in the control	FontUnit enumeration properties (Medium, Small, Large, and so on) or Point method
Height, Width	Size of the control	Unit enumeration object, Pixel or Point method
ToolTip	Text in a yellow pop-up window that appears when the user hovers mouse pointer over the control	string
Visible, Enabled	Whether control is visible and usable	true or false. Default: true

Common TextBox Server Control Properties (See Chapters 8 and 10)

Property	What It Specifies	How You Set It
Text	Contents of the textbox. A default value or get a value the user entered.	string
ReadOnly	Disallow user entry or modification of	true or false. Default: false
TabIndex	Where this co as the user tal	...er
TextMode	Which kind of	...BoxMode enumeration values ...leLine, Password, MultiLine). ...lt: SingleLine
MaxLength	The maximum number of characters that can be entered into this textbox	integer. Default: 0 (meaning unlimited)
Columns, Rows	The physical width and height (in characters) of the textbox	integer
AutoPostBack	Whether the page should return to the server when the user modifies the textbox value and then presses Tab or clicks away. Used with TextChanged event.	true or false. Default: false

D1367088

ASP.NET For Dummies®

Cheat Sheet

Common Button Server Control Properties (See Chapters 8 and 10)

Property	What It Specifies	How You Set It
Text	The text that appears on the button	string
Enabled	When set to false, turns off button. Any text on button turns gray, and the onclick event is not triggered.	true or false. Default: true
Visible	When set to false, causes button to disappear from page completely.	true or false. Default: true

Common ListBox Server Control Properties (See Chapter 11)

Property	What It Specifies	How You Set It
Items(x).Selected	Whether or not the listbox item with the index of x is selected	true or false. Default: false
Items(x).Text	The line of text in the listbox for the item with the index of x	string
Items(x).Value	The value associated with the item in the listbox with the index of x	string
SelectionMode	Whether the user can select only one item or multiple items in the listbox	ListSelectionMode enumeration value (Multiple, Single).Default: Single
Rows	The height of the listbox in rows	integer. Default: 4
SelectedIndex	The index number of the currently selected item in the listbox	integer
SelectedItem	The ListItem object of the currently selected item in the listbox	ListItem object

Common ListBox.Items Methods (See Chapter 11)

Method	What It Does
Items.Add(string1)	Adds a row to the end of the list using string1 as its text
Items.Insert(integer1,string1)	Adds a row at integer1 index location in the list using string1 as its text
Items.Remove(string1)	Removes item from the list that has the text string1
Items.RemoveAt(integer1)	Removes item from the list that has the index integer1
Items.Clear()	Removes all items from the list
Items.FindByText(string1)	Finds the item in the list with text that matches string1
Items.FindByValue(string1)	Finds the item in the list with the value that matches string1

Hungry Minds™

For Dummies: Bestselling Book Series for Beginners

by Bill Hatfield

Hungry Minds™

Best-Selling Books • Digital Downloads • e-Books • Answer Networks • e-Newsletters • Branded Web Sites • e-Learning

New York, NY ◆ Cleveland, OH ◆ Indianapolis, IN

ASP.NET For Dummies®

Published by
Hungry Minds, Inc.
909 Third Avenue
New York, NY 10022
www.hungryminds.com
www.dummies.com

Library of Congress Control Number: 2001092888

ISBN: 0-7645-0866-0

Printed in the United States of America

10 9 8 7 6 5 4 3 2 1

1B/RW/RQ/QR/IN

Distributed in the United States by Hungry Minds, Inc.

Distributed by CDG Books Canada Inc. for Canada; by Transworld Publishers Limited in the United Kingdom; by IDG Norge Books for Norway; by IDG Sweden Books for Sweden; by IDG Books Australia Publishing Corporation Pty. Ltd. for Australia and New Zealand; by TransQuest Publishers Pte Ltd. for Singapore, Malaysia, Thailand, Indonesia, and Hong Kong; by Gotop Information Inc. for Taiwan; by ICG Muse, Inc. for Japan; by Intersoft for South Africa; by Eyrolles for France; by International Thomson Publishing for Germany, Austria and Switzerland; by Distribuidora Cuspide for Argentina; by LR International for Brazil; by Galileo Libros for Chile; by Ediciones ZETA S.C.R. Ltda. for Peru; by WS Computer Publishing Corporation, Inc., for the Philippines; by Contemporanea de Ediciones for Venezuela; by Express Computer Distributors for the Caribbean and West Indies; by Micronesia Media Distributor, Inc. for Micronesia; by Chips Computadoras S.A. de C.V. for Mexico; by Editorial Norma de Panama S.A. for Panama; by American Bookshops for Finland.

For general information on Hungry Minds' products and services please contact our Customer Care Department within the U.S. at 800-762-2974, outside the U.S. at 317-572-3993 or fax 317-572-4002.

For sales inquiries and reseller information, including discounts, premium and bulk quantity sales, and foreign-language translations, please contact our Customer Care Department at 800-434-3422, fax 317-572-4002, or write to Hungry Minds, Inc., Attn: Customer Care Department, 10475 Crosspoint Boulevard, Indianapolis, IN 46256.

For information on licensing foreign or domestic rights, please contact our Sub-Rights Customer Care Department at 212-884-5000.

For information on using Hungry Minds' products and services in the classroom or for ordering examination copies, please contact our Educational Sales Department at 800-434-2086 or fax 317-572-4005.

For press review copies, author interviews, or other publicity information, please contact our Public Relations Department at 317-572-3168 or fax 317-572-4168.

For authorization to photocopy items for corporate, personal, or educational use, please contact Copyright Clearance Center, 222 Rosewood Drive, Danvers, MA 01923, or fax 978-750-4470.

Hungry Minds™ is a trademark of Hungry Minds, Inc.

About the Author

Bill Hatfield is the best-selling author of several computer books, including two editions of *Active Server Pages For Dummies* (on Classic ASP) as well as *Visual InterDev For Dummies* and *Creating Cool VBScript Web Pages* (all from Hungry Minds, Inc.). He is also the editor of *.NET Developer* and *ActiveWeb Developer*, two technical journals from Pinnacle Publishing for professional developers using Microsoft technologies. He's an independent corporate trainer and maintains a Web site (www.edgequest.com) dedicated to helping developers solve problems. He works from his home in Indianapolis, Indiana, where he now has a real baby (and therefore he can stop dressing up the cat in little outfits).

Dedication

This book is dedicated to Bryce Christopher Hatfield, born on Monday, August 13th, 2001 — just as this book was wrapping up.

Bryce, seeing your birth was one of the most profound and powerful experiences of my life. You've already enriched my life and Melanie's life more than you'll ever know. And we pledge to return the favor every chance we get.

We're really looking forward to introducing you to this crazy world and experiencing its discovery afresh through your eyes. You've just begun a fantastic journey, and it's our privilege to help you prepare for it.

Always hang on to that wide-eyed wonder that I can already see glimmering in your eyes when you look at me. No matter what happens, never let them take that away from you. . . .

Author's Acknowledgments

Many thanks to Chris Webb, acquisitions editor; I really appreciate your responsiveness, concern, and professionalism. To John Pont, project editor: Your experience, thoroughness, and our occasional chats made this project an enjoyable experience. To Greg Guntle, my technical editor, for a great eye and great insights, as always. And thanks, too, to all the rest of the Hungry Minds staff that helped make this book possible.

To my wife, who had to deal with both a pregnancy and a very-busy, sometimes-crabby (who me?) husband: Your patience and tolerance of all my projects and activities in a time when I should be focused on supporting you is appreciated more than I can express. The coming weeks are for us — all three of us, I promise. I love you, Melanie. . . .

Thanks to my parents for your love and support. You keep me grounded in a world where everything else is flying around.

Thanks to my good friends: Brad, Mike, Curtis and Dee, Wayne and TaKiesha. Mondays are the highlight of my week for one reason — you!

Publisher's Acknowledgments

We're proud of this book; please send us your comments through our Hungry Minds Online Registration Form located at www.dummies.com.

Some of the people who helped bring this book to market include the following:

Acquisitions, Editorial, and Media Development

Project Editor: John W. Pont

Acquisitions Editor: Chris Webb

Technical Editor: Greg Guntle

Editorial Manager: Constance Carlisle

Permissions Editor: Laura Moss

Media Development Specialist: Greg Stephens

Media Development Coordinator: Marisa Pearman

Media Development Manager: Laura VanWinkle

Media Development Supervisor: Richard Graves

Editorial Assistants: Amanda Foxworth, Jean Rogers

Production

Project Coordinator: Maridee Ennis

Layout and Graphics: Karl Brandt, Brian Drumm, Joyce Haughey, Jacque Schneider, Betty Schulte, Julie Trippetti, Jeremey Unger

Proofreaders: TECHBOOKS Production Services

Indexer: TECHBOOKS Production Services

General and Administrative

Hungry Minds, Inc.: John Kilcullen, CEO; Bill Barry, President and COO; John Ball, Executive VP, Operations & Administration; John Harris, Executive VP and CFO

Hungry Minds Technology Publishing Group: Richard Swadley, Senior Vice President and Publisher; Mary Bednarek, Vice President and Publisher, Networking; Joseph Wikert, Vice President and Publisher, Web Development Group; Mary C. Corder, Editorial Director, Dummies Technology; Andy Cummings, Publishing Director, Dummies Technology; Barry Pruett, Publishing Director, Visual/Graphic Design

Hungry Minds Manufacturing: Ivor Parker, Vice President, Manufacturing

Hungry Minds Marketing: John Helmus, Assistant Vice President, Director of Marketing

Hungry Minds Production for Branded Press: Debbie Stailey, Production Director

Hungry Minds Sales: Michael Violano, Vice President, International Sales and Sub Rights

Contents at a Glance

Cartoons at a Glance

By Rich Tennant

page 277

page 357

page 11

page 141

On the CD

page 315

page 371

page 35

page 105

Cartoon Information:
Fax: 978-546-7747
E-Mail: richtennant@the5thwave.com
World Wide Web: www.the5thwave.com

Table of Contents

Introduction

· ·

*W*elcome to *ASP.NET For Dummies,* the book that shows you how to make your Web pages come alive and interact with the people who visit your Web site. And, best of all, you can do it without dedicating a large portion of your life to your Web site!

I Know Who You Are . . .

Because you've picked this book up off the shelf and are flipping through it, I can make some pretty good guesses about the kind of person you may be:

- ✔ You may be a Web site or intranet developer working for a company.
- ✔ You may have a personal or small-business Web site.
- ✔ You may be a Classic ASP developer who has worked with ASP 1.0, 2.0, or 3.0 and is interested in discovering what's new with .NET.
- ✔ Or, you may be one of those folks who just *has* to get in on all the hot, new technologies.

In any case, you're probably looking for ways to make your job easier and your Web site a lot cooler. I'd guess that . . .

- ✔ You know how to use Windows .NET, Windows 2000, or Windows NT, and you know how to use Internet Information Server (IIS), at least well enough to get around. (Or, the company that hosts your Web site takes care of all that.)
- ✔ You're familiar with HTML. Maybe you've played around with some advanced tags.
- ✔ You have at least a little experience with a scripting language like JavaScript, VBScript, or Perl.
- ✔ You may have worked with a macro language that you'd find in a spreadsheet or other application — possibly VBA.
- ✔ Perhaps you've actually done some programming in Visual Basic, Java, C/C++, or COBOL.

But don't worry if you aren't a programmer or an HTML guru. This book and ASP.NET make interactive Web pages easy.

About ASP.NET

Your Web pages are simple and informative, but not very exciting. You'd like to make them more interactive. Maybe add a survey or a trivia question or a game. Or perhaps something more serious like a mortgage payment calculator. Maybe you could even retrieve information from the corporate database to make your pages a truly valuable resource.

Unfortunately, you can't do all that nifty stuff with HTML alone. Of course you're interested in exploring new technologies, but you don't want to spend months and months figuring out complex programming languages and esoteric relational database concepts. As quickly as possible, you want to get a handle on all the stuff you need to start making all those cool ideas buzzing around in your head a reality.

ASP.NET makes it possible. You'll start creating interesting pages right away. And the more you discover, the more you can do. With ASP.NET, your creativity is the only limit to the kinds of pages you can create!

About ASP.NET For Dummies

The book you're holding in your hands is your key to the world of ASP.NET. It unlocks the secrets of the easy-to-use Visual Basic .NET programming language to make your Web pages more intelligent. It helps you transform your pages from a lecture format into a two-way conversation. You'll engage your visitors by making them part of the action!

Although ASP.NET is a relatively simple technology, many books and magazines would have you believe that it's only for people with PhDs in Computer Science. They use buzzwords and complex descriptions. They make lots of assumptions about what you already know.

This book is different. It's designed for you. It uses plain English to explore all the exciting features of ASP.NET with an eye toward creating practical and fun pages that will keep your visitors coming back to your site again and again. No jargon, no big assumptions, and no esoteric bunny-trails — I promise!

How This Book Is Organized

This book is divided into several parts, and each part is divided into several chapters. The book first explores the basics and then moves on to the tougher stuff.

Here's a brief rundown of the book's parts and what each part covers.

Part I: Getting Started

In this part, you find out how to set up your computer so that you can start creating your own ASP.NET pages and trying them out right away. You even create your very first ASP.NET page.

Part I also gives you a deeper understanding of ASP.NET and its place in the world of Web development. In this part, I define some terms that you're bound to hear tossed around all the time by developers, books, and magazines. I also give you a context for understanding how ASP.NET fits into the big picture.

Part II: Speaking the Language

¿Habla Visual Basic .NET? You will after you read the chapters in this part! Through numerous examples and plain-English descriptions, you discover all the essential aspects of programming with Visual Basic .NET to create cool ASP.NET Web pages.

Part III: Classy Objects and Methodical Properties

Object-oriented programming is one of those buzzwords that can send chills down your spine! No need to fear — it's not nearly as difficult as everyone tries to make you think it is. In this part of the book, you discover not only *what* it is, but also what *good* it does for you in your Web page development. You also find out how to use a few of ASP.NET's built-in objects to do some very cool stuff.

Part IV: Creating Interactive Web Applications

Making your pages interactive means giving the user a chance to chime in. That's exactly what you do in this part. Uncover the controls that enable your users to enter information and find out how to make your page respond intelligently to that information.

You also explore advanced controls that look slick and do all the drudgery work for you. Imagine a complete monthly calendar with all the standard functions built into one control — and no coding necessary!

Finally, you uncover ways to easily *validate* what your users type in — to help them find typos and things they forgot to fill in before they send it to you.

Part V: Casting a Wider ASP.NET

After you have the basics down, it's time to dive in! Fortunately, the water is deep and you're just beginning to discover all the possibilities that ASP.NET offers.

In this part, you build on your knowledge of objects and find a toy box full of functionality in the .NET Framework Class Library. Find out how you can make your applications do all kinds of neat tricks like send e-mail, ferret around on the server's hard drive, and even bake cookies!

Discover options for enhancing your applications in a variety of ways to make them more powerful and flexible. And find out how to configure Web server settings that apply to your application alone — and all without a system administrator anywhere in sight!

Part VI: Tapping the Database

From users of corporate intranets to home-shopping customers, everyone needs access to information stored in a database. And Part VI takes you from where you are now to turbo-guru in no time. You find out how to retrieve information and display it in a variety of ways. You also discover how to add, update, and delete database information directly from your own ASP.NET pages.

Part VII: Really Cool ASP.NET Applications

All these new capabilities are interesting by themselves. But the really interesting stuff happens when you start to pull together these capabilities to create real Web applications. In Part VII, I give you a quick look at two complete applications that I've written and included on the CD-ROM in the back of the book: a real-time chat room and a classified-ads site. Looking for more depth? Check out Bonus Chapters 1 and 2, included on the CD. These chapters provide detailed descriptions and source-code walkthroughs for both of these applications.

Part VIII: The Part of Tens

There's so much to explore! Find out all the places you can go to get more information about ASP.NET, including the top ten ASP.NET Web sites. Flipping back to The Part of Tens before you read the rest of the book is a little like eating dessert before the main course. I highly recommend it!

Bonus Part: Napoleon (Get It?) — On the CD

Well, bad pun or no, you can't beat *free* — and that's exactly how much this power-packed Bonus Part is! Think it can't be worth much if you get it for free? Think again.

In this part, you get detailed, blow-by-blow descriptions on how each page of the Café Chat Room and Classy Classifieds applications works. You also get a Guestbook application and a detailed description of how that application is constructed. In all, you get more than 80 pages of information showing you all the tricks you need to make ASP.NET sing.

But wait! There's more! I don't have mail-order knives, but I do have an on-CD chapter specifically written for Classic ASP developers. If you've worked with ASP 1.0, 2.0, or 3.0, this is the place you should start. Pull up this chapter and get a fast-paced overview of all the key changes you need to consider. Then use this bonus chapter as a roadmap that shows you what you can skip and what you need to pay attention to. And that's not the end of my dialog with you Classic ASP-ers! Check out the Classic ASP icon listed at the end of this introduction. Then keep an eye out for sidebars marked with that icon, which indicates that I'm talking to you directly about what has changed, what hasn't, and what you need to know about the topic at hand.

Finally, in case you've never worked with a database before, or you need a quick refresher, I've provided one for you here. It's a great stop before you tackle Chapters 18, 19, and beyond.

You sure got your money's worth with this book, didn't you?

On the CD

In addition to the Bonus Part described in the preceding section, the CD located in the back of this book includes all the source code for all the major examples in this book — and lots of the smaller examples, too! It also includes useful software from various developers — some demo versions, shareware, and freeware.

You can read all about the CD's contents, the system requirements, and the installation instructions in the "About the CD" appendix.

How to Use This Book

Using this book is quite simple, really: You read the first page, then proceed to the second, and go on like that until there are no more pages.

What?!? You don't read books from cover to cover? You skip around? Egad!

All right, I guess it's just a fact of life. Some people (you know who you are!) prefer not to read books from front to back. But if you're going to skip around, let me help you out a bit.

I cover the core stuff you need to know in Parts I, II, and III, and Chapters 8 and 9 of Part IV. With those topics under your belt, you can begin creating dynamic, interactive Web applications to do all sorts of stuff. Another good spot to hit is Chapter 16, which explores the .NET Framework Class Libraries. You'll find all kinds of fun stuff there.

How quickly you spin through those first few chapters depends heavily on how much programming and Web development experience you have. Not much? No problem — this book starts at the beginning. A little or a lot? Great! You'll move through some of these chapters more quickly. But be careful skipping any of the early chapters entirely — .NET offers many unique features that you may never have seen before.

Beyond that, it's up to you. Want to find out more about Visual Basic .NET? Check out Chapter 15. Want to create richer user interfaces? Chapters 10 and 11 can help you do it. Want to play with cool Calendar and Ad Rotator controls? See Chapter 12. Interested in working with a database? Chapters 18, 19, and 21 are key. By the way, if you've never worked with a database before, be sure to check out Bonus Chapter 5 (on the CD) before you tackle the other database chapters.

Regardless of your experience level, do yourself a big favor: Don't just read the examples — *try them out!* It's a lot more fun that way and you'd be amazed at how much more you absorb by playing around with it than you do when you just read about it.

Finally, when you've exhausted this book and are thirsty for more, head to Chapters 22 and 23. They'll point you in the right direction.

ASP Me, I Might . . .

If you want to send me feedback about the book, I'd love to hear from you! My e-mail address is

```
BillHatfield@EdgeQuest.com
```

My Web site is

```
www.EdgeQuest.com
```

And for a Web site completely dedicated to this book, check out

```
www.AspDotNetForDummies.com
```

Here, you find cool ASP.NET applications, the latest book corrections, news, and links to other great ASP.NET sites.

Help! It Doesn't Work!

In case you run into any problems while reading this book, go to the Web site dedicated to this book and look for the Frequently Asked Questions section:

```
www.AspDotNetForDummies.com
```

At the site, you find reader questions and answers to all sorts of ASP.NET and book-related issues.

If you still need more help, Chapter 22 lists the Ten Best Places to Get Answers. From books and magazines to newsgroups, user groups, and ASP.NET nerds, you have lots of options out there!

Conventions Used In This Book

Here are a few things that you should know about the way I format the text in the book and exactly what it's supposed to mean when I do that.

When I want to show you the HTML from a Web page or some source code for an example, it will look something like this:

```
<html>
<head>
<title>Hello and Welcome Page</title>
</head>
<body>
. . .
```

Sometimes, I refer to something from a page or a source code listing or something that you see on the screen. When I do, I set it off by using a monofont typeface, like this:

Set the Budget variable to the value 25.

Suppose I need to refer to items on a menu bar. I want to say, for example, that you should click to pull down the Edit menu and then choose the option called Cut. Here's how I do that: Choose Edit⇨Cut.

Icons Used In This Book

Throughout this book, I use icons to set off important information. Here's a quick description of the meaning of each icon:

These sidebars are for those who've used Classic ASP before. If you are new to ASP, you definitely want to skip these sidebars. They'll only confuse you! However, if you are a Classic ASPer, these sections will spell out clearly the changes, similarities, and differences from what you're used to. This should ease your path into the brave new world of .NET.

This icon points to features you can find on the companion CD.

When you see this icon, read the text carefully and tuck the information away in a safe place in your brain where you can easily find it later. You'll need it.

Sometimes I get carried away and go off on a tangent about some technical bit of trivia that is completely unessential to the topic at hand. But don't worry. If I do, I label it with this icon so that you know you can safely skip over it, if you want.

This icon highlights a quick idea or technique that will make your life a little better.

If I'm exploring a new topic, I always enjoy it more if I can actually try it out while I'm reading. So I include lots and lots of little examples throughout the book for you to try. When you see this icon, don't just read it — do it!

If you see this icon, always read and follow the accompanying directions. This information can keep you from having a very bad day.

Sometimes things just don't work the way any normal, rational person would expect them to work. And it's those goofy things that trip you up every time. When you see this icon, watch for weirdness ahead.

Where to Go From Here

You've read this book through and understand every word. You've stolen the Café Chat Room and the Classy Classifieds, and adapted them for use on your own site. In short, you've graduated from _ASP.NET For Dummies_. Congratulations! What's next?

Well, fortunately for you, your journey isn't over. In fact, it's just beginning! You'll find a host of things to discover and explore in ASP.NET and the .NET Framework. Here are a few suggestions for places you can go to uncover the mysteries that await you.

First, the Web is a great source of information on ASP.NET. If you haven't already, check out all the sites I list in Chapter 23. From there, go to the links sections of those sites and, well, let's just say you could blow a day or two just exploring.

Next, if you're looking for something on a more monthly basis, check out Pinnacle Publishing's technical journals. Pinnacle is known for providing hard-core content in the form of tips, techniques, articles, and code for professional developers. I edit two of these technical journals: *ActiveWeb Developer* and *.NET Developer*. Find them at: www.pinnaclepublishing.com.

Finally, Hungry Minds, the publisher of this and all the books in the *For Dummies* series, also has books for the more intermediate and advanced ASP.NET developer. Check out the *ASP.NET Bible,* by Anju Sani, Rick Lassan, and Peter Macintyre, as well as *Visual Basic .NET Database Programming For Dummies,* by Richard Mansfield. For something specifically focused on database applications, look for *ASP.NET Database Programming Weekend Crash Course,* by Jason Butler and Tony Caudill.

Part I
Getting Started

The 5th Wave   By Rich Tennant

"Just how accurately should my Web site reflect my place of business?"

In this part . . .

You're off to a running start as you discover the wonders of interactive Web applications created with ASP.NET technology. You begin by figuring out the requirements and setup you need to get going with ASP.NET. I walk you through every step in the process of creating, running, and testing your first ASP.NET page. That way, you can read the rest of the book with your fingers on the keyboard, trying out — and tearing apart — every example you see!

But getting set up to create pages is just half of it. You don't have to look at too many articles and books on Web development before the hodge-podge of buzzwords and confusing technologies makes your head spin! But don't worry. In this part, I also set your mind at ease by giving you some *context* — a quick tour of the Web technologies and an understanding of how ASP.NET fits in the puzzle.

Chapter 1

ASP.NET — Let's Do It!

. . . .

In This Chapter

▶ Identifying and installing the software you need to work with ASP.NET

▶ Understanding which computer languages are available and what's right for you

▶ Creating an environment for developing and testing ASP.NET pages

▶ Walking through a detailed, step-by-step plan to create and execute a page

▶ Exploring some simple and commonly used Visual Basic .NET commands

▶ Modifying, retesting, and creating new pages, and converting old ones

. . . .

I'm going to turn the traditional philosophy of chapter-order sequence on its head. Most books (especially about .NET, it seems) give you lots of concepts and theories and detailed, boring analysis before they ever let you jump in and play with the stuff.

In this book, I start by getting you set up and creating your first ASP.NET page in *this* chapter. There's no teacher like experience!

Then, if you like, you can head for Chapter 2, where I take a step back and put what you've seen into context. There, I show you how ASP.NET came about and how it differs from other technologies you may have heard about. If questions pop up in your mind as you're going through this chapter, hang on! I probably address them in Chapter 2.

Everything You Need to Get Started

ASP.NET isn't a software package that you can just pick up at your local software store. ASP.NET is a *technology,* which is a fancy way of saying it's a cool feature that's built into some *other* piece of software. That other piece of software, in this case, is the .NET Framework. The .NET Framework is a product that Microsoft gives away for free. It's the foundation for a new approach to software development, and ASP.NET is a key component of that. For more information on the .NET Framework, see Chapter 2.

To set up a machine for creating and testing ASP.NET pages, you need three things:

- An operating system that supports Internet Information Server (IIS) — for example, Windows .NET Server, Windows XP Professional, Windows 2000 Server/Professional, or Windows NT 4.0 (with Service Pack 6a or higher)

- Internet Information Server

- The .NET Framework

How do you get all this cool software? Windows .NET Server, Windows 2000 Server, and Windows NT 4.0 Server install IIS automatically, by default. Windows XP and Windows 2000 Professional may not install IIS by default, but you can install it from the Windows installation disks.

The .NET Framework is included with Windows .NET Server. It is available for other operating systems from Microsoft at no charge. You can download it at `www.microsoft.com/net`, `www.asp.net`, or `www.gotdotnet.com`. You will also find instructions at those sites telling you all you need to know about downloading and installing the .NET Framework.

You do not need an active Internet connection in order to create and test ASP.NET pages. IIS can also process and serve Web pages to you locally on the server itself or over a Local Area Network (LAN).

The hosting option

If you don't want to go through the hassle of setting up your own Web server, you may want to find a Web site hosting service that supports ASP.NET.

Hosting services are companies that provide room on their Web server for you to place your site. You can even get a domain name (like `www.mywebsite.com`) that jumps right to your hosted site.

However, hosting services aren't all created equal. So, be sure to ask about all the things that are important to you:

- Do they host on Windows .NET/2000/NT machines? Many hosting services use some form of Unix operating system and, at least for now, ASP.NET doesn't run on Unix.

- Do they support ASP.NET development? If they say they support ASP, they may be referring to Classic ASP. Be sure to ask specifically about ASP.NET.

- Do they provide Microsoft Access or SQL Server database support?

A hosting service may charge a setup fee and then usually a monthly fee of anywhere from $10 up to hundreds of dollars, depending on what you want. Most services offer various packages at increasing price/feature levels. In some cases, you can add features à la carte for an added setup fee and monthly rate.

There are lots of hosting services out there and it pays to shop around. In fact, if you just want a simple ASP.NET site to practice on, you may find a few that offer minimal space (5MB or 10MB) for free!

For a list of ASP.NET hosting options and instructions on how to use them, go to

```
www.AspDotNetForDummies.com/
hosting
```

What about Personal Web Server?

You can run Classic ASP with a much more modest setup. You could use Windows 95/98/ME or Windows NT Workstation along with a scaled-down version of IIS called Personal Web Server (or, for NT, Personal Web Services).

ASP.NET, however, doesn't work with Personal Web Server. It will only work with IIS. So the requirements for IIS are also the requirements for ASP.NET. And that means larger scale software and hardware.

If you don't have the time, inclination, or money to set up a server-class machine, see the sidebar titled "The hosting option," in this chapter.

After you have the operating system, IIS, and the .NET Framework installed, you are ready to go!

Watch Your Language!

Before you begin on your ASP.NET journey, you need to decide which programming language you want to use for creating ASP.NET pages. Many possibilities exist.

The .NET Framework comes with Visual Basic .NET, C#, C++, and JScript (a form of ECMA Script or JavaScript). But those aren't your only options.

Third-party companies are hard at work developing new languages to plug in to the .NET Framework. You'll find (either now or in the near future) many, many languages, including COBOL, Perl, Python, SmallTalk, Pascal, Scheme, Eiffel, Haskell, Mercury, and Oberon! And you can create ASP.NET pages by using any language that plugs in to the .NET Framework.

Feeling overwhelmed? Don't. Flexibility is nice, but in all likelihood, you'll find a language that suits you and stick with it. So, which language suits you?

If you're looking for an easy-to-learn, easy-to-use programming language that will get you up to speed as quickly as possible, you can't beat Visual Basic .NET. In fact, Visual Basic .NET is the most popular computer language ever created. It's very English-like and straightforward.

On the other hand, if you already have some programming experience in a C-type language, like C, C++, Java, or JavaScript, you may want to consider one of those languages, or, perhaps even better, the new language from Microsoft called C# (pronounced *see-sharp*). It has lots of exciting features, uses a C/C++-type syntax, and is specially designed for the .NET Framework.

What happened to VBScript and JavaScript?

Although other options existed, most Classic ASP developers used either VBScript or JavaScript.

VBScript is not available in ASP.NET. If you've used VBScript to create Classic ASP pages (as most Classic ASP developers did), Microsoft expects you to upgrade to the full-blown Visual Basic .NET language. The Visual Basic .NET language is much more powerful and a bit more complicated than VBScript. You may need to make some changes in your Classic ASP VBScript pages to get them to work in ASP.NET.

Bonus Chapter 4 (on the CD) describes many of those changes.

However, ASP.NET does directly support JavaScript. And it is compatible with the JavaScript used in Classic ASP. It has even been enhanced with many new features. However, if you used JavaScript to create Classic ASP applications, you may want to upgrade to C# when you do ASP.NET applications. C# is a C-like language like JavaScript, but it is much more powerful.

In this book, my examples use Visual Basic .NET, the most popular ASP.NET programming language.

If you already know C, C++, Java, or JavaScript, you probably have enough programming under your belt that you'll be able to translate the Visual Basic .NET examples into your language of choice.

Where's the Development Environment?

For most computer languages, you can buy a complete development environment that puts at your fingertips every tool you need to write, run, and test applications that you create.

What happened to Visual InterDev?

Gone! Outta here! See ya! That's right, Visual InterDev, Visual Studio 6.0's Internet development environment for creating Classic ASP pages, is no more.

Many of you may say, "Good riddance!" Visual InterDev isn't a favorite among Classic ASP developers. However, for those of you who are

concerned, you should know that you can find most of its functionality in Visual Studio .NET. Visual Studio .NET is no longer a hodge-podge collection of different development tools all thrown into one box, as it has been in the past. It is now a single, coherent development environment for creating all types of applications in any language supported by the .NET Framework.

Visual Basic .NET — the product versus the language

You may be familiar with a product that Microsoft sells called Visual Basic .NET. Do you need that product to do ASP.NET?

No. The product called Visual Basic .NET, which you can buy at your local computer store (and as a part of Visual Studio .NET), is a complete software development environment for creating Windows applications. You can also use it to create ASP.NET pages, but it is not required.

When I refer to Visual Basic .NET in this book, unless specified otherwise, I'm referring to

Visual Basic .NET, the *language*. Visual Basic .NET, the language, is built into the .NET Framework and can be used directly to create your ASP.NET pages — nothing else is required.

By the way, Visual Basic .NET, the language, is the language that's used in the product called Visual Basic .NET. So if you ever want to pick up that tool, it will be a breeze after you understand ASP.NET development.

ASP.NET is different. It is a development technology that is built in to the .NET Framework. You can easily create great ASP.NET applications with nothing more than Notepad or your favorite editor.

Or, if you prefer to work in a development environment, you'll probably have plenty to choose from. Microsoft Visual Studio .NET provides one development environment for ASP.NET pages, and Microsoft expects that many third parties will come out with their own development tools for ASP.NET, too.

But remember, you don't need lots of complex tools and mystical icons to make ASP.NET work. ASP.NET is a simple language combined with standard HTML. What could be more elegant?

Preparing to Develop and Test Your ASP.NET Pages

You need to think about a few things after you get everything installed and before you create your first ASP.NET page.

Deciding on an ASP.NET Web server

First, you need to figure out what server you will use to test the pages you create. You may use an existing server at your company, set up your own server, or use a hosting service.

If you use an existing server at your company, there are probably procedures in place regarding how you can add new pages, where you can and cannot put test pages, and so on. Be sure you fully understand and follow those guidelines.

If you set up your own system, at work or at home, you're responsible for installing everything and getting it up and running. You're in complete control, but it can be a big task, requiring knowledge of server operating systems and IIS.

Perhaps the easiest solution is to use a Web hosting service that supports ASP.NET. The host will give you the information you need to know to create new folders on your site, send files you create to the site, and test those files. And best of all, the hosting service handles all the installation and maintenance for you! For more information on this option, see the sidebar titled "The hosting option," in this chapter.

Setting up the environment

If you are working directly with the Web server (*not* through a hosting service), you need to know a little about IIS and where it looks for its pages.

IIS creates a folder on the server's hard drive with the default name inetpub. The inetpub folder contains a subfolder called wwwroot. The wwwroot folder is the root for the Web site.

If you place a new Web page in wwwroot or any of its subfolders, your Web server has access to the page, and you can link to it from other pages on your site.

So when you begin a new project, create a folder under wwwroot for your application and then, within that folder, create the pages you need. If you have lots of pages, you may want to create subfolders inside your application's folder to help organize things.

Saving your pages: The .aspx extension

Always save your ASP.NET pages with the .aspx extension. That's how the Web server knows it should process the page as an ASP.NET page.

You may be wondering why the extension for ASP.NET is .aspx. Well, a long time ago, during the development of ASP.NET, it was referred to inside Microsoft as ASP+. Now, you can't use a + symbol in a filename, but if you turn that plus sign about 45 degrees, it looks a lot like an x. So, Microsoft chose .aspx as the extension for ASP+. After the name was changed to ASP.NET, Microsoft didn't bother to change the extension.

.ASP versus .ASPX

Classic ASP pages use the .asp extension. ASP.NET pages use the .aspx extension. You can have both types of pages running and active on a Web server at the same time. In this way, you can easily migrate your site, with some old applications still using Classic ASP while new applications are written in ASP.NET. Just be sure to keep those extensions right!

If you use Notepad as your editor to create ASP.NET files, be aware that Notepad almost *insists* that you name your files with a .txt extension. In fact, if you try to create a new file and save it as test.aspx, the file's name will end up test.aspx.txt. Here's how you fix that problem: When you type in the filename, put it in quotes — for example, "test.aspx". Notepad saves the file with exactly the filename you give it.

If you accidentally save a file with the wrong extension, just go out in Explorer and rename the file. Notepad only pulls this trick if you're creating new pages. After you edit an existing page, Notepad always saves the page with the name it had originally.

Many versions of Windows, by default, hide known extensions from you. This can be a problem if Notepad saves your file as test.aspx.txt because the file may show up in Explorer as test.aspx (hiding the .txt extension). It looks right, but the .txt extension will keep your Web server from recognizing it as an ASP.NET page. Of course, this can be very confusing. Turn off this option in Windows Explorer by choosing Tools⇨Folder Options. Then click the View tab and scroll down until you find the option labeled Hide File Extensions for Known File Types. Make sure that checkbox is *not* checked.

Testing your pages

You need to break some old habits when you're ready to start creating and testing your ASP.NET pages. In the past, when testing HTML pages or pages that included client-side script, you may have opened the page by simply dragging and dropping it onto the Internet Explorer browser. Or you may have used the browser's File⇨Open command to open the page. You can't use either of those techniques for testing ASP.NET pages. Both techniques open up the page directly without any Web server involvement. Because ASP.NET works on the server side, you have to let the server find the page, run the code, and then send the results to the browser.

To test your ASP.NET pages, open a browser window, type the address of the page into the Address line, and press Enter. That makes the browser request the page from the server and gives the server the opportunity to process the ASP.NET code on the page.

Getting Your ASP in Gear: Creating Your First ASP.NET Page

After you have your environment set up to edit files on your Web site (see the preceding section), you can create your first ASP page:

1. **Create a folder under** `wwwroot`. **Name it** `hello`.

   If you're using a hosting service, you won't see `wwwroot`. Just create a folder in your root directory. Again, your hosting service can tell you how to do this.

2. **Create a new page in Notepad or the editor of your choice.**

   Most HTML editors work fine, as long as they let you work with the raw HTML tags and don't try to hide them from you. If you're using Microsoft Front Page, click the HTML tab at the bottom of the window to edit the HTML directly and add your scripts. If your editor puts any tags or other stuff in the page automatically, delete all that so you start with a blank slate.

3. **Enter the following code:**

```
<%@Page Language="VB" Debug="True" %>
<html>
<head>
<title>Hello and Welcome Page</title>
</head>
<body>
<center>
<% Dim TextSize As Integer %>
<% For TextSize = 1 To 7 %>
<font size = <%=TextSize%>>
Hello and Welcome!<br>
</font>
<% Next %>
</center>
</body>
</html>
```

   Be sure to type it exactly as it is listed. Don't worry about whether something is entered in upper- or lowercase. It will work either way.

4. **Locate the** `hello` **folder you created. Save the page with the name** `welcome.aspx`.

   If you're using Notepad, remember to put quotes around the name so that Notepad doesn't add the `.txt` extension.

   If you are using a hosting service, save the file to a spot on your local hard drive and then send it to the server.

5. **Minimize your editor and open your browser. Open the page you created by typing** http://localhost/hello/welcome.aspx **into the Address line at the top of the browser.**

   If you are not working on the Web server machine itself, access your page by simply typing the intranet URL. Usually, you just type the name of the server in place of `localhost`, as in `http://bigserver/hello/welcome.aspx`.

   If your Web site is on a hosting service, use the address the service gave you or your own domain name to access your page, as in `http://www.mydomain.com/hello/welcome.aspx`.

   You should see the page you created in the browser. It looks a lot like Figure 1-1.

Figure 1-1: The Welcome. aspx page.

If you don't see this page, go back and check to make sure you entered the page exactly as it appears in Step 3.

How Does It Work?

In the preceding section, I show you how to create a Web page so that you'll understand the *process* for creating and testing pages. Unless you already know Visual Basic .NET or are a proficient programmer, you probably don't understand exactly how the page works just by looking at it. I explain exactly what it does here. For more information on any of the commands I use in this page or Visual Basic .NET commands in general, see Chapters 3, 4, and 5.

The Visual Basic .NET commands always appear inside <% and %> symbols. Those symbols are called *delimiters*. They keep the Visual Basic .NET commands separate from the HTML tags.

The very first line in the listing is a page header:

```
<%@Page Language="VB" Debug="True" %>
```

This isn't required, but including it at the top of any ASP.NET page is a good idea. It does two things: It specifies that the ASP.NET language used in this page will be Visual Basic .NET, and it sets Debug to True. The Debug setting helps by providing more detailed error messages for you if you make a mistake.

The first Visual Basic .NET command on this page is Dim. Dim is used to create variables. Here, it creates a variable named TextSize:

```
<% Dim TextSize As Integer %>
```

A *variable* is a place to store information to be used later. The As Integer at the end of that line indicates that this variable will hold whole numbers. No information is put into the variable, yet.

The next line identifies the beginning of a For...Next *loop*. A loop provides a way to repeat the same commands (or HTML) over and over again. This loop will repeat the lines between the For line and the Next line. These lines (shown here in bold) are referred to as the *body* of the loop:

```
<% For TextSize = 1 To 7 %>
<font size = <%=TextSize%>>
Hello and Welcome!<br>
</font>
<% Next %>
```

When does a loop stop looping? Well, there are different kinds of loops, but a For loop decides when it's done by counting. In this case, it counts from 1 to 7. The loop sets the value of the TextSize variable to 1 the first time through the loop. Then, the body of the loop is executed. Next identifies the end of the loop, so you jump back up to the top again. The second time through the loop, `TextSize` is set to 2; the third time, it is set to 3; and so on through 7, when the loop ends.

In the body of the loop, the `<font>` tag sets the size of the text. The size is set equal to `<%=TextSize%>`. What's that? The `<%` and `%>` are the normal delimiters, but there are no commands inside! Just an = sign followed by the `TextSize` variable name. This special syntax is used to get at the *value* of the variable. So the first time through the loop, the HTML `<font>` tag that's generated looks like this: `<font size=1>`. The second time through, it looks like this: `<font size=2>`. Each time through the loop, the font size is set to the value of `TextSize`.

Then, `Hello and Welcome!` is displayed on the page. Because the font's size is set to a bigger number each time the loop executes, the same line is printed again and again in increasingly larger sizes. And that's exactly what you see in Figure 1-1.

If you choose View⇨Source from the Internet Explorer menu while looking at this page, you see the following HTML:

```
<html>
<head><title>Hello and Welcome Page</title>
</head>
<body>
<center>
<font size=1>
Hello and Welcome!<br>
</font>
<font size=2>
Hello and Welcome!<br>
</font>
. . .
<font size=7>
Hello and Welcome!<br>
</font>
</center>
</body>
</html>
```

As you can see, there's no indication of a loop in the HTML that was sent. In fact, there's no code at all — just pure HTML. One of the beauties of ASP.NET is that the code is executed on the server and *produces* the HTML that is sent to the browser.

Don't feel like you need to completely understand this example before you go on. You'll get a better understanding of ASP.NET itself in Chapter 2. And I cover Visual Basic .NET commands in Chapters 3, 4, and 5. For now, just make sure you understand the process used to create and test an ASP.NET page.

Modifying, Retesting, and Creating New Pages, and Converting Old Pages

If you want to modify `welcome.aspx` and then test it again, follow these steps:

1. **Make your changes in the editor.**

2. **Save the file. Save the file. Don't forget to save the file.**

3. **Go back to your browser window.**

4. **Click Refresh in the browser window.**

If you make changes and don't notice a difference when you click Refresh, check to make sure you saved the file! It's easy to forget.

Whenever you want to create a new ASP.NET page:

1. **Create the page in your editor and save it with the `.aspx` extension to the appropriate folder. (Don't forget to put quotes around the name if you're saving from Notepad!)**

2. **Type the page's address into the browser's Address line and then press Enter.**

   The page is retrieved and processed, and the results are sent to your browser.

Later, after you're ready to start working on your own Web site, you'll probably want to convert some of your existing HTML pages into ASP.NET pages. That's easy, too:

1. **Rename the file. Change the `.htm` or `.html` extension to `.aspx`.**

2. **Edit the page in your editor and add any Visual Basic .NET commands you like.**

The only difference between normal HTML files and ASP.NET files is that the extension is different. That's how the Web server knows to process the ASP.NET pages differently. If you find that your code isn't executing, make sure you remembered to set the extension to `.aspx`!

Chapter 2

Putting ASP.NET in Its Place

*I*n Chapter 1, I demonstrate how to set up your environment and then create and test an ASP.NET page. In this chapter, I step back a moment and put it all in context for you.

ASP.NET is a major leap forward in the development of Active Server Pages (ASP). Classic ASP (ASP 1.0, 2.0, and 3.0) makes dynamic, interactive Web pages easy to create and maintain. ASP.NET builds on that foundation and provides a much more complete environment for creating everything from simple brochure sites to complex e-commerce and intranet application sites.

In this chapter, I give you a bird's-eye view of the more important technologies that have transformed the Web from a document-viewing technology into something more interactive. My goal in this chapter is to give you a framework for understanding ASP.NET's purpose, where it fits in the industry, and what all those buzzwords mean!

Boring, Dumb, Static HTML

Think about how a simple Web page works:

1. In your browser's Favorites menu or Bookmarks menu, you click your favorite site's name — perhaps it's called "ASP.NET For Dummies." The URL associated with it is

```
www.AspDotNetForDummies.com/page1.htm
```

2. Your browser sends out a request to the `AspDotNetForDummies.com` server, asking for the page named `page1.htm`.

3. The server finds that page on its hard drive and sends it back to your browser.

4. After your browser gets the page, it looks at what's inside. The browser reads all the HTML tags and then converts them into a beautifully formatted page. The page also may have links to other pages. If you click one of those links, the process starts all over again.

This example shows how the World Wide Web was originally conceived. In its earliest form, the Web provided a very easy way to access and navigate information made of text and pictures. Today, this type of page is referred to as *static HTML*.

Forms and CGI

The problem with static HTML is that the communication works only one way. You can't send information back to a Web server. To fix this problem, *forms* and *CGI* (the Common Gateway Interface) were created.

Forms are HTML tags that enable you to include controls, such as textboxes, checkboxes, and radio buttons, in your pages. That way, the user can type in information. Forms also provide a Submit button that sends the information off to the server.

But after the user submits the information, what happens then? In order to handle information sent back to the server, you have to write a program that runs on the Web server machine and communicates with the Web server software. That's where CGI comes in.

CGI is not a computer language. It is a standard *interface* to the Web server software. It is the *telephone,* if you will, that a software application can use to communicate with the Web server software. You can write an application that uses CGI in any language, but often programmers use C/C++ or Perl.

So, you can write an application that works with the Web server (via CGI) to accept information entered by the user in a form. When the application receives the form information, it can save that information to a text file, store it in a database, or do whatever else you want to do.

This system works fine for simple forms, but if you get lots of traffic, it can bog down your Web server. For every person who accesses your server, a separate copy of your application must be running. If 100 people submit form information at once, 100 copies of the application run at the same time. This is a great way to make a popular Web server fall to its knees and crawl.

Software applications, programming languages, source code, and the like . . .

I use various programming terms in this section and regularly throughout the book, and I want to make sure we're all on the same page about what they mean.

Software applications make your computer useful. They *do* something. Word and Excel, for example, are software applications.

You write software applications using *programming languages,* such as C, C++, or Visual Basic .NET. Just as Spanish and English (human languages) offer different ways of communicating with people, programming languages offer different ways of communicating with the computer.

Each programming language has its own vocabulary of commands. As a programmer,

you write these commands in the order you want them followed. A list of commands like this is referred to as *source code*, or just *code*.

After the source code is complete, you put it through a process called *compilation.* Compiling translates the high-level commands in the source code into low-level commands that the computer can directly understand. The result is an *executable* or *EXE file*. After you create the executable, you can run (or execute) it directly to perform the tasks you wrote it to do.

For more information on these topics, see Chapter 3.

Server APIs

Because of the problems with CGI applications slowing everything down, server APIs were born. API stands for Application Programming Interface. The Microsoft server API is called ISAPI, which stands for the Internet Server Application Programming Interface. (Clever, no?)

Like CGI, ISAPI provides a way for an application to communicate with the Web server. But ISAPI is much more efficient than CGI. It doesn't launch a separate copy of your program each time someone sends back information from a form. And ISAPI gives the application developer a lot more flexibility in determining how the server responds to the browser. ISAPI applications are often written in C or C++.

However, ISAPI doesn't solve all the problems. You still have to write separate computer programs that have complex interfaces to your Web server and that work closely with your Web pages. ISAPI isn't very intuitive, and creating and maintaining ISAPI applications can be difficult. Because of these problems, few businesses go to the trouble of creating truly engaging, interactive Web applications. It just takes too much time.

Web applications

You know what a software application is, but what's a *Web application?* Is it like a Web page or a Web site?

A Web application is really just a set of Web pages that work together to do something. Usually, some sort of software is also involved to coordinate the pages, accept information submitted through forms, and retrieve information that the pages will display. You can implement this software using one of the many technologies out there, including CGI, ISAPI, or ASP.NET.

You've probably used many Web applications on the Internet yourself already, but hadn't thought of them that way. A Web auction, like eBay, is a Web application. A Web-based chat room is a Web application. And when you go shopping on the Internet, the catalog and shopping cart you use are Web applications.

As you may have noted, these examples work like a traditional Windows application might — the only difference is that they use Web pages to communicate with their users rather than windows.

Lofty ASPirations

In November, 1996, Microsoft introduced a new solution for creating Web applications: ASP. (That's "Active Server Pages," *not* the snake that killed Cleopatra.) This solution offers the efficiency of ISAPI applications, along with a new level of simplicity that makes ASP easy to understand and easy to use.

With CGI or ISAPI, you have to write a computer program that has complex interface code connecting it to the server. Then, you have to compile the application and associate it with the appropriate HTML Web pages.

With ASP, however, you simply write your code *in* the HTML page itself. The HTML tags and your source code are side by side. You write the code in a language that's easy to learn and use. Then, you save the page to your Web site, and it's ready to go!

As you can imagine, ASP made a big splash. Hundreds of thousands of developers migrated to it and began using it extensively for all their Web site development needs. You'll find ASP used by many big names, including the Web sites of Barnes & Noble, Dell, Merrill-Lynch, and Nordstrom, just to name a few!

ASP: Good, But Not Perfect

In some ways, ASP's success was also its Achilles heel. The more people used it, the more they loved it. ASP developers could easily implement interesting, interactive Web sites and then easily modify and maintain those sites. So people began to develop bigger and better ideas — new ways of adding complex and subtle interactivity to their Web sites.

As Web applications grew bigger and more complex, the number of lines of source code in ASP applications also increased dramatically. Some applications had so much code interacting in such complex ways that developers began referring to it as *spaghetti code*. ASP made possible a whole new level of Web development — a level for which ASP itself wasn't quite ready.

The New ASP: ASP.NET

ASP.NET isn't a simple upgrade or the latest version of Active Server Pages. ASP.NET redesigns the whole process. It's still simple to grasp for the beginner (as I show you in this book), but it provides many new ways of managing projects as they grow in complexity. ASP.NET . . .

- Drastically reduces the amount of code required to build large projects.

- Provides support for *Web farms* — many machines working together as one Web server — and *Web gardens* — one large multiprocessor machine acting as a Web server.

- Makes for easy deployment. No need for registering components because the configuration information is built in!

- Is virtually crash-proof. The Web server software watches the various pages, components, and applications running on the server machine. If it notices memory leaks, infinite loops, or other non-kosher activities, it seamlessly kills and restarts the offending software.

- Makes development simpler and easier to maintain with (warning — geek talk ahead!) an event-driven, server-side programming model.

- Validates information entered by the user without writing a line of code.

- Easily works with database information using the data-binding and page formatting features.

- Runs faster and scales to larger volumes of users without hurting performance.

You don't need to understand all the specifics of these features to get the picture. Microsoft has really put lots of thought into ASP.NET, and this technology is more than ready for primetime. In fact, many people believe that it will be recognized as *the* way to create real-world Web sites for corporate intranets, business-to-business (B2B) e-commerce sites, and a whole host of Web applications that will make up the Internet of the future.

The Bigger Picture: Microsoft's .NET Framework

ASP.NET is not an island unto itself. In fact, all of Microsoft's technologies are coming together under one banner: *The .NET Initiative* (sometimes referred to as *Microsoft.NET*). This combining and integrating of Microsoft's technologies, products, and operating systems will take some time. But its foundation — and the foundation of ASP.NET — is available now: the .NET Framework.

What is the .NET Framework? It's a large library of code that Microsoft makes available for developers to build on.

Imagine you're a real-estate developer building two dozen houses on a few acres of land that you just bought. You want to build various types of homes to meet the needs of different families.

Now suppose a company came along and provided a very flexible foundation system. You could use this same foundation and adapt it for almost any kind of home you'd like to build. Would you be interested? Of course! If you don't have to think about the foundation for each home, you're that much farther ahead of the game. You can build 'em faster and with less expense than your competitors!

That's what the .NET Framework does for software developers. It's a very flexible foundation on top of which you can build business applications that do all kinds of things. It provides unprecedented support for software development. In fact, it doesn't just lay the foundation, it does the software equivalent of the plumbing and electrical work, too!

But don't confuse the .NET Framework with other frameworks or design-time/run-time libraries you may have seen. The .NET Framework is much more extensive and complete than anything ever attempted before.

For example, the .NET Framework provides a complete set of tools for creating user interfaces (both for standard Windows applications and for the Web). It provides a set of tools for accessing data in almost any database. And it makes working with XML (eXtensible Markup Language) and other new technologies pretty simple.

The .NET Framework also enables you to work in almost any programming language you like! The Framework comes with several commonly used languages, like Visual Basic .NET and C++, as well as a new language called C# (pronounced *see-sharp*). And the Framework is modular, so third-party developers can create new languages that just plug right in to the Framework. In fact, dozens of such languages are available now or are in the works.

And because ASP.NET is built on top of this framework, you can create ASP.NET pages using any of the built-in languages or any of those created by third parties. And you have access to all the features and capabilities of the .NET Framework with no additional work required.

ASP, as Easy as 1, 2, 3

I start this chapter by describing how an HTML page is processed. Here, I do the same thing for an ASP.NET page so you can see what's different:

1. You click your favorite site's name in your browser's Favorites or Bookmarks menu. Imagine the URL associated with it is

   ```
   www.AspDotNetForDummies.com/page1.aspx
   ```

2. The browser sends out a request to the `AspDotNetForDummies.com` server, asking for the page named `page1.aspx`.

3. The Web server receives the request, locates the page, and looks at it. Because the filename has an `.aspx` extension at the end, the server understands that this page is an ASP.NET page.

4. The server checks to see if it has a compiled version of this page. A Web server can't run an ASP.NET page until that page is compiled, so if the server doesn't have a compiled version, it compiles the page.

5. The server executes the compiled version of the page, running the source-code parts of the page and sending the HTML parts of the page to the browser. None of the source code itself is sent. Only pure HTML is returned to the browser.

6. The server saves the compiled version of the page for use next time the page is requested.

This arrangement has lots of advantages:

✔ ASP.NET pages are easy to write and maintain because the source code and the HTML are together.

✔ The source code is executed on the server, so your pages have lots of power and flexibility.

✔ You don't have to worry about compiling the code yourself — it's done for you the first time the page is requested.

✔ Execution is fast because the Web server only has to compile the page the first time it is requested (the server saves and re-uses the compiled version of the page), and your ASP.NET pages continue to work well even when you have lots of traffic on the server.

✔ Only the HTML produced by the page is returned to the browser, so your proprietary application source code can't be easily stolen.

✔ Because only pure HTML is sent back, your ASP.NET pages work with any browser running on any computer.

How Does ASP.NET Differ from Client-Side Technologies?

You've probably seen all the books on the market teaching JavaScript and VBScript. How do these scripting languages differ from ASP.NET?

You can use JavaScript and VBScript in your Web pages to do *client-side scripting. Client-side* refers to the browser and the machine running the browser, as opposed to *server-side,* where the Web server is running.

ASP.NET runs on the server-side. Client-side scripting works a little differently:

1. You choose a Favorite or click a link in your browser to go to an HTML page that includes client-side scripting code.

2. The Web server locates the page and sends it back to your browser.

3. The browser interprets the HTML tags and, at the same time, executes any client-side scripting code that it encounters.

4. Some code isn't executed immediately. Instead, it waits until you do something like clicking a button before it runs.

Client-side scripting and ASP.NET code are similar in that they both enable you to write code right alongside your HTML and have that code executed when the page is requested. And in many cases, you can do the same thing using either client-side scripts or ASP.NET code.

Client-side scripting and ASP.NET code do have some important differences, though:

✔ A client-side script executes in the browser *after* the page has been received. ASP.NET code executes on the server *before* the page is sent to the browser. The server executes the ASP.NET code to produce pure HTML that is then sent to the browser.

✔ A client-side script is downloaded as part of the page, and you can see the script in your browser by simply viewing the source code for the page. Consequently, others could steal the code you worked so hard to develop and use it in their own site!

✔ A client-side script can only run on browsers that support scripting and specifically support the scripting language that you use. For example, if you use client-side VBScript in your Web page, and someone accesses the page using Netscape Navigator (which only supports JavaScript), the script will not execute at all. With ASP.NET code, you don't have to worry about the browser's capabilities because the code runs on the server and only pure HTML is finally sent to the browser.

However, you don't have to pick between client-side scripting and ASP.NET. You can use both, even in the same page! I don't discuss client-side scripting in this book, but plenty of books on the topic are available.

But client-side script isn't the only technology out there to keep your browser entertained. You can use Java applets, ActiveX controls, and Netscape plug-ins. All these technologies work basically the same way: A small application is written to do something cool. That application is referenced in a Web page and automatically downloaded along with the page. Then, the application runs and presents its output on part of the page.

What do these technologies do? They may provide a control, like a special kind of listbox. Or, they could enable you to explore three-dimensional worlds, view an animation, or see live video as it is broadcast from a Web site. Flash and Shockwave, for example, are two popular ActiveX controls that are designed to show animations and enable you to play simple games over the Web.

How do these technologies differ from ASP.NET? Again, with these technologies, the little application is downloaded to the client and executed there. This may require long download times and it may not even work if the browser doesn't support it or the machine runs an operating system other than the one that's expected.

ASP.NET is purely server-side technology, so you always know what hardware and software it will be running on. And it produces pure HTML when communicating with the browser, so the type of browser or operating system on the client doesn't matter — it just works!

Part II
Speaking the Language

The 5th Wave   By Rich Tennant

"Give him air! Give him air! He'll be okay. He's just been exposed to some raw HTML code. It must have accidently flashed across his screen from the server."

In this part . . .

ASP.NET brings together standard HTML with a real programming language to make your Web applications work as well as your Windows applications do! But before you can build those Web applications, you have to understand that programming language. Fortunately, the most popular ASP.NET language is also probably the easiest programming language to learn: Visual Basic .NET.

In this part of the book, you find out how programs store and shuffle information around. Although that may not sound very exciting, it's probably the most important thing that computer programs do. You also explore the different ways Visual Basic can make decisions and repeat parts of its code again and again and organize its code into manageable pieces. This is where things get interesting.

Every page is full of examples, so take your keyboard and mouse in hand and get ready to have some fun!

Chapter 3

VB.NET Essentials: Juggling Information and Firing Off Functions

ASP.NET enables you to combine your HTML with code you write in a simple programming language. Although you can use any language supported by the .NET Framework in your ASP.NET pages, Visual Basic .NET is an excellent choice if you're just getting started. It is the most popular programming language for ASP.NET and, in fact, the most popular programming language ever created — primarily because it is so productive and easy to use.

In this chapter, you begin to explore the Visual Basic .NET language and discover how to put it to use creating ASP.NET pages. Visual Basic .NET has a vast array of commands and capabilities. Fortunately, you don't have to know them all to create useful pages. In this chapter, Chapter 4, and Chapter 5, I show you the key elements of the language that you'll use most often.

Getting Started with Programming

If you have very little or no computer programming experience, review the next couple of sections. They define some terms and describe some basic concepts that you need to know to get started. If you've done some programming, feel free to skim or skip these sections. Pick up reading again with "The ASP.NET Process."

What is a programming language?

A computer *programming language* is a lot like a human language. Like a human language, each computer language has a vocabulary of words. Likewise, each language has syntax rules for putting the words together in meaningful ways.

However, unlike human languages, computer languages are very precise. Human languages may have five different words that mean the same thing, whereas a computer language has only one. And, in a human language, you can put together the same sentence in several ways, reordering the words or even bending the rules of syntax now and then, and still be understood. Computers require that you follow their syntax to the letter. If you don't, the computer won't understand and will generate an error.

Also, human language is designed for two-way communication, whereas programming is a one-way street: You tell the computer exactly what it's supposed to do and how it should respond to every situation. Instead of a conversation, it's more like a recipe or a to-do list. The computer then simply follows your instructions. The computer can't argue with you. (However, when it throws error messages your way, you may feel like it's being argumentative!)

That's why the words in a computer language's vocabulary are often called *commands* or *statements*. When you put a series of commands together, the result is referred to as *source code,* or simply *code*. When you bring all the source code together, you have a computer *program* or *application*.

Compiling and running

After you create an application, you still have one problem: The computer can't read the source code directly. The computer really only understands binary numbers — ones and zeros. A series of commands given to the computer in binary form is called *machine code*. After you finish writing and debugging your source code, you run a piece of software called a *compiler,* which translates your source code into machine code.

You only need to compile your program once. After that, you *run* or *execute* the program, causing the computer to carry out your commands. You can run the compiled code again and again. You don't need to compile it again unless you change the source code.

The machine code usually takes the form of an *.EXE* file, or *executable.* This file is distributed to those who need to use the application, people who are fondly referred to as *users* or, in the case of Web sites, *visitors.*

The ASP.NET Process

For an ASP.NET Web page, the programming process is just a bit more interesting than the one I describe in the preceding sections of this chapter.

You create an ASP.NET page by typing in HTML and Visual Basic .NET source code. When you finish the page, you copy it to the Web server where it can be accessed.

The first time a user requests the ASP.NET page, the Web server notices that the page has not been compiled and automatically compiles it and then executes it. From then on, the compiled version is executed whenever the page is requested. If you change the page, the Web server notices when the next request for that page comes and again automatically compiles and executes it.

The upshot of all this is that the Web server takes care of compiling your ASP.NET pages for you, when necessary. You should know that it is happening, but you don't have to worry about doing it yourself!

Stepping up to a real programming language

Classic ASP pages use VBScript or JavaScript as their language. These are *scripting* languages, and you don't have to compile your scripts before you run them. Instead, when your scripts run, they are *interpreted.* Interpreted scripting languages run much slower than compiled programming languages, so ASP.NET works better than Classic ASP on high-traffic sites.

Scripting languages also are not as powerful as full-blown programming languages like Visual Basic .NET. ASP.NET provides you with all the features of Visual Basic .NET. Although the changes do require some getting used to, the power and speed you get in return is more than worth the effort.

Power — In Time . . .

Using ASP.NET provides many powerful capabilities. But when you're first discovering Visual Basic .NET in the context of ASP.NET, you are somewhat limited in what you can do. For example, the applications you create in this chapter and the next aren't very interactive. I show you how to accept input from the user in Chapter 8. If I tried to present everything at once, it would be very confusing!

So, as you read this chapter, some of the examples may seem a little contrived. Don't judge yet! These commands and their power will become much clearer as you discover more about ASP.NET in the next few chapters.

Delimiters — Keeping Your Tags and Your Code Apart

Because your Visual Basic .NET code is a part of your HTML page and coexists right alongside the HTML tags, you need some way to separate the HTML from the Visual Basic .NET code. That's what delimiters do. Here's the example from Chapter 1:

```
<%@Page Language="VB" Debug="True" %>
<html>
<head>
<title>Hello and Welcome Page</title>
</head>
<body>
<center>
<% Dim TextSize As Integer %>
<% For TextSize = 1 To 7 %>
<font size = <%=TextSize%>>
Hello and Welcome!<br>
</font>
<% Next %>
</center>
</body>
</html>
```

The tags appear and work in the document just as they would in a normal HTML page. The only difference between this ASP.NET page and an HTML page are the lines of Visual Basic .NET code that are interspersed throughout the page. The <% and %> signs that surround these lines of code are the *delimiters*.

Up your case!

When you type in the page header and other Visual Basic .NET commands, variable names, and so on, you can use upper- and lowercase characters however you like. Each of these headers would work just fine:

```
<%@PAGE LANGUAGE="VB" DEBUG="TRUE" %>

<%@page language="vb" debug="true" %>

<%@PaGe LaNgUaGe="Vb" DeBuG="tRuE" %>
```

However, even though case doesn't affect how the code works, you shouldn't get careless. Pick a standard and stick to it. Throughout this book, I capitalize the first letter of each Visual Basic .NET command. The capitalization makes the VB.NET commands stand out and keeps the code easy to read, and it's also similar to the way lots of other Visual Basic .NET developers write their code.

Delimiters can contain more than one line. For example, I could have written the first two lines of Visual Basic .NET code in the body of the page like this:

```
<% Dim TextSize As Integer
For TextSize = 1 To 7 %>
```

Or like this:

```
<%
Dim TextSize As Integer
For TextSize = 1 To 7
%>
```

You decide how you organize your delimiters and your code. The code will work as long as you keep all Visual Basic .NET code *inside* the delimiters and all HTML tags *outside* the delimiters.

The ASP.NET Page Header

The page header often appears at the top of an ASP.NET page. Although not required, including it is always a good idea. Make sure it's on the very first line:

```
<%@Page Language="VB" Debug="True" %>
```

The syntax for the header requires that the entire line appear inside the `<%` and `%>` delimiters (discussed in the preceding section) and that it begins with @ Page. Following that, you can specify various things about the page. For example, you can specify which computer language you use in this page. VB is the abbreviation for Visual Basic .NET.

My sample header also assigns the value "True" to Debug. Include this setting when you create and debug your pages. It ensures that you get detailed error messages if you make a mistake. After your pages are complete and ready to use on a real Web server, you can remove Debug="True" from the page header to increase the performance of your page.

Creating and Using Variables

Think of variables as named boxes that you use to temporarily hold information so you can use it later. After you create a variable, you can put information inside it and then use the variable anywhere you'd normally use that information. Variables are very handy in all kinds of situations. For example, you can use one to store the result of a calculation until you have a chance to show it to the user.

Making your own variables with objects you can find around the house

In VB.NET, you *create* (or *declare*) a new variable by using the Dim statement.

Create a page, type in the following listing exactly as it appears here, and then use the process I describe in Chapter 1 to test it. (By the way, don't expect to actually *see* anything in the browser when you try this one — I tell you why later in this section.)

```
<%@Page Language="VB" Debug="True" %>
<html>
<body>
<%
Dim Cost, Tax, Total As Integer
Cost = 40
Tax = 2
Total = Cost + Tax
%>
</body>
</html>
```

After the page header and the opening tags, the <% delimiter separates the VB.NET code from the rest of the page. After the delimiter, the first line of code begins with Dim and creates three variables named Cost, Tax, and Total. You can give the variables any name you want, but choose names that will remind you of what they hold.

All three variables are identified As Integers, which means they can hold whole numbers. (For more information on this topic, see "She's not my data type," later in this chapter.)

> # What *not* to name your variables
>
> VB.NET keeps several keywords for its own use. These are called *reserved words*. VB.NET doesn't allow you to use these words as variable names because it already uses them for something else. For example, `Dim` is a reserved word. You'd be pretty confused if you saw a variable declaration like this:
>
> ```
> Dim Dim As Integer
> ```
>
> I don't have room to list all the reserved words here, but as you discover more and more of VB.NET's built-in commands, keep in mind that the names used for those commands are usually reserved words, so don't use them as variable names.

After they are created, `Cost` and `Tax` are immediately assigned values of 40 and 2, respectively. Then, the values held by `Cost` and `Tax` are added, and the sum is placed in the variable `Total`. Simple enough.

You can do this kind of math with any combination of numbers and variables. You use the normal + and – signs for addition and subtraction, respectively. Multiplication uses the * symbol, and division uses the / symbol. Exponents are created using the ^ symbol.

Table 3-1 summarizes some of the math operators you can use with numbers or variables that hold numbers.

Table 3-1	Common Math Operators
Symbol	*Description*
+	Addition
–	Subtraction
*	Multiplication
/	Division
^	Exponents (Raise to the power)

So, what does this page do when you run it? Absolutely nothing. Or at least that's the way it seems. If you haven't already, try it out!

Actually, the page does exactly what it's told to do. The page creates three variables, assigns values to two of them, and then adds them and puts the sum in the third variable. You never told the page to display any values, though. I show you how to do that in the next section!

Displaying variable values

In the preceding section, I show you a page that does some math, but doesn't display its result. Change that page (or create a new page) to look like this:

```
<%@Page Language="VB" Debug="True" %>
<html>
<body>
<%
Dim Cost, Tax, Total As Integer
Cost = 40
Tax = 2
Total = Cost + Tax
%>
<%=Total%>
</body>
</html>
```

What happens when you run it now? The number 42 appears in the upper-left corner of an otherwise blank page.

But how did you do that? What kind of funky syntax does the second-to-last line contain? That line has the normal delimiters <% and %> surrounding a variable name with an equal sign in front of it:

```
<%=Total%>
```

This little shortcut enables you to replace that short section of code with the value in the variable. So if you choose View⇨Source in the browser, you see this:

```
<html>
<body>
42
</body>
</html>
```

What DIMwit came up with that idea?

Dim? What the heck is Dim? Wouldn't something like Variable or Var be a better command for creating new variables? Yes, it would!

Dim stands for DIMension. Why? It's a long and boring story, but suffice to say that it's a holdover from way back, when they were carving Basic programs on cave walls. And now we're stuck with it. Sorry.

Using this syntax is a very handy technique. Not only can you use it to print the value in a variable, but you can also use it within HTML tags themselves:

```
<%@Page Language="VB" Debug="True" %>
<html>
<body>
<%
Dim TextSize As Integer
TextSize = 5
%>
<font size = <%=TextSize%>>
All creatures, big and small . . .<p>
</body>
</html>
```

When you try this page out, you see the phrase All creatures, big and small . . . printed on the page in the font size specified in the TextSize variable.

Using View⇨Source in your browser, you can see what happened:

```
<html>
<body>
<font size=5>
All creatures, big and small . . .<p>
</body>
</html>
```

The <%=TextSize%> was replaced by the *value* in the TextSize variable: 5.

Change the number, save the page, and then refresh the browser to see the result.

Can you use a variable you didn't create?

Do you always have to create a variable using the Dim statement before you can use it in your code? Actually, no, you don't. If you just start using a variable name that's never been used before, VB.NET automatically creates it for you. Is this a good idea? Absolutely *not*!

Bye, bye <% Option Explicit %>

In Classic ASP, if you want to force yourself to declare your variables before you use them, you put the command <% Option Explicit %> at the top of your page. In ASP.NET, that command doesn't work. Instead, you must place the Explicit="True" clause in the page header.

With these simple pages, using a variable that's never been created probably isn't a big deal. But when pages start to get complicated, figuring out what all the variables are and what they do can be a real pain. If you start using variables that you haven't even created, the code gets even more complicated. As a general rule, always declare your variables with `Dim` before you use them.

Forcing the point

VB.NET has a way that you can force yourself to always create your variables before you use them. In the page header, set an option called `Explicit`. Just modify your header so that it looks like this:

```
<%@Page Explicit="True" Language="VB" Debug="True" %>
```

After you make this change, you get an error if you try to use a variable that you haven't created.

Why would you want to do this? Well, if you set the `Explicit` option on and then you accidentally misspell a variable name in your code, VB.NET flags the misspelled variable as an error. If you don't have the `Explicit` option on, VB.NET just assumes that you are trying to make a new variable and goes on.

Always use the `Explicit` option in your page header.

She's not my data type

Here's a snippet of code from a previous section in the chapter (see "Making your own variables with objects you can find around the house"):

```
<%
Dim Cost, Tax, Total As Integer
. . .
%>
```

Types for the typeless

Classic ASP uses VBScript, which doesn't support data types. With Classic ASP, you simply create all variables with a `Dim` statement and use them however you like. With ASP.NET, you can still omit the `As Integer` or `As Single` clause from the `Dim` statement, and the variables will work, more or less, as they do in Classic ASP. As tempting as that may sound, I strongly recommend that you use types with your variables. They make your code clearer and your variables easier to manage. They also make your code run faster and more efficiently.

Why not use Single for every number?

Perhaps you're thinking, "Hmm . . . a `Single` variable can hold numbers with decimal places. Even numbers like 3.0, right? So, why not use `Single` as the data type for *all* my number variables, just to keep it simple?"

Well, that may be simple for you, but it's not simple for Mr. Computer. The computer allocates a whole lot more space to hold a variable of type `Single` than it does for an `Integer`. In addition, math calculations are much more complex with a `Single`, and thus take more time.

So if you're working with whole numbers, but you put them in `Single` variables, the computer will work with them as though they were decimal numbers, whether they are or not. To save your computer headaches, and to make your programs run faster, always use variable types that match your data as closely as possible.

As I explain in that section, you use `Dim` to create variables, and this line identifies three new variables as integers. So, these variables have an integer *data type*.

If you think of a variable as a box for holding data, you can imagine that different boxes have different sizes and shapes. A box's size and shape determine what the box can hold. This "size and shape" is analogous to a variable's *data type* — that is, the type of data the variable can contain. Just as you can't put a pair of shoes in a matchbox so you shouldn't try to store someone's last name in a variable that's supposed to store a number.

A variable declared as an `Integer`, as these three are, can contain whole numbers (that is, numbers *without* a decimal point). You can also create variables to hold other types of numbers — for example:

```
<%
Dim Pi As Single
Pi=3.14159
%>
```

Variables with the data type `Single` can hold what are called *single-precision* values. That's a confusing way of saying that a `Single` can hold a number that *has* a decimal point and digits after the decimal.

Where does the term *single-precision* come from? Well, it refers to the fact that variables of this type can hold numbers with a decimal point, but some numbers are too small for it to keep track of accurately. As you might expect, you also can declare *double-precision* variables, which use the `Double` data type. `Double` variables can hold very, very small numbers accurately. But, really, unless you are doing seriously complex scientific calculations, you probably can get by with the `Single` data type.

So, now you know what data type to use for a variable to hold almost any number you want. If it's a whole number, use `Integer`. If it includes a decimal point, use `Single`.

For information on more data types designed to hold numbers, see Chapter 15.

Don't string me along . . .

In addition to holding numbers, variables can hold *strings*. A string is a bunch of letters put together to form words or sentences. Or maybe just nonsense:

```
<%@Page Explicit="True" Language="VB" Debug="True" %>
<html>
<body>
<%
Dim FirstName, LastName, WholeName As String
FirstName = "Bill"
LastName = "Gates"
WholeName = FirstName & LastName
%>
<%=WholeName %>
</body>
</html>
```

Strings are always enclosed by quotation marks so you know exactly where they begin and end, even though the quotes aren't actually a part of the string. In this example, the variable `FirstName` is assigned the string `Bill`, and `LastName` is assigned `Gates`. `WholeName` is assigned to be equal to both `FirstName` and `LastName`. Notice the & separating the `FirstName` and `LastName` variables on the right side. In VB.NET, & sticks two strings together, or *concatenates* them.

Always put spaces on either side of the & in your code when you use it. You'll get an unusual error if you don't. (Go ahead; try it!)

What's wrong with this page?

```
BillGates
```

There's no space between the first and last names. You have to add the space when you stick them together.

Change the line that assigns a value to `WholeName` in the preceding page to look like this:

```
WholeName = FirstName & " " & LastName
```

This time, *three* strings are concatenated: the one in FirstName, a space, and then the one in LastName. You can see the result:

```
Bill Gates
```

Give it a value when you create it

TRY THIS

Here's a shortcut for you. Instead of declaring all your variables and then assigning values to them as a separate step, you can do it all at once!

```
<%@Page Explicit="True" Language="VB" Debug="True" %>
<html>
<body>
<%
Dim FirstName As String = "Bill"
Dim LastName As String = "Gates"
Dim WholeName As String = FirstName & " " & LastName
%>
<%=WholeName %>
</body>
</html>
```

This handy technique can save you a few keystrokes.

Cantankerous Constants

A constant is like a variable except that you give it a value once, when you create it, and from then on, you're not allowed to change its value.

If you have a common number that you'll be using in several places throughout your page, you can assign that number to a constant at the top of your page and then use the constant name everywhere you'd normally use the number. This has two advantages:

✔ Because you're giving the number a meaningful *name,* the code is more understandable.

✔ If that number ever changes in the future, you won't have to hunt it down everywhere you use it on the page. You can simply change the constant declaration, and you're ready to go!

You declare a constant in much the same way you declare a variable, replacing Dim with Const:

```
Const Temperature As Single = 98.6
Const CompanyName As String = "Colonial Systems, Inc."
```

You may want to create a naming standard to differentiate between constants and variables so that you can keep them straight. For example, you may put constants in all uppercase, while using mixed case for variables. Or, you may want to put a prefix before all constant names, like con.

Keep Your Comments to Yourself

Comments, also called *remarks,* are the way you include notes to yourself or others inside your page without changing the way the page works.

In HTML, you use <!-- and --> to enclose comments that you want to include in the page, but don't want to display in the browser.

With ASP.NET, you can still use the HTML comment symbols in your pages. But if you want to comment VB.NET code as you create it, you can also use the VB.NET-style comment, as in the following example:

```
<%@Page Explicit="True" Language="VB" Debug="True" %>
<%
' This page calculates
' the total cost by adding
' the price and tax.

Total = Cost + Tax
%>
. . .
```

Instead of enclosing the comment with two different symbols as HTML does, the VB.NET comment always begins with an apostrophe (or single quote) and ends at the end of the line. So, you need a new apostrophe at the beginning of each new comment line.

You can also put a comment on the same line as code. Again, the comment starts with the apostrophe and ends at the end of the line:

```
<% TextSize = 1 ' Sets TextSize to 1 %>
```

Although this works fine for normal lines of VB.NET code, you can't use comments inside the special syntax that's used to display variables:

```
<%=Total    ' This comment causes an error %>
```

You'll get the following error:

```
Expected ')'
```

Because that error message doesn't make much sense in this context, it can be very confusing!

The VB.NET comments, like all the rest of the ASP.NET code, are removed before the page is sent to the user's browser. So, unlike the HTML comments, these comments can't be seen when the person browsing your page chooses View⇨Source from the Internet Explorer menus.

During testing of a new page, you can temporarily disable some lines you've written, but still easily get them back later if you need to. Rather than delete a line of code, simply put an apostrophe in front it. The apostrophe turns the line into a comment. The line of code no longer affects the way the page works, but it's there if you want to bring it back. To put that line of code back into service, simply remove the apostrophe. Adding an apostrophe is called *commenting-out* a line of code. Removing the apostrophe is referred to as *uncommenting* the code.

Understanding How Functions Function

Commands in VB.NET come in two flavors: statements and functions. A statement is a command that stands on its own and simply does something. Dim, which declares variables, is a statement:

```
Dim Artist, CD As String
```

A function, on the other hand, returns a value for you to use in your code. In this section, I describe how functions work and introduce you to some functions that are handy when dealing with dates.

Getting a date

The following code shows how you can use the Today function:

```
<%@Page Explicit="True" Language="VB" Debug="True" %>
<html>
<body>
<%
Dim CurrentDate As String
CurrentDate = Today
%>
The current date is <%=CurrentDate %>.<br>
</body>
</html>
```

In this code, the variable CurrentDate is created and then assigned the value that is returned from the Today function. Then, the value of CurrentDate is used within a sentence to inform the user of the current date.

What do you mean it "returns a value"?

If you haven't used a computer language with functions before, the concept of a function returning a value can be confusing. When I say a *value is returned,* what do I mean?

You *call* the built-in VB.NET function Today when you use its name in the code. When it's called, the function goes out to the system clock and finds out the current date. Then, the function sends that current date back to *this* code and places the value in the code *right where the* Today *function appears.* The date returned by the function is then assigned to the Current Date variable:

```
CurrentDate = Today
```

So this line does *two* things:

- ✔ It calls the Today function.
- ✔ It assigns the date returned from the Today function to the CurrentDate variable.

You may think that Today looks like a variable that simply isn't declared. And you're right, it does look like that. However, you know it's not a variable because it's not declared and because you happen to know that Today is a built-in function with a special meaning in VB.NET. (Okay, you may not have known that before, but you do now!) You'll discover more built-in functions as you explore VB.NET.

Let the arguments commence!

A function can also have *arguments* (sometimes referred to as *parameters*). An argument is a value that you can send to the function when you call it. By passing an argument to a function, you give the function information to work on. For example, take a look at the Weekday function:

```
<%@Page Explicit="True" Language="VB" Debug="True" %>
<html>
<body>
<%
Dim ThisDay, ThisDate As String
ThisDate = Today
ThisDay = Weekday(ThisDate)
%>
It is day number <%=ThisDay %>.<br>
</body>
</html>
```

First, ThisDay and ThisDate are declared as strings.

The next line calls the Today function. The Today function gets the system date and returns it. The value returned is assigned to ThisDate.

The next line calls the Weekday function and passes the value of ThisDate as an argument. Weekday uses this date to determine the weekday on which the date falls. Notice that you pass arguments by placing them after the function name and putting them in parentheses. If this function had taken two arguments, you would put them both inside parentheses and separate them with a comma.

The value returned is a number from 1 to 7, indicating Sunday through Saturday.

If you want to make this code more concise, you could do it this way:

```
<%@Page Explicit="True" Language="VB" Debug="True" %>
<html>
<body>
<%
Dim ThisDay As String
ThisDay = Weekday(Today)
%>
It is day number <%=ThisDay %>.<br>
</body>
</html>
```

The Today function is called first and then the value it returns is immediately sent to the Weekday function as an argument.

Rolling Dice and Cutting Cards — Using Functions in Formulas with Rnd and Int

One of the handier things about functions and the way they return their values is that you can use them right in the middle of larger formulas. To illustrate how this works, I'm going to introduce you to two new functions: Rnd and Int:

```
<%@Page Explicit="True" Language="VB" Debug="True" %>
<html>
<body>
<%
Dim RandNum As Single
Randomize
RandNum = Rnd
%>
<%=RandNum%>
</body>
</html>
```

Why Randomize?

Okay, here's the deal. You know about right-brained and left-brained people, right? Right-brained people are creative and usually become starving artists. Left-brained people are analytical and usually become accountants. Well, computers are left-brained, with a vengeance. The Rnd function is about as creative as computers can get. But even picking a number out of the air isn't easy for the computer.

The computer actually goes through a complex formula to generate a "random" number. But the computer needs a number to stick into the formula to kick it off — what programmers call a *seed* value. If you don't use the Randomize statement, the computer always starts with the same seed. And, therefore, the computer ends up with the same series of "random" numbers every single time. Not very random, right?

Randomize goes to the system clock and gets the numbers that it uses as the seed for the complex formula. That way, the seed and the random numbers are different every time you run your page.

Look at the resulting page in your browser. Now click Refresh. Click it again. If everything went well, you see a new number pop up in the upper-left corner of your page each time you click Refresh. Because the number is random, I don't know exactly what number you'll see, and you get a different number every time you click Refresh. But the number probably looks something like this:

```
0.1525385
```

The Randomize statement and the Rnd function work together to generate random numbers. Randomize needs to appear in any page where you plan to use the Rnd function — before you use it. Randomize gets the ball rolling. (See the sidebar titled "Why Randomize?" for more information on why Randomize is necessary.)

Then, Rnd returns decimal numbers that are greater than 0 but less than 1. You get a different number each time you display the page. Random numbers come in very handy when you're creating games and some types of cool graphics.

But these random numbers between 0 and 1 aren't very useful, are they? For example, if you wanted to create a program that simulates drawing cards or rolling dice, you would want numbers between 1 and 13 or between 1 and 6.

Unfortunately, VB.NET doesn't provide any other random-number functions. So you have to use this one and tweak it a little. Take a look at this code:

```
RandNum = (Rnd * 6) + 1
```

This line calls the Rnd function, which returns a decimal value between 0 and 1. Then, that value is multiplied by 6. Now you have a decimal value between 0 and 5. So you add 1 to get a decimal value between 1 and 6. That number is then assigned to the RandNum variable.

The parentheses help VB.NET decide which calculations it does first. In this case, it multiplies 6 times the number returned from Rnd first because that's in parentheses. (Actually, in this case, even if the parentheses weren't there, VB.NET would always do the multiplication before the addition, but the parentheses make it clearer.)

Try plugging the preceding line of code into your page in place of the RandNum = Rnd line. Save it and click Refresh in your browser. See what you get. You get a number that looks something like this:

```
4.167642
```

Now click Refresh again. You should continue to see numbers like that between 1 and 6. Great! That's what you wanted, right? Well, yes, except for that annoying decimal part of the number. If only you could just chop off that decimal part.

And, of course, you can. Just use a function called Int, which stands for integer. Just as the Integer data type enables you to create variables that hold whole numbers, so the Int function takes a number with a decimal part (like the ones you're getting here) and returns an integer. The Int function expects one argument: a number with a decimal part. Int returns the exact same number with the decimal part chopped off.

Notice I didn't say that Int rounds the number off — it doesn't. Int simply, unceremoniously chops off any decimal part and returns the whole number.

Replace the RandNum = (Rnd * 6) + 1 line in your page with this new one:

```
RandNum = Int(Rnd * 6) + 1
```

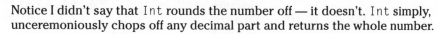

Save and then click Refresh in your browser. I can't predict exactly what number you'll see, but it should look something like this:

```
2
```

Click Refresh again. Each time you should see whole numbers between 1 and 6. Perfect! Now you can create random numbers between 1 and any number you like.

Want to simulate pulling cards off a deck? Use this line:

```
RandNum = Int(Rnd * 13) + 1
```

The 1 is an Ace, 11 through 13 are Jacks through Kings, and the rest are number cards. Easy enough.

Want to simulate flipping a coin? Use this line:

```
RandNum = Int(Rnd * 2) + 1
```

This code generates either a 1 or a 2. Call 1 heads and 2 tails and you're ready to go!

Finally, if you want to generate random percentages, use this line:

```
RandNum = Int(Rnd * 100) + 1
```

More Common Functions

This section introduces you to some of the more commonly used functions in VB.NET. If you've read the previous sections in this chapter, you've seen a few of these functions already, but most of them, you haven't.

You certainly don't have to memorize them all. You don't even have to read through them all. But if you at least skim over them, you get a good idea of many things VB.NET can help you do. And you know where to look when you want to read more detail.

Also, keep in mind that this isn't an exhaustive list of functions — not by a long shot. And even with the functions I do list here, I won't bore you with every last detail.

Think of this section as a quick overview to get you off and running with the more common commands and functions in VB.NET.

And, if you need more information, you can check out the VB.NET documentation, which comes with the .NET Framework.

Playing with string

Strings are letters, words, and numbers that can be stored in a variable. For example, names, addresses, and book titles are stored in the computer as strings. Because strings are so important, many commands and functions exist to deal with them. I describe some of the more important ones here.

Len

Len is short for length. When you send a string to this function as an argument, it returns the number of characters in the string.

Here's an example:

```
<%@Page Explicit="True" Language="VB" Debug="True" %>
<html>
<body>
<%
Dim MyString As String
Dim MyLength As Integer
MyString = "Butter side down"
MyLength = Len(MyString)
%>
This string: <%=MyString%><br>
Is <%=MyLength%> letters long.<br>
</body>
</html>
```

MyLength is 16 — that's how many letters are in the string.

LCase, UCase

LCase and UCase both take one string as an argument. They both return that same string converted to lower- or uppercase, respectively:

```
LCase("This Is A Scary Story") returns "this is a scary story"
UCase("This Is A Scary Story") returns "THIS IS A SCARY STORY"
```

LTrim, RTrim, Trim

The trim functions — LTrim, RTrim, and Trim — each receive a string as an argument and return a string. The string returned is the same as the string sent except

✔ LTrim chops off any spaces that appear on the left side of the string (at the beginning). These are often referred to as *leading spaces*.

✔ RTrim chops off any spaces that appear on the right side of the string (at the end). These are often referred to as *trailing spaces*.

✔ Trim chops off both leading and trailing spaces.

For example:

```
LTrim("   Hello!   ") returns "Hello!   "
RTrim("   Hello!   ") returns "   Hello!"
Trim("   Hello!   ") returns "Hello!"
```

Space

With the Space function, you can easily create a string with lots of spaces in it. Just send a number indicating how many spaces you want, and Space returns a string of that length, filled with spaces:

```
Space(15) returns "               " (15 spaces)
```

Left, Mid, Right

Left, Mid, and Right are very useful. They enable you to tear apart a string into smaller strings.

Left takes two arguments: a string and a number. It returns a string that consists of the left-most characters of the string sent:

```
Left("Dog bones",3) returns "Dog"
Left("Rubble",4) returns "Rubb"
```

Right works exactly the same way, but it takes the characters from the right side of the string:

```
Right("Dog bones",5) returns "bones"
```

Mid takes characters from anywhere within a string. The first argument is the string you want to work with. The second argument determines where in the string to begin, and the third argument determines how many characters to use. Mid returns the string that results:

```
Mid("Quick brown fox",7, 5) returns "brown"
```

It starts with the seventh character ("b") and takes five characters total (including the seventh).

InStr

InStr is a really handy function. It searches for a shorter string within a long string. If it finds the shorter string, InStr returns the position within the larger string where the shorter string can be found.

In other words, InStr returns the character position at which it finds the second argument within the first argument.

Here's an example:

```
<%@Page Explicit="True" Language="VB" Debug="True" %>
<html>
<body>
<%
Dim BigString, FindString As String
Dim Position As Integer
BigString = "I do not like green eggs and ham."
FindString = "eggs"
Position = InStr(BigString, FindString)
%>
This string: <%=FindString%><br>
Appears inside this string: <%=BigString%><br>
At position <%=Position%><br>
</body>
</html>
```

Position holds the value 21, because "eggs" starts at the 21st position in BigString.

Replace

Replace goes a step further than InStr. It looks for a small string inside a larger one, and when the small string is found, it is replaced with another specified string.

Here's an example:

```
<%@Page Explicit="True" Language="VB" Debug="True" %>
<html>
<body>
<%
Dim BigString as string
BigString = "Mary had a little lamb"
%>
<%=Replace(BigString, "little", "big")%><br>
</body>
</html>
```

This page displays the following line:

```
Mary had a big lamb
```

Format

Format enables you to take a date, time, or number and format it the way you want it to look. You send two arguments. The first can be a date, a time, or a number. Or, you can use a variable holding a date, time, or number. The second argument can hold many different values depending on what you're trying to format and how you want it to look. Here's an example:

```
<%@Page Explicit="True" Language="VB" Debug="True" %>
<html>
<body>
<%=Format(0.675,"p")%><br>
<%=Format(55102,"n")%><br>
<%=Format(1552,"c")%><br>
<br>
<%=Format(Now,"g")%><br>
<%=Format(Now,"d")%><br>
<%=Format(Now,"t")%><br>
<br>
<%=Format(Now,"MMM dd, yyyy")%><br>
</body>
</html>
```

Tangled strings

Although most of the string functions will look familiar to you, Format may seem a little suspicious. In Classic ASP, you have a whole slew of formatting functions like FormatCurrency, FormatDateTime, FormatNumber, and FormatPercent. Thankfully, Format takes over the role of all these functions!

You also may notice that the String function is missing. It is no longer available.

Here's the result this page produces:

```
67.50 %
55,102.00
$1,552.00

5/18/2001 3:35 PM
5/18/2001
3:35 PM

May 18, 2001
```

As this example shows, you can use many letters for the second argument, and each letter has a predefined meaning. Table 3-2 lists common examples of the letters you can use for this argument.

Table 3-2	Common Format Arguments
Letter	*What It Means*
p	Percentage
n	Standard
c	Currency
g	General date/time
d	Short date
t	Short time

You can also enter your own format using certain letters in combination, as the last Format line in the example shows. For more details and options, see the .NET Framework documentation.

Now what?

The Now function works exactly like it does in Classic ASP. However, the Date and Time functions have new names, as you can see: Today and TimeOfDay.

If you wanna date, I got the time . . .

These VB.NET functions provide key date and time access and manipulation functions.

Today, TimeOfDay, Now

Today, TimeOfDay, and Now are functions that take no arguments and each returns a single value, swiped from the system clock:

- ✔ Today returns today's date.
- ✔ TimeOfDay returns the current time.
- ✔ Now returns the date and time together.

Weekday, WeekdayName

Weekday accepts a date as an argument. It returns a number between 1 and 7, indicating the number of the day on which that date falls.

WeekdayName conveniently accepts a number argument between 1 and 7 and returns the name of the associated weekday:

```
<%=WeekdayName(Weekday(Today)) %>
```

Whose time is it?

If you plan to put the current date and time on your Web page, be aware that Today, TimeOfDay, and Now in an ASP.NET page return the date and time from the *server's* system clock, not the client machine where the browser is running. So, if people from other time zones access your site, you're probably giving them misleading information.

The better way to put the current date and time on your page is to use functions like these in a client-side script using JavaScript. That way, you pull the information from the client machine, which is much more likely to have the correct local time.

This line would display the current day of the week in the browser.

Other date and time functions

VB.NET provides a broad variety of date and time commands and functions. Here are some date and time functions you may find interesting:

- `DateDiff`: Returns how many days, weeks, months, or years exist between two dates.

- `DateAdd`: Adds a certain number of days, weeks, months, or years to a date and returns the new date.

- `Day`, `Month`, `Year`: Each takes a date and returns a number, which indicates the part of the date associated with the function's name. For example, if `MyDate` holds `10/5/67`, then `Month(MyDate)` returns 10, `Day(MyDate)` returns 5, and `Year(MyDate)` returns 67.

- `MonthName`: Takes a month number (1 to 12) and returns the name of the month ("January" through "December").

Chapter 4

VB.NET Essentials: Asking Questions and Jumping Through Loops

. . . .

In This Chapter

▶ Asking questions with simple and compound If...Then statements

▶ Using ElseIf to ask several questions at once

▶ Cleaning up your code with Select Case

▶ Counting with For...Next loops

▶ Doing a loop While a condition is true

▶ Repeating a loop Until something happens

▶ Nesting loops inside other loops

▶ Repeating a set of tasks For Each element in an array

. . . .

*I*n Chapter 3, you discover some fundamentals of Visual Basic .NET programming, such as creating variables to hold different types of information, displaying the value of a variable in a Web page, and using various common functions.

In this chapter, you continue your exploration of VB.NET. You discover *conditionals,* which enable you to ask questions and do different things based on the answer. You also discover *loops,* which you use to repeat certain parts of your code again and again.

Decisions, Decisions, Decisions: Using If...Then

Your Web pages can make decisions on their own based on information they gather. But first you have to tell your Web pages which decisions to make and how to make them. The keywords you use to do that, naturally enough, are If and Then:

```
If condition Then
    statement
End If
```

This If...Then structure is often called a *conditional.* A conditional has two parts:

- ✔ The *condition,* or the question part
- ✔ The *statement,* or the thing-to-do part

The End If just tells you when the statement part is over.

IF you want cool Web pages, THEN use conditionals

So, how do you use conditionals in your Web pages? Good question. Here's an example. The computer spins a wheel that has five sections numbered 1 through 5, and I bet on number 3 coming up:

```
<%@Page Explicit="True" Language="VB" Debug="True" %>

<html>
<body>
<%
Dim Wheel, Won As Integer
Randomize
%>
<p>My favorite number is 3. I'm spinning the wheel!</p>
<% Wheel = Int(Rnd * 5) + 1 ' Random number: 1-5 %>
<p>The Wheel landed on <%=Wheel%>.</p>
<%
If Wheel = 3 Then
    Won = 50
%>
```

```
<p>It landed on my number!</p>
<p>I win $<%=Won%></p>
<% End If %>
<p>All done.</p>
</body>
</html>
```

First, I display a little text to explain the premise of the game. I spin the wheel by generating a random number between 1 and 5. Then, I display the value that the wheel landed on. (For more information on Randomize, Rnd, and this formula used to generate random numbers, see Chapter 3.)

Next up is the If...Then statement. The condition part of the If...Then asks the question, "Does the Wheel variable hold a value that equals 3?"

Everything between the Then and the End If is part of the statement portion, whether it is additional VB.NET commands or HTML.

If the condition is true, the statement portion is performed. If the condition is not true, the statement portion is ignored. So, in this case, if Wheel equals 3, two things happen:

- The Won variable is set to 50.
- This HTML becomes part of the Web page that is sent back (after evaluating the value of Won):

  ```
  <p>It landed on my number!</p>
  <p>I win $50</p>
  ```

When you create an ASP.NET page, you are not creating the Web page itself. You are creating a set of instructions that tells the server *how to create* the Web page.

Now, if you haven't already, try out this example. After you bring it up in your browser, click Refresh several times. Depending on what number is generated, you should see one of the two possibilities that I describe in the next two sections.

If the condition is true

If the random number generated is 3, the final Web page sent to the browser looks like this (which you can see by choosing View➪Source):

```
<html>
<body>
<p>My favorite number is 3. I'm spinning the wheel!</p>
```

```
<p>The Wheel landed on 3.</p>
<p>It landed on my number!</p>
<p>I win $50</p>
<p>All done.</p>
</body>
</html>
```

Note: If you keep clicking Refresh, you'll notice that the Won variable doesn't accumulate an additional $50 every time you win. That's because the page (and therefore the variable) is reset every time you click Refresh. I explain how to create variables that last from one refresh to another in Chapter 10.

If the condition is false

If the random number generated is not 3, the page sent from the server looks something like this:

```
<html>
<body>
<p>My favorite number is 3. I'm spinning the wheel!</p>
<p>The Wheel landed on 1.</p>
<p>All done.</p>
</body>
</html>
```

Using Boolean variables with conditions

In Chapter 3, you discover three different data types for variables: Integer and Single to hold whole numbers and decimal numbers, and String to hold letters, words, and sentences.

Another data type you may use from time to time is called Boolean (named after George Boole, a famous mathematician who brought together math and logic). A variable with a Boolean data type can have only one of two possible values: True and False.

You can use these variables in an If...Then statement, too:

```
<%
Dim AccountBalanced As Boolean
. . .
AccountBalanced = True

. . .
If AccountBalanced = True Then
%>
. . .
```

TIP

In fact, when you are working with `Boolean` variables like this, you don't even need the `= True` part!

```
<%
Dim AccountBalanced As Boolean
. . .
AccountBalanced = True
. . .
If AccountBalanced Then
%>
. . .
```

Why does this work? The condition part of the `If...Then` statement is looking for a True or False anyway. You can just use the variable by itself. If the variable holds the value True, the statement part is executed. If the variable holds the value False, it is not.

Inequalities: A fact of life

`If...Then` statements can use what math professors call *inequalities*. Inequalities are ways of comparing numbers to see if they are greater than or less than each other. And, to keep it simple, VB.NET uses the same symbols as you did in your sixth-grade math class:

- ✔ This symbol means *greater than*: >
- ✔ And this symbol means *less than*: <

How do you keep them straight? My sixth-grade teacher explained it to me this way: Think of the symbol as an alligator's big mouth opening. And just remember, the alligator always eats the bigger number. Silly? Yes. But I've never forgotten it!

Here's an example that shows how inequalities work in an `If...Then` statement:

TRY THIS

```
<%@Page Explicit="True" Language="VB" Debug="True" %>
<html>
<body>
<%
Dim Grade As Integer
Grade = 95
If Grade > 90 Then
%>
<p>You get an A!</p>
<% End If %>
</body>
</html>
```

The happy result:

```
You get an A!
```

Because the variable Grade holds a value greater than 90, the message You get an A! appears. Suppose you don't get greater than 90, but you get 90 right on the nose. Shouldn't that be an A, too?

Try changing the preceding code so that Grade = 90. Save and Refresh the browser. The page is blank.

It doesn't work. How do you fix that? Well, here's one way: Change the If...Then line to look like this:

```
If Grade > 89 Then
```

But sticking with round numbers makes more sense. A better way would be to use another symbol, >=, which means *greater than or equal to*.

Change the If...Then line so that it looks like this:

```
If Grade >= 90 Then
```

That's better.

```
You get an A!
```

As you may expect, you also can use a <= symbol, which means *less than or equal to*. These symbols are a little different from the ones you learned in sixth-grade math, but these are easier to remember anyway.

You can use one more symbol to compare variables: <>, which means *does not equal*. Here's an example:

```
<% If Grade <> 100 Then %>
<p>You did not get a perfect score.</p>
<% End If %>
```

Table 4-1 summarizes the comparison symbols you use in If...Then statements.

Table 4-1	Comparison Operators for If...Then Statements
Symbol	**What It Means**
=	Equals
>	Greater than

Symbol	What It Means
<	Less than
>=	Greater than or equal to
<=	Less than or equal to
<>	Does not equal

Creating a compound If...Then

You can also use what programmer-types like to call a *logical expression* in an If...Then condition. This simply means that you can put more than one question together inside the same condition by using an And or an Or to separate them. This creates a *compound* If...Then statement.

A compound If...Then statement works just like you may expect. If an And separates the two conditions, the statement succeeds only if both conditions are true. If either one or both is false, then the statement portion is ignored. If an Or separates the two conditions, the statement succeeds if either condition (or both) is true.

You can connect together as many conditions as you like as long as an And or an Or separates each condition from the others:

```
<% If Temperature <= 32 And Liquid = "Water" Then %>
<p>Looks like ice...</p>
<% End If %>
```

Of course, too many conditions can make your statement very confusing. When you're creating Web pages, one rule always applies: As much as possible, keep it simple.

Lies! All lies! Or, what to do if it isn't true

In the previous sections of this chapter, all the If....Then statements only tell the computer what to do if a condition is true. What if you want it to do something else when the condition is not true? That's where Else comes in:

```
<%@Page Explicit="True" Language="VB" Debug="True" %>
<html>
<body>
<%
Dim Grade As Integer
```

```
Randomize
Grade = Int(Rnd * 100) + 1 ' Random number between 1 and 100
%>
<p>Your grade is <%=Grade%>.</p>
<% If Grade >= 60 Then %>
<p>You passed!</p>
<% Else %>
<p>You failed...</p>
<% End If %>
</body>
</html>
```

After you try this page, click Refresh in your browser several times. You should see both the passing and failing results.

So, with If...Then, you can choose whether to include some HTML, based on a condition. By adding Else to the mix, you can go one step further, choosing to include one bit of HTML if the condition is true and a different chunk of HTML if it isn't.

As I was saying: line continuation

In some cases, a line of code gets really long and a little difficult to deal with, especially when you're using a compound If...Then. Fortunately, you can break your line in two without confusing VB.NET into thinking it's supposed to treat that code as two separate lines. Here's an example:

```
<%
If Weekday(Today) > 3 And _
    Weekday(Today) < 6 Then
%>
```

You find the underscore character (_) on your keyboard on the same key as the dash — just press Shift along with it. The underscore at the end of the line tells the ASP.NET to consider the next line as an extension of this one. Although you may often use the underscore with a compound If...Then, that's not the only place. In fact, you can use it in any statement. Just place the underscore in the line just before you break it. You can break a line anywhere you'd normally put a space.

If you use the underscore, indent the second line three spaces or so to make it clear that the second line is a continuation of the previous line.

In some cases, you may want to break a long string and put part of it on a second line. You can use the underscore character to do that, too, but you also need to use the & concatenation character with it:

```
Desc = "This is a " & _
    "long description."
```

You put a final quote at the end of the string on the first line and a new string with quotes around it on the second line. You still need the underscore, but you also need the & to join the two strings together. Also, be careful to put a space between the & and the underscore. You'll get an error that says "Expected an identifier" if you don't.

Handling multiple conditions

You can ask one question, why not more? Of course, you can always just
write one `If...Then` statement after another. For example, if you want to
translate a percentage grade to a letter grade, you may write code that looks
like this:

```
<%@Page Explicit="True" Language="VB" Debug="True" %>
<html>
<body>
<%
Dim Grade As Integer
Dim LetterGrade As String
Randomize
Grade = Int(Rnd * 100) + 1 ' Random number between 1 and 100
%>
<p>Your grade is <%=Grade%>.</p>
<% If Grade >= 90 Then %>
<% LetterGrade = "A" %>
<p>You got an A! Congratulations.</p>
<% End If %>
<% If Grade >= 80 And Grade < 90 Then %>
<% LetterGrade = "B" %>
<p>You got a B. Good job.</p>
<% End If %>
<% If Grade >= 70 And Grade < 80 Then %>
<% LetterGrade = "C" %>
<p>You got a C. Not bad.</p>
<% End If %>
<% If Grade >= 60 And Grade < 70 Then %>
<% LetterGrade = "D" %>
<p>You got a D. Try harder next time.</p>
<% End If %>
<% If Grade < 60 Then %>
<% LetterGrade = "F" %>
<p>You failed. I'm sorry.</p>
<% End If %>
</body>
</html>
```

The preceding code has two major problems: It's wordy, and you end up
repeating yourself a lot. To make the process easier, VB.NET includes another
statement to help you in situations like this: `ElseIf`. If you use `ElseIf`, your
page begins to look simpler and is easier to understand:

```
<%@Page Explicit="True" Language="VB" Debug="True" %>
<html>
<body>
<%
Dim Grade As Integer
Dim LetterGrade As String
Randomize
```

```
Grade = Int(Rnd * 100) + 1 ' Random number between 1 and 100
%>
<p>Your grade is <%=Grade%>.</p>
<% If Grade >= 90 Then %>
<% LetterGrade = "A" %>
<p>You got an A! Congratulations.</p>
<% ElseIf Grade >= 80 Then %>
<% LetterGrade = "B" %>
<p>You got a B. Good job.</p>
<% ElseIf Grade >= 70 Then %>
<% LetterGrade = "C" %>
<p>You got a C. Not bad.</p>
<% ElseIf Grade >= 60 Then %>
<% LetterGrade = "D" %>
<p>You got a D. Try harder next time.</p>
<% Else %>
<% LetterGrade = "F" %>
<p>You failed. I'm sorry.</p>
<% End If %>
</body>
</html>
```

Now the whole thing is part of one big, long If...Then. You know that because the code has only one End If — all the way at the end.

Here's the way the If...Then...ElseIf works:

1. If the Grade is greater than or equal to 90, the LetterGrade variable is set to A, the first HTML statement is displayed, and then the statement ends. The rest of the conditions are ignored after a condition is met.

2. If the first condition is false, the second condition is checked. Here you only have to check whether the Grade is 80 or better. You don't have to specify that it is less than 90 because if it had been 90 or greater, you wouldn't be executing this condition. Right?

3. Likewise for the third and fourth conditions.

4. If you get through all the conditions and you still don't have a match, the Else catches everything else — which, in this case, is bad news.

Developing your nesting instincts

You also can put an If...Then inside of another If...Then. Programmers call this *nesting*. Here's an example:

```
<%@Page Explicit="True" Language="VB" Debug="True" %>
<html>
<body>
<%
Dim Card, Total As Integer
Total = 15 ' Total value of cards so far
Card= 1 ' Your next card
If Card=1 Then ' If it's an ace
    If Total + 11 <= 21 Then ' Will 11 make you bust?
        Total = Total + 11 ' If not count ace as 11
    Else
        Total = Total + 1  ' Else count ace as 1
    End If
End If
%>
<p>The card you drew was <%=Card%></p>
<p>That makes your total <%=Total%></p>
</body>
</html>
```

In the card game 21 (or Blackjack), the goal is to draw enough cards to get as close as you can to 21 without going over (or busting). Face cards count as 10, and aces can count as either 1 or 11 — your choice. You normally count an ace as 11 unless it would make you bust; then, you count it as 1.

In this code, Total holds the value of your hand so far. Card is the next card you are dealt. In this case, you are dealt an ace.

The If...Then evaluates what card you just got and, if it was an ace, checks whether it should be counted as 11 or 1. If you can add 11 to your total without busting, it adds 11. Otherwise, it adds 1.

The If...Then that checks the Card gets executed first. Only if that condition is true does the second If...Then get executed.

Change the starting Total from 15 to 8. Save and click Refresh in your browser.

You also can nest an If...Then inside the Else or ElseIf portion of an If...Then statement:

```
<%@Page Explicit="True" Language="VB" Debug="True" %>
<html>
<body>
<%
Dim Card, Total As Integer
Randomize
```

```
Total = 15 ' Total value of cards so far
Card = Int(Rnd * 13) + 1 ' Your next card
If Card=11 Or Card=12 Or Card=13 Then ' If it's a face card
   Total=Total + 10
ElseIf Card=1 Then ' If it's an ace
   If Total + 11 <= 21 Then
      Total = Total + 11
   Else
      Total = Total + 1
   End If
Else
   Total = Total + Card   ' It's a numbered card (2-10)
End If
%>
<p>The card you drew was <%=Card%></p>
<p>That makes your total <%=Total%></p>
</body>
</html>
```

I've changed this code so that the next card you draw is random. And I've changed the If...Then structure to calculate the updated Total for whatever card you draw. When you try this page out, click Refresh several times and note the result of the different cards on the total.

The first condition checks to see if the card is one of the face cards. If so, the total is increased by 10. However, if this condition fails, an ElseIf clause checks another condition. If the card is not a face card, but it is an ace, the total is checked, as before, to see how the ace should be calculated. Finally, if it is neither a face card nor an ace, then it must be a numbered card, in which case, you can simply add the number to Total.

You can nest If...Then statements inside the Then, ElseIf, or Else portions of other If...Then statements. And they can also have additional If...Then statements nested within them! You can go as deep as you like with this nesting.

TIP

Indenting makes everything clearer

Notice how I indent the lines of code when I use an If...Then statement? I indent all the lines in the Then and Else portions of the examples about three spaces. Then, in the nested If...Then, I indent the Then and Else portions an additional three spaces. VB.NET doesn't require you to indent at all, but doing so makes the code much easier to read. Indenting also makes clear which If goes with which Else and End If.

However, if you have lines of HTML inside the Then or Else portions of your If...Then statement, you may not want to indent them, because in some cases, this may throw off your formatting. You can just leave them as they are.

Get Off My Case!

Like the If...Then statement, the Select Case statement is used for decision-making. Select Case enables you to do various comparisons against one variable that you use throughout the whole statement.

A simple case

Here's a simple Select Case statement that checks an employee's status and displays the result to the user:

```
<%@Page Explicit="True" Language="VB" Debug="True" %>
<html>
<body>
<%
Dim EmployeeStatus as String

EmployeeStatus = "L"

Select Case EmployeeStatus %>
<% Case "G" %>
<p>Employee is employed in good standing.</p>
<% Case "L" %>
<p>Employee is on leave.</p>
<% Case "F" %>
<p>Employee no longer works here.</p>
<% End Select %>
</body>
</html>
```

Here's how this Select Case statement works:

1. Always begin your Select Case statements with the words Select Case. (Easy enough?)

2. After that comes a variable name. Here, the variable is EmployeeStatus. This variable is used throughout the rest of the Select Case statement.

3. Next comes a series of lines that each contain the word Case followed by a value. Select Case automatically compares the first value ("G") to the variable at the beginning of the Select Case statement (EmployeeStatus) to see if they are equal.

4. If the first value is equal to the variable at the beginning, the line after Case "G" and before Case "L" is executed. After that line is finished, the statement is done and any other Case lines are ignored. Anything after the End Select gets processed next.

5. If the first value isn't equal to the variable at the top, the next `Case` statement is checked (`Case "L"`) and that value is compared with the variable at the beginning (again, `EmployeeStatus`). If a match exists, the lines under `Case "L"` are executed. If not, VB.NET proceeds to the next `Case` statement.

It's possible that none of the `Case` statements may match. If that happens, none of the lines within the `Select Case` get executed, and you just go on after the `End Select`. This situation would happen in the preceding statement if the `EmployeeStatus` was something other than "G," "L," or "F."

Notice that you don't need to repeat the variable name or even the equal sign again and again as you would in an `If...Then...ElseIf`. Both are automatically assumed. This strategy makes the `Select Case` much cleaner and easier to understand if you are continually comparing against one variable.

A tougher case

The `Select Case` statement is very flexible. It can do more than simple checks for equality. Like `If...Then` statements, it can do inequalities (with the <, >, <=, >=, and <> operators, which I discuss in the section "Inequalities: a fact of life," earlier in this chapter).

Here's the letter grade calculator I demonstrate in the section "Handling multiple conditions," earlier in this chapter. However, instead of using `If...Then...ElseIf`, I've converted the code to use `Select Case`:

```
<%@Page Explicit="True" Language="VB" Debug="True" %>
<html>
<body>
<%
Dim Grade As Integer
Dim LetterGrade As String
Randomize
Grade = Int(Rnd * 100) + 1 ' Random number between 1 and 100
%>
<p>Your grade is <%=Grade%>.</p>
<% Select Case Grade
Case Is >= 90
    LetterGrade = "A" %>
<p>You got an A! Congratulations.</p>
<% Case Is >= 80
    LetterGrade = "B" %>
<p>You got a B. Good job.</p>
<% Case Is >= 70
    LetterGrade = "C" %>
<p>You got a C. Not bad.</p>
<% Case Is >= 60
    LetterGrade = "D" %>
```

```
<p>You got a D. Try harder next time.</p>
<% Case Else
    LetterGrade = "F" %>
<p>You failed. I'm sorry.</p>
<% End Select %>
</body>
</html>
```

Notice that when comparing to see if something is equal in a Select Case, you only have to put the value on the Case line:

```
Case "G"
```

However, when you check for inequality, you have to use the keyword Is and you have to include the inequality operator you want to use:

```
Case Is >= 90
```

Using the keyword Is here may seem odd, but that's how it works!

You can also do some other fancy comparisons in the Case line. For example, if you were checking a value that could be any integer between 1 and 6, you might have a case line that looks like this:

```
Case 3 To 6
```

This will match if the variable is 3, 4, 5, or 6. If you want to specify several values, use commas:

```
Case 2, 4, 6, 8
```

You can even combine the two techniques:

```
Case 1,3, 4 To 6
```

This would match on 1, 3, 4, 5, or 6.

When Should You Use Select Case Instead of If...Then...ElseIf?

As you may have noticed, you can create an If...Then...ElseIf that works very much like a Select Case statement, and vice versa. So, which one should you use?

In some cases, it doesn't matter. You can use either one. But remember that `If...Then...ElseIf` is more flexible. `Select Case` restricts you to doing comparisons to only *one value* — the one that comes after `Select Case`. In an `If...Then...ElseIf`, you can use compound conditions to compare against two or three values, or as many as you like.

So, if you're doing several comparisons against one variable, using the `Select Case` is probably easier. But if you need to do more complex comparisons, resort to `If...Then...ElseIf`.

Updating Your Site — Automagically!

`If...Then` statements can help you to make your site's content dynamic. You can check conditions and then change the page's appearance on the fly based on the results. In this section, I present a real-world example to show you how it's done.

If you want to attract new people to your Web site and keep them coming back often, you absolutely must keep your site updated on a regular basis.

Have you ever gone to a site that had text like this?

> *Don't forget about our contest — sign in with our Guest Book by December 1st and get a chance to win $100 cash in our Guest Book drawing!*

Great idea. Except that it's December 15th, and they obviously haven't bothered to update their site in several weeks. Why should you waste your time here if they don't even keep it up-to-date?

On the other hand, if you're the person who must keep a site constantly updated, you know it's quite a task, especially with a big site. Why not use ASP.NET to help?

Speed champ: Select Case versus If...Then...ElseIf

In some computer languages, the `Select Case` statement actually runs faster than an `If...Then...ElseIf`. If you have programmed in C or C++, you know that this is true for those languages — and because of that factor, you are encouraged to use `Select Case` whenever possible. In VB.NET, you'll find no significant difference in execution speed between the two statements. So use whichever makes your code easier to understand.

Take a look at this welcome page:

```
<%@Page Explicit="True" Language="VB" Debug="True" %>
<html>
<head><title>Welcome</title></head>
<body>
<h1>Hello and Welcome to My Site</h1>
<p>We're happy you came to visit us.</p>
<h3>Important Information:</h3>
<% If Today < CDate("12/1/2001") Then %>
<p>Don't forget about our contest - sign in with our
Guest Book by December 1st and get a chance to win
$100 cash in our Guest Book drawing!</p>
<% ElseIf Today = CDate("12/1/2001") Then %>
<p>Today's the last day you can sign in with our
Guest Book for a chance to win $100 cash. Don't
put it off a moment longer!</p>
<% Else %>
<p>Our drawing to win $100 cash by signing in with
our Guest Book is officially over. Keep watching!
We'll be announcing the winner soon...</p>
<% End If %>
</body>
</html>
```

As you try out this page, change the dates so they are before, during, and after your current date to see the different outcomes.

Instead of just entering the message and then expecting that I'll have time to come back and update it in the future (yeah, right!), I put an If...Then...ElseIf statement around three different messages: one for before the drawing, one for the exact day of the drawing, and one for after the drawing. That way, the site updates itself, and the content always looks current — even if I forget to do the actual drawing on December 1st!

The only thing new in this page that you probably haven't seen before is the CDate function. It accepts a string as an argument and turns it into a date. You need to perform that step before your code compares the specified date and the date returned from the Today function (which returns today's date) and figures out which one comes later, or if they are the same. (For more information on comparing dates, see Chapter 15.)

This page demonstrates a very useful technique. In fact, you should consider using this technique anywhere on your Web site where time-sensitive information is present.

Figure 4-1 shows the page before the drawing, and Figure 4-2 shows it on the day of the drawing.

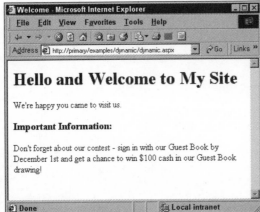

Figure 4-1:
The dynamically updated page before the drawing.

Figure 4-2:
The dynamically updated page on the day of the drawing.

Loop the Loop

Loops enable you to execute the same commands (or HTML) again and again. VB.NET has two types of loops. The For...Next loop counts off a certain number of times and then quits. The Do...Loop uses a condition similar to an If...Then statement to determine whether it should continue looping each time or not.

Counting with For...Next

With the For...Next loop, you can easily execute some commands a set number of times while keeping track of how many times you've gone through the loop. Here's an example similar to the one in Chapter 1 (the only significant difference is the addition of Explicit="True" to the @ Page directive):

```
<%@Page Explicit="True" Language="VB" Debug="True" %>
<html>
<head><title>Hello and Welcome Page</title>
</head>
<body>
<center>
<% Dim TextSize As Integer %>
<% For TextSize = 1 To 7 %>
<font size=<%=TextSize%>>
Hello and Welcome<br>
</font>
<% Next %>
</center>
</body>
</html>
```

This code displays the same line seven times at seven different font sizes. The result looks something like Figure 4-3.

Figure 4-3:
Hello and
Welcome.

The For line marks the beginning of the loop. For also identifies the *index variable* (in this case, TextSize), the number of the first loop (1), and the number of the last loop (7). The index variable holds the number of the current loop.

The line that contains Next marks the end of the loop. Everything between the For line and the Next line is a part of the loop's *body* — that is, the stuff that gets executed again and again.

The first time through the loop, `TextSize` is set to 1. The second time, it's set to 2, and so on, up through 7.

You can use any `Integer` variable as an index variable in a `For...Next` loop. The index variable is simply assigned the loop value each time the `For` line is executed. You can use the index variable as I do in the example. You can even display it in your page, if you like. But remember that *changing* its value is never a good idea. The `For` loop really gets confused when you do that.

Most loops start with 1. But they don't have to. You can create a loop like this:

```
For Items = 10 To 100
```

This loop sets the variable `Items` to 10 the first time through, to 11 the second time through, and so on, up to 100. This loop executes 91 times.

Here's another example:

```
For Counter = 0 To 5
```

Again, the first time through, `Counter` is set to 0, then to 1, and so on, up to 5. This loop executes 6 times.

You can even do this:

```
For Coordinate = -5 To 5
```

The first time through, the loop is set to –5, then to –4, then on up through 0 and ending with 5. This loop executes 11 times (counting 0).

Watch where you Step

By using the keyword `Step` with your `For...Next` loops, you can tell VB.NET what number the `For` loop counts by. Here's an example:

```
For Num = 2 To 10 Step 2
```

In this loop, the first time through, `Num` is assigned 2, then 4, then 6, then 8, and finally 10. Here's another example:

```
For Weeks = 0 To 35 Step 7
```

`Weeks` is assigned 0 the first time, then 7, then 14, 21, 28, and 35.

You can even step backward! Here's an extended version of the "Hello and Welcome" example to demonstrate:

```
<%@Page Explicit="True" Language="VB" Debug="True" %>
<html>
<head><title>Hello and Welcome Page</title>
</head>
<body>
<center>
<% Dim TextSize As Integer %>
<% For TextSize = 1 To 7 %>
<font size=<%=TextSize%>>
Hello and Welcome<br>
</font>
<% Next %>
<% For TextSize = 6 To 1 Step -1 %>
<font size=<%=TextSize%>>
Hello and Welcome<br>
</font>
<% Next %>
</center>
</body>
</html>
```

The result looks something like Figure 4-4.

Figure 4-4:
Hello and
Welcome —
small to big
and back
again.

In this example, I've added another loop after the first one to count down from 6 to 1, counting by –1. It's okay to re-use an index variable in another loop after you're completely done with the first loop.

Nesting loops

Just as you can nest an `If...Then` statement inside another `If...Then` statement, you can nest a loop inside another loop:

```
<%@Page Explicit="True" Language="VB" Debug="True" %>
<html>
<body>
<%
Dim OuterLoop, InnerLoop
For OuterLoop = 1 To 3
    For InnerLoop = 1 To 5
%>
<p>
OuterLoop = <% =OuterLoop %>, InnerLoop = <% =InnerLoop %>
</p>
<%
    Next
Next
%>
</body>
</html>
```

The result in your browser looks like Figure 4-5.

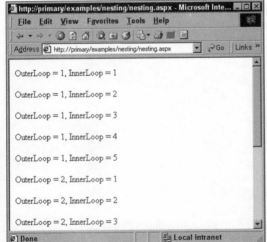

Figure 4-5:
The result of nesting an inner loop within an outer loop.

`OuterLoop` begins at 1, as does `InnerLoop`. The information is displayed and then you run into `Next`. The first `Next` goes with the *inner* loop. That's why I indented it to line up with the inner loop's `For` line. The `Next` causes control to jump back up to the inner loop's `For` line and execute again. The inner loop executes all five times before the outer loop can continue. Then the outer loop is incremented by one and the inner loop executes five more times.

So, when you have a loop within a loop, the innermost loop executes all its times and ends before the outer loop has a chance to loop a second time.

Did you try this example? The HTML for this page looks like this:

```
<html>
<body>
<p>
OuterLoop = 1, InnerLoop = 1
</p>
<p>
OuterLoop = 1, InnerLoop = 2
</p>
<p>
OuterLoop = 1, InnerLoop = 3
</p>
<p>
OuterLoop = 1, InnerLoop = 4
</p>
<p>
OuterLoop = 1, InnerLoop = 5
</p>
<p>
OuterLoop = 2, InnerLoop = 1
</p>
. . .
```

You see no indication of a loop at all in the HTML — that's all done on the server in VB.NET. Only the results get sent to the browser.

Doobee-Doobee-Do...Loop

The VB.NET Do...Loop is a very different kind of looping structure from the For...Next loop. Do...Loop enables you to loop while a condition is true or while a condition is false (until it *becomes* true).

Do While and Do Until

A Do...Loop looks like this:

```
<%@Page Explicit="True" Language="VB" Debug="True" %>
<html>
<body>
<%
Dim Amount As Single
Dim Quarters As Integer
Amount = 3.85
Quarters = 0
Do
    Quarters = Quarters + 1
```

```
     Amount = Amount - .25
Loop While Amount >= .25
%>
<p>You can buy <%=Quarters%> $.25 gumballs</p>
</body>
</html>
```

The result?

```
You can buy 15 $.25 gumballs
```

As you might expect, the loop begins with Do and ends with Loop. Everything in-between is the body of the loop.

You'll notice in this example that Loop is immediately followed by the keyword While. This keyword indicates that a condition will follow and that the loop will continue executing as long as the condition remains *true*. When the condition is tested and is false, the loop stops repeating.

You can change the Do line to use Until, instead:

```
Loop Until Amount < .25
```

Until is the logical opposite of While. If you use Until, the loop continues as long as the condition remains *false*. When the condition is tested and is true, the loop stops repeating.

So, to change this program to use Until, I have to change the condition so that the program still works the same way.

Top-tested loops

The gumball counting program has just one problem.

Set Amount to .17. Now try running the program again:

```
You can buy 1 $.25 gumballs
```

Hmm. It still says you have enough to buy one gumball. And that's not true. You don't have $.25, so the result should be 0. Why did this happen?

Well, when While or Until appears on the Loop line at the bottom of the loop, you can always be sure that the body of the loop will be executed once. That's because the condition after the While or Until isn't checked until you get to the Loop line — after you've gone through all the lines in the body. This is called a *bottom-tested loop*.

In this case, it counts off one quarter and subtracts the .25 from Amount. Of course, Amount has a negative number at that point, but the quarter has already been added in.

To fix this, you can switch to a *top-tested loop*. It's easy. Just move the `While` or `Until` and the condition to the top of the loop, after the `Do` keyword:

```
<%@Page Explicit="True" Language="VB" Debug="True" %>
<html>
<body>
<%
Dim Amount As Single
Dim Quarters As Integer
Amount = .17
Quarters = 0
Do Until Amount < .25
    Quarters = Quarters + 1
    Amount = Amount - .25
Loop
%>
<p>You can buy <%=Quarters%> $.25 gumballs</p>
</body>
</html>
```

This time, the condition is checked first thing, before the body of the loop ever executes. This loop is to execute until `Amount` is less than .25. In other words, after the value goes below .25, the loop should stop. And because `Amount` starts out at .17, the loop stops before it ever starts and none of the lines in the loop get executed. You simply jump over the entire loop and begin with whatever follows `Loop`:

```
You can buy 0 $.25 gumballs
```

So, is a top-tested loop always better than a bottom tested loop? Not necessarily. The best method depends on what you're doing and how you want to set it up. In some cases, you want the loop to execute at least once. Use whatever works best for your situation.

Exit, stage left

You may discover, right in the middle of a loop, that you want to get out of the loop entirely — no matter what else is happening. VB.NET makes this possible with the `Exit` command:

```
For Count = 1 To 100
    . . .
    If Temp > Threshold Then
        Exit For
    End If
    . . .
Next
```

Usually, you find `Exit For` within an `If...Then` statement that checks for some special case why the loop needs to end. You can use `Exit Do` in exactly the same way to exit a `Do...Loop`.

If you're inside a nested loop, an `Exit` only pops you out of the inner loop. It won't pop you out of the outer loop, too.

Arrays: Information Juggling Revisited

In this section, I leave the topic of loops and conditions for a moment and revisit the topic of creating and using variables. (For more information about creating and using variables, see Chapter 3.)

Creating and using arrays

An *array* is a way of declaring a whole group of variables at once. An array declaration looks like this:

```
Dim Friends(10) As String
```

This single line creates 10 different variables. Each of these 10 variables, or *elements* as they're sometimes called, has the same name: `Friends`. You refer to each variable individually by using its number. For example, you can assign a value to `Friends`, element number 3, by using this syntax:

```
Friends(3) = "Brad Jones"
```

But why would you want to do this at all? Why not create 10 different variables the normal way?

```
Dim Friends1, Friends2, Friends3, Friends4 As String
Dim Friends5, Friends6, Friends7, Friends8 As String
Dim Friends9, Friends10 As String
```

Well, being able to refer to variables by number has a couple of advantages. One advantage is that you can search through them one-by-one, using a loop:

```
<html>
<body>
<%
Dim Friends(10) As String
Dim CurrentFriend As Integer
Dim Found As Boolean

Friends(1) = "Curtis Dicken"
Friends(2) = "Dee Townsend"
```

```
Friends(3) = "Brad Jones"
Friends(4) = "Wayne Smith"
Friends(5) = "TaKiesha Fuller"
Friends(6) = "Mike Lafavers"
Friends(7) = "Farion Grove"
Friends(8) = "Troy Felton"
Friends(9) = "Steve Barron"
Friends(10) = "Marc Nelson"

Found = False
For CurrentFriend = 1 To 10
    If Friends(CurrentFriend) = "Mike Lafavers" Then
        Found = True
        Exit For
    End If
Next
If Found = True Then
%>
<p>I found Mike Lafavers!</p>
<% Else %>
<p>I didn't find Mike Lafavers.</p>
<% End If %>
</body>
</html>
```

This code creates a couple of variables. Then, the values for all ten array elements are set. A little later on in the page, you search through the entire array using a `For...Next` loop to find the element that matches a particular name. The first time through the loop, `CurrentFriend` is 1 and so when you refer to `Friends(CurrentFriend)`, you're looking at the first element of the array. The next time through the loop, you're looking at the second element, and so on.

In fact, using a `For...Next` loop with an array is so common that VB.NET has a special version of the `For...Next` loop designed for arrays: the `For Each...Next` loop.

Starting at zero

Actually, when you create an array, VB.NET starts counting at 0 rather than at one:

```
Dim Friends(10) As String
```

This line creates an array of 11 elements — numbered 0 through 10. In this example, I ignore that 0th element. You can do that, but you should be aware of the fact that number 0 is there.

Using For Each...Next with arrays

The For Each...Next statement works just like a For...Next loop, except for one thing. Instead of specifying the numbers, you simply specify the array's name, and it knows to go through all the elements — no matter how many there are.

Try changing the example in the previous section to use a For Each...Next loop by modifying the lines to look like this:

```
Dim CurrentFriend As String
. . .
For Each CurrentFriend In Friends
    If CurrentFriend = "Mike Lafavers" Then
        Found = True
        Exit For
    End If
Next
. . .
```

Three things change:

- ✔ The CurrentFriend variable is declared as a string instead of an integer. I explain why in the next bullet.

- ✔ The For line changes to For Each. This works a little differently from a normal For...Next loop. For Each assumes that you're going to work your way through an array. So you don't need to tell For Each where to start and end. You just need to give it the array to work with (after the In keyword) and a variable to assign the value of the current element in the array. Notice that CurrentFriend won't hold the *number* of the loop this time. Instead, it holds the *value* of the current array element (like "Curtis Dicken" or "Dee Townsend").

- ✔ Because CurrentFriend actually contains the value of the current array element, the If statement inside the loop simply checks CurrentFriend to see if it equals what we're looking for.

For Each is handy to use and is safer than For...Next in the long run. If, in the future, the number of elements in Friends changes, you won't have to change this loop. For Each automatically goes through all of them, no matter how many there are.

For Each goes through all the elements in the array, and arrays actually start at 0, so the loop in the preceding code actually checks the 0th element first. That string doesn't have anything in it, so the loop never matches on it. So, it doesn't affect the way this example works. But it may affect your code when you use For...Each if you're not aware of the fact that the 0th element is there.

Chapter 5

Divide and Conquer: Structured Programming

*A*fter you get the hang of it, writing small programs is easy. But big programs get complex fast! Even the most experienced programmers get confused. So, lots of time and effort have been spent trying to find ways to simplify and organize the way people write programs. Most solutions to this problem involve different ways of breaking big programs down into a bunch of smaller programs and then organizing those smaller programs in a way that makes sense.

The first major effort to apply these principles to software development was called *structured programming*. The ideas of structured programming have left their mark in all major programming languages today and in the minds of everyone who creates software — either for Windows or the Web.

Structured programming breaks down programs into smaller pieces. That makes each piece easier to understand. It has another benefit, too. If you write a program that breaks down into lots of pieces, when I write my program, I may be able to use some of the pieces you've already written! That's called *code reuse* and it's one of the more important ways of reducing software development time and increasing the quality of the final application.

In this chapter, you see how structured programming affects VB.NET and how you can apply its principles to your pages. This is important not only to help organize your own pages, but also in helping you understand how the .NET Framework is organized and how you make use of it.

Wrestling with Monolithic Applications

To best understand how programming works today, it's helpful to know what programming was like in the beginning.

When people wrote computer programs for some of the earlier computers (way back in the '60s and '70s), those machines didn't have much memory, so most of the programs were pretty small. The programmers just wrote one command after another in the order they wanted those commands completed. And that worked pretty well, for a while.

But as computers grew in complexity and gained more memory, the programs began to get longer and longer. Simply stringing together a bunch of commands in a long list grew cumbersome. The code was difficult to follow, and one programmer might take weeks or months to become familiar with a program that someone else had written.

Something had to be done.

Simplifying Your Life: Structured Programming and Functions

How do you make a complicated list of commands easier to understand? By applying one of the simpler and more effective problem-solving tools:

If you have a big problem, break it down into a bunch of little problems and solve each of them.

This was the core idea of structured programming. Its practical result was the introduction of a new concept in programming languages — the *function*. In previous chapters, you can see and play with various functions — Rnd, Len, Today, and so on. Those functions are built into the VB.NET language. But you can create your own functions, too.

A function is simply a group of commands that has a name. Whenever the program needs to have those lines executed, it can simply call that function by name, and the commands are performed. When the function completes its work, the computer returns back to its original location within the main program.

With this simple tool, programmers can slice up a program into many different pieces, give each piece a name that makes sense, and then just call each piece as needed. This technique greatly simplifies large computer programs and it's a great way to write any program.

Giving Your Functions a Place to Live: The Script Tag

ASP.NET offers a special place for you to put your functions: inside of an HTML <script> tag. This snippet shows how you use the <script> tag:

```
<%@Page Explicit="True" Language="VB" Debug="True" %>
<html>
<script runat="server">
' My functions here
. . .
</script>
<body>
. . .
</body>
</html>
```

The <script> tag must appear before the <body> tag in your page. It has an attribute called runat, which you set to the value "server". This attribute indicates that this tag contains ASP.NET code that runs on the server (as opposed to JavaScript code that runs in the browser).

Only ASP.NET code is allowed inside the <script> tag. Because you can't put HTML tags in there, you don't need to use the <% and %> delimiters. In fact, you'll get an error if you try to.

Also, the <script> tag is specifically designed for you to write your own functions. Inside the tag, don't write code that isn't part of a function.

Finicky function placement

In Classic ASP, little difference exists between using the <script> tag to hold ASP code and simply using the <% and %> delimiters. In ASP.NET, a definite distinction exists. The <script> tag must precede the body of the page, and if you have any functions, subroutines, or class definitions, they *must* appear inside the <script> tag. However, no other code (besides variable declarations) may appear inside the <script> tag.

Creating Functions

In Chapter 3, I show you a formula that you can use to generate random numbers between 1 and any number you like. For example, this line generates a number between 1 and 6:

```
RandNum = Int(Rnd * 6) + 1
```

That's handy if you want to simulate rolling a die. But wouldn't it be nice if you had a `RollDie` function that simply returned the random number so you didn't have to remember and write out that formula every time? VB.NET doesn't have a built-in `RollDie` function, but you can make your own!

```
<%@Page Explicit="True" Language="VB" Debug="True" %>
```

```
<html>
<script runat="server">

Function RollDie As Integer
    Dim Roll As Integer
    Randomize
    Roll = Int(Rnd * 6) + 1
    Return(Roll)
End Function

</script>

<body>
<p>I'll roll two dice; let's see what
we get!</p>
<%
Dim FirstRoll, SecondRoll As Integer
FirstRoll = RollDie
SecondRoll = RollDie
%>
First roll: <%=FirstRoll%><br>
Second roll: <%=SecondRoll%><br>
</body>
</html>
```

I put the `<script>` tag at the top of the page, before the `<body>` tag. Inside the `<script>` tag, you see a line that begins `Function` and one a little later that says `End Function`. All the code between those lines is referred to as the *body* of the function. These commands are executed when the function is called. (In this listing, I indent these lines to show clearly that they are the body of the function. Although not required, this indentation makes the code more readable.)

After the keyword `Function`, the first line has the name you want to give your function — in this case, `RollDie`. Like variables, you can give functions any name you like. But, also like variables, the name you give each function should somehow indicate what that function does.

The name of the function is followed by `As Integer`. It's almost as if you were declaring a variable! But you're not. Instead, you are specifying what kind of value this function will return. I describe how functions return values in the next section.

Because the commands in the function appear first in the page, you may think they're executed right away. But that's not so! A function's body is not executed until the function is specifically called.

Calling Functions

How do you call a function? The same way you call your dog! Just say its name:

```
. . .
<body>
<p>I'll roll two dice; let's see what
we get!</p>
<%
Dim FirstRoll, SecondRoll As Integer
FirstRoll = RollDie
SecondRoll = RollDie
%>
First roll: <%=FirstRoll%>
Second roll: <%=SecondRoll%>
</body>
</html>
```

This code creates two integer variables: `FirstRoll` and `SecondRoll`. Then, the function is called by invoking its name: `RollDie`. The function's body is executed:

```
Function RollDie As Integer
    Dim Roll As Integer
    Randomize
    Roll = Int(Rnd * 6) + 1
    Return(Roll)
End Function
```

The function creates a variable called `Roll` and assigns it the value from the random number formula. Now `Roll` has a value between 1 and 6.

The last line of the function body indicates what value the function will return. In this case, the function returns the number that's in the `Roll` variable. The value returned must match the type at the end of the `Function` line — in this case, `As Integer`.

After the function is done, you go back to the place where the function was called. The value returned from the `RollDie` function is assigned to the variable `FirstRoll`:

```
FirstRoll = RollDie
```

To clarify, the preceding line does two things:

✔ It calls the `RollDie` function you just created in the `<script>` section at the top of the page. All the lines in the body of the function are executed.

✔ After the function is called, the value returned effectively replaces the name of the function in the code. So in this case, the function generates a random number between 1 and 6, and that number comes back and gets assigned to the `FirstRoll` variable.

The `RollDie` function is called again on the next line to put another random number in the `SecondRoll` variable:

```
SecondRoll = RollDie
```

Finally, both values are displayed in the page:

```
First roll: <%=FirstRoll%>
Second roll: <%=SecondRoll%>
```

As you try this example, click the Refresh button several times. You get a different roll each time. Figure 5-1 shows the results.

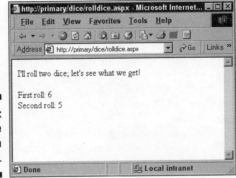

Figure 5-1:
Rolling the dice with a function.

You can create as many functions as you like. Each can contain any number of commands, and you can call these functions from anywhere in your program as many times as you like. You can even call functions from within other functions.

Opening Arguments

In some cases, you need to give a function some information so that it can do its job. You pass information to a function using *arguments*.

To demonstrate this concept, I'll go back to the drawing board for generating random numbers. The example in the preceding section uses a RollDie function. You could create a FlipCoin function and a DrawCard function, each returning random numbers within different ranges. Or you could create a more generalized random number function:

```
<%@Page Explicit="True" Language="VB" Debug="True" %>
<html>
<script runat="server">

Function RandNum(Limit As Integer) As Integer
    Dim Num As Integer
    Randomize
    Num = Int(Rnd * Limit) + 1
    Return(Num)
End Function

</script>
<body>
<h1>Random Numbers</h1>
<p>And now, the multi-talented RandNum function!</p>
A Die Roll: <%=RandNum(6)%><br>
A Card Draw: <%=RandNum(13)%><br>
A Coin Flip: <%=RandNum(2)%><br>
</body>
</html>
```

Again, the Function and End Function lines surround the indented body of the function. The name of the function is RandNum. But this time, parentheses follow the function name and something that looks like a variable declaration (without the Dim) appears inside. What's going on there?

When you call this RandNum function, you'll use the integer variable Limit to refer to the information that you pass into this function as an argument.

The As Integer that *follows* the parentheses looks a little out of place now, but it's the same As Integer that appears immediately after a function name when there are no parentheses (like the RollDie function created in the previous section). Again, it indicates that this function will return an integer value.

All the rest of the function looks the same as the previous example except for one thing. I use Limit in the random number formula to indicate the highest random number generated. So, if the user passes in a 5, the function generates a random number between 1 and 5. If the user passes in 500, the function returns a random number between 1 and 500.

However, the body of the function isn't executed until the function is called. That happens in the body of the page. In this example, I don't bother with creating variables, calling the function, assigning the returned value to the variable, and then displaying the variable, as I do in the previous example. Instead, I just call the function and immediately display whatever it sends back:

```
. . .
A Die Roll: <%=RandNum(6)%><br>
A Card Draw: <%=RandNum(13)%><br>
A Coin Flip: <%=RandNum(2)%><br>
. . .
```

You can see the result in Figure 5-2. Click Refresh in your browser several times to make sure that each number returned by the function falls within the appropriate range.

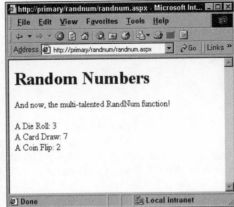

Figure 5-2:
RandNum
does it all!

Functions in All Shapes and Sizes

You can create as many functions as you like inside the `<script>` tag at the beginning of your page:

```
<%@Page Explicit="True" Language="VB" Debug="True" %>
<html>
<script runat="server">
Function RollDie As Integer
   . . .
End Function

Function FlipCoin As Integer
   . . .
End Function

Function RandNum(Limit As Integer) As Integer
   . . .
End Function
</script>
<body>
   . . .
</body>
</html>
```

If a function has an argument, you simply put a variable declaration (minus the `Dim`) inside parentheses on the `Function` line, after the name, as in the `RandNum` function that I describe in the preceding section. Don't forget the `As` keyword after the parentheses to indicate the type of value the function returns!

If a function has more than one argument, just put each declaration inside the parentheses, separated by commas:

```
Function AddNums(A As Integer, B As Integer) As Integer
   Return(A + B)
End Function
```

Then, when you *call* the function, you include the arguments in parentheses — either values or variables that hold values:

```
Sum = AddNums(MyNum, 5)
```

The values passed should be of the same type as the arguments you specified when you created the function. For example, `AddNums` expects you to pass two integers. If you pass numbers with a decimal value, they get rounded to integers and then added.

For arguments, you can send any type of data you want. And you can also return any type. Here's a function that accepts a string and an integer and returns a string:

```
Function Greet(Name As String, Age As Integer) As String
    Return("Hi, I'm " & Name & " and I am " & Age & "!")
End Function
```

Creating and Using Subroutines

In addition to functions, VB.NET supports another feature for chopping up your code: subroutines. But don't worry; subroutines aren't complicated.

In fact, they are identical to functions except for one thing: A subroutine doesn't return a value.

You specify a subroutine using the Sub and End Sub keywords:

```
Sub DisplayIngredient (Amount As Single, Units As String)
. . .
End Sub
```

You specify your arguments inside parentheses after the subroutine's name, just as you do with a function.

Unlike a function, a subroutine has no As clause after the parentheses on the first line because no return value exists. That also means, of course, that you won't see Return in the body of the subroutine.

When you call the subroutine, you simply use the name of the subroutine and include the arguments you want to pass inside parentheses, just as you do for a function:

```
DisplayIngredient(3,"cups")
```

To use parentheses, or not to use parentheses . . .

In Classic ASP, with VBScript, a confusing difference exists in the syntax you use for calling functions as opposed to subroutines. If you called a function, you always put parentheses around your arguments:

```
x = GetValue(a,b)
```

But when you called a subroutine, you did not use parentheses:

```
ShowValue a,b
```

Fortunately, ASP.NET fixes all that confusion. You use parentheses in all calls.

If you want to send back a value, use a function. If you just want to do some work and don't need any information returned, you can use a subroutine.

Making a Quick Exit

Sometimes, you're in the middle of a function or subroutine and you realize that you need to get out — now. VB.NET makes that possible with Exit Function and Exit Sub:

```
Function CalculateValue(Age As Integer)
If Age < 1 Then
    Exit Function
End If
. . .
```

This function accepts an argument — a person's age. First, the function checks to see if the age is less than 1. If it is, Exit Function is called. This causes the function to end right away and return to the code that called the function. The Exit Sub command works exactly the same way for subroutines.

Oh! The Places Your Variables Will Go . . .

You need to know one more thing about functions and subroutines: *Where* you create your variables can make a big difference in how you can use them.

Three places to create variables

The best way to illustrate this difference is with an example. This example creates variables in the three different places where they can be created and then uses the variables wherever they can be used. It does not, however, produce any output in your browser. (However, if you try to use a variable somewhere you shouldn't, you will see an *error* message in the browser!)

```
<%@Page Explicit="True" Language="VB" Debug="True" %>
<html>
<head></head>
<script runat="server">
Dim GlobalVar As Integer = 1
```

```
Sub SomeSubroutine
    Dim LocalVar As Integer = 1

    LocalVar = 99
    GlobalVar = 99
End Sub

</script>
<body>
<%
Dim BodyVar As Integer = 1

SomeSubroutine

BodyVar = 55
GlobalVar = 55
%>
</body>
</html>
```

Three places exist where you can put a Dim statement to create variables. This placement has an impact on a variable's *scope* — that is, where you can use the variables.

The preceding listing includes three Dim statements in the three different possible locations:

- ✔ BodyVar is created in a Dim statement in the body of the HTML page — that's where you're used to seeing Dim statements.

- ✔ LocalVar is created in a subroutine. Previous examples in this chapter show you variables created in functions and subroutines.

- ✔ GlobalVar is created *inside* the <script> tag at the top of the page (where the functions and subroutines go), but *outside* any individual function or subroutine. This may be the first time you've seen a Dim statement here.

Two places you can use variables

A page has two places where you can write code and use a variable: in the body of the page and in a function or subroutine.

In the *body* of a page, you can use

- ✔ **Body variables:** Variables that were created in the body of the page. In the previous example, BodyVar is a body variable.

- ✔ **Global variables:** Those created inside the <script> tag but outside of any function or subroutine. In the previous example, GlobalVar is a global variable.

You *cannot* use variables that were created inside of a function or subroutine (like `LocalVar` in the previous example), even after you call the function or subroutine. Local variables are just that — local. In other words, you can only use them in the function or subroutine where they are created.

That leads me to the next place where you can write code and use variables. Inside *functions* or *subroutines,* you can use

- ✔ **Local variables:** Those declared inside the function or subroutine where you're writing code.
- ✔ **Global variables:** Again, those created inside the `<script>` tag but outside any function or subroutine.

You *cannot* use variables that were declared in the body of the page. So, in the previous example, inside `SomeSubroutine`, you can change the value of `LocalVar` and `GlobalVar`, but not `BodyVar`.

Finally, if you have two subroutines, you can't use the local variables from one subroutine in the other subroutine. You can only use local variables in the function or subroutine where they were created. Further, a local variable only lives as long as the subroutine or function is being executed. After the subroutine or function is done, the variable goes away. If you call that same subroutine or function again, the variable is created anew and doesn't have the same value it did when the subroutine or function was called last.

What does it all mean?

So where should you put your `Dim` statements? You may be tempted to say in the `<script>` tag — after all, global variables can be accessed anywhere!

However, that's a bad idea. For simple pages, it doesn't make much difference, but when you start creating more complex pages, you end up with lots of variables floating around. And if they're all global, you could accidentally change the value of a variable in one part of your page and have it affect something totally different somewhere else. This can be a big debugging headache.

More complicated scope

In Classic ASP, you declare variables either inside a function or subroutine, in which case they're local, or outside any function or subroutine, in which case they're global to the entire page. As you can see, scope is a bit more complicated in ASP.NET.

So, here's the best guideline to use: Create your variables where you're going to use them. If you use a variable in the body of your page, declare it there. If you're only going to use it in a function or subroutine, declare it there.

If you really, really need to access a variable everywhere, you can consider a global variable. But before you do, ask yourself, "Do I have another option?"

For example, you can always pass information to your functions and subroutines using arguments. And functions can send information back. That should be your usual way of sharing information.

But if you find yourself passing the same variable in and out of several different functions, it may be a good candidate to become a global variable. I'm not saying that you shouldn't use globals, I'm just saying, "Don't make them your first choice!"

Part III

Classy Objects and Methodical Properties

The 5th Wave®   By Rich Tennant

THE GREAT THING ABOUT OBJECT-ORIENTED PROGRAMMING IS, IT'S MADE APPLICATION DEVELOPMENT AS EASY AS PUTTING ONE FOOT IN FRONT OF THE OTHER.

In this part . . .

Visual Basic .NET can make your pages smart. But to make your pages cool, you need objects. Objects are a way of organizing code so that it's more intuitive and easier to understand. And although you may have heard of object-oriented programming (OOP), you probably never had any idea that it's all about making things simpler, not more complex! It's true, and I'll show you how in this part.

And after you know what objects are, you can put them to use! You'll uncover a variety of objects that ASP.NET makes available to enable you to communicate with both the Web server and the user's browser.

Chapter 6

OOPs — No Mistake Here!

*A*s I explain in Chapter 5, structured programming helps developers make their code much more readable and maintainable. But, as you might expect, programmers continue to write longer and more complex programs.

To handle this complexity, many programmers have turned to a new way of organizing their code: object-oriented programming (OOP). However, OOP doesn't replace structured programming. Instead, this new technique was built on top of structured programming.

What is OOP? Well, if you ask most programmers, they usually start waving their arms and throwing around even bigger buzzwords like *encapsulation* and *polymorphism*. (Say that three times fast!) It's just one of those topics that some people like to make more complex than it really is.

In reality, the fundamental concepts of OOP are simple! That's the very reason why it works so well. And because it works so well, Microsoft has made OOP the very foundation on which ASP.NET and the whole .NET Framework are built.

This chapter helps you understand OOP's basic concepts. The next chapter provides many examples of how you can use those concepts to do very cool stuff in your ASP.NET pages.

A Real-World Example: My Car

Objects are everywhere! Your chair is an object, your computer is an object, and even your mother-in-law is an object. An object is just a thing that you give a name. Most objects have characteristics or properties that describe them, and most objects can do things and even interact with other objects. You deal with these kinds of real-world objects every day.

To help you understand software objects, indulge me for a moment while I provide a more detailed, real-world object example.

There's a car in my driveway. It's exactly the kind of car you'd expect a famous, big-shot computer-book author would drive, too: a Toyota Camry.

Now that car didn't appear out of nowhere. Far from it! A few years ago, several men and women in long white lab coats stood around a table. On that table lay the plans for what would, one day, be my car.

If I'd shown up that day, sat on the table, and tried to drive those plans out of the room, they would've called security and had me hauled out with no questions asked. You can't drive these plans. They're just a detailed description of what the car will be. They aren't the car itself.

In order to turn that plan into a real car, you have to go through a process. In this case, the process is called manufacturing.

Now that my car has been manufactured, I can appreciate many things about it, such as its fetching burgundy color, its fake leather interior, and its roomy trunk. Table 6-1 lists these *properties* of the car.

Table 6-1	Properties of My Car
Property	*Value*
Color	Burgundy
Interior	Fake Leather
Trunk	Roomy

The other thing you'll notice about my car is that it can *do* certain things, if you ask it to. For example, if you ask it to Go, by pressing the gas pedal, it will, in fact, move forward. If you ask it to Stop, by pressing the brake pedal, it will stop.

Oh, Great Master, What's the Meaning of This Parable?

All right, enough speaking in riddles. What's this all about? Well, this real-world object example actually goes a long way toward explaining the key concepts of software objects used in OOP.

First, the plans used to create the car are referred to in OOP terms as a *class*. A class is a detailed description. A description of what? A description of an object! The car itself is an object. Just as the plans are a detailed description of a car, so a class is a detailed description of an object. But what does a class describe? What's inside of an object?

An object contains two things:

- ✔ **Properties** hold information about the object. Think of them as a description of different aspects of the object. Color, Interior, and Trunk are the names of three properties of the Car object. The values those properties hold are Burgundy, Fake Leather, and Roomy, respectively.

- ✔ **Methods** are actions that the object can do. Go and Stop are the two methods of the car that I mentioned. (You might be thinking, "Perhaps I'm missing something, but *method* seems like a really strange term to use for that." You aren't missing anything. It is a strange term.)

Programming Objects

So far so good, but how does all this apply to programming and organizing your code? Well, you already know what a variable is. And you know what a function is. So, imagine taking a bunch of variables, functions, and subroutines that all work together and putting them in a big bag, as shown in Figure 6-1.

That bag is an object. The variables in the bag are properties, and the functions and subroutines in the bag are methods. There's nothing special about a property or a method. They're just variables, functions, and subroutines that are *associated with* a particular object.

By packaging up the data and code in your application, you create a new way of dividing up your application. You still use functions, but you then put them together with other functions, and the variables they use, and create a higher-level division: an object.

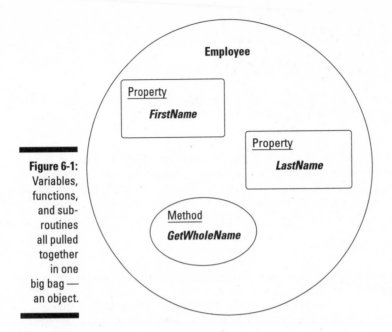

Figure 6-1:
Variables,
functions,
and sub-
routines
all pulled
together
in one
big bag —
an object.

Creating a Class

The following page demonstrates how to create a class, how to use a class to make an object, and how to work with the properties and methods of an object:

```
<%@Page Explicit="True" Language="VB" Debug="True" %>

<html>
<head></head>
<script runat="server">

Class Employee
    Public FirstName, LastName As String

    Function GetWholeName As String
        Dim Whole As String
        Whole = FirstName & " " & LastName
        Return(Whole)
    End Function
End Class
```

```
</script>
<body>
<%
Dim Emp1 As Employee
Emp1 = New Employee
Emp1.FirstName = "Bob"
Emp1.LastName = "Smith"
%>
Whole Name: <%=Emp1.GetWholeName%><br>
</body>
</html>
```

And here's the result.

```
Whole Name: Bob Smith
```

Objects are a great way to help you organize your functions and variables. So, how do you create an object? Well, the first step to creating a car is to draw up the plans for it. So, the first step to creating an object is to create a class that describes it.

Like functions, you put classes in the <script> tag at the top of the page. The words Class and End Class surround the class's body. Following the word Class, you see the class's name: Employee.

In the body of the class, this example declares two string variables: FirstName and LastName. Instead of Dim, this declaration uses the keyword Public.

Public indicates that you can use variables outside the class (as I show you in a moment).

In addition to the variables, the class contains a function named GetWholeName. This function doesn't accept any arguments, but it does return a string. Basically, it just sticks the first and last names together with a space in the middle and returns that.

Using the Class to Make an Object

Like a function, a class doesn't actually do anything until you use it in the body of your page. So, that's the next step:

```
<body>
<%
Dim Emp1 As Employee
Emp1 = New Employee
```

This code creates a new variable: Emp1. It isn't an Integer or a String. It's an Employee. What's that? That's the class you just created. So, Emp1 is a variable that's designed to hold an Employee-type thing.

So, the next step is to put an Employee-type thing in it! But how do you create an Employee object? You use the New keyword.

The last line of the preceding code assigns a value to Emp1. The value is New Employee. New is a special keyword that takes a class and makes an object out of it. In this case, it takes the Employee class and creates an Employee object and then puts that object in the Emp1 variable. From that point on, the page can refer to the new object by the name Emp1.

You can even combine these two lines into one:

```
Dim Emp1 As Employee = New Employee
```

Using the Properties and Methods in an Object

After you create an object, you can work with its properties and methods:

```
Emp1.FirstName = "Bob"
Emp1.LastName = "Smith"
%>

Whole Name: <%=Emp1.GetWholeName%>
</body>
</html>
```

The variables inside Emp1 are FirstName and LastName. You know that because you created Emp1 from an Employee class, and all Employee class objects have those variables in them.

The syntax you use to access properties and methods is called *dot notation*. Because the variables are inside an object, you must use the object's name first, then a dot (period), and then the name of the variable — for example, Emp1.FirstName.

The same goes for calling a function that's inside an object. In this case, Emp1 is the object name, followed by the dot, and then the function GetWholeName. This calls the function and returns the whole name, which appears in the browser.

VBScript's got class, too!

Are classes new to ASP.NET? Nope. But if you don't have IIS 5.0, then it's a good bet you've never used them in your ASP pages before. The `Class` keyword and the ability to create and use your own classes was added to VBScript 5.0, which is included with the version of ASP that comes with IIS 5.0. Of course, now you have to pay attention to data types and other such details, but otherwise it doesn't differ much from Classic ASP.

Creating Multiple Instances

You may wonder why you have to create a class separately and then create an object from that class before you use the object. Why the extra step? There's a good reason: You may want more than one `Employee`-type object.

Replace the body of the previous page (everything between and including the `body` tags), with this code:

TRY THIS

```
<body>
<%
Dim Emp1, Emp2 As Employee
Emp1 = New Employee
Emp2 = New Employee
Emp1.FirstName = "Bob"
Emp1.LastName = "Smith"
Emp2.FirstName = "Abbey"
Emp2.LastName = "Hatfield"
%>
Emp1 Name: <%=Emp1.GetWholeName%><br>
Emp2 Name: <%=Emp2.GetWholeName%><br>
</body>
```

The new page looks like this:

```
Emp1 Name: Bob Smith
Emp2 Name: Abbey Hatfield
```

What's the difference? This version of the code creates two `Employee`-type objects. One is stored in `Emp1` and the other in `Emp2`. They are assigned different names and then the names are presented to the user.

When you create multiple copies, or *instances,* of a class, each has its own set of properties. That is, Emp1 and Emp2 both have their own FirstName and LastName properties, and Emp1.FirstName can hold a different value from Emp2.FirstName. And the methods of Emp1 (like GetWholeName) work with the properties of Emp1.

Jargon Watch

OOP is full of jargon. I try to avoid jargon when I can, but you just have to put up with some of it because that's how programmers talk. Here are some OOP-related words and phrases that you'll encounter in other books and magazines.

The Emp1 and Emp2 variables that hold objects are called *reference variables.* That's because each one holds a reference to the object. This jargon differentiates them from normal variables that just hold numbers and strings.

The term *instantiation* refers to the process of creating a new object using the New keyword. This fancy term simply means *making an instance of* — that is, you make an instance of the class. In the code from the preceding section, you actually make two instances of the same class. The words *instance* and *object* are more-or-less interchangeable here.

Finally, the word *members* is commonly used to refer collectively to all the stuff in a particular object — all its properties and methods.

Get Out! This is Private Property

To help you get a clearer understanding of classes, objects, properties, and methods, here's another example.

Suppose you want to create an object that works like a simple counter. It starts at 0. You can add one to it (increment) or you can subtract one from it (decrement). You can also check its current value. How would you create a class to implement that object?

```
<%@Page Explicit="True" Language="VB" Debug="True" %>
<html>
<head></head>
<script runat="server">

Class Counter
    Private CounterValue As Integer = 0
```

```
    Sub Increment
        CounterValue = CounterValue + 1
    End Sub

    Sub Decrement
        CounterValue = CounterValue - 1
    End Sub

    Function GetValue As Integer
        Return(CounterValue)
    End Function
End Class

</script>
<body>
<%
Dim Count1 As Counter
Count1 = New Counter
%>
Count1 = <%=Count1.GetValue%><br>
<%
Count1.Increment
Count1.Increment
Count1.Increment
Count1.Decrement
%>
Count1 = <%=Count1.GetValue%><br>
</body>
</html>
```

This class is different from the example in the previous sections of this chapter. It has only one property: CounterValue. And instead of Public, I use the keyword Private in place of Dim.

In the previous example, I mention that Public enables you to use the variable outside the object. Private means just the opposite. Only functions and subroutines inside the class can access properties that you declare as Private. But what good is a variable if you can't get to it?

Well, in this case, you want to create a simple counter. You don't want people to simply assign any value they want to it. It should start at 0 and then it can be incremented and decremented. The code provides two subroutines to do those tasks. You can call those subroutines from outside the object, and those subroutines can, in turn, change the private variable. So, there is a way to work with the value held by the private variable. But by providing access only through these functions, you specifically limit how the outside world works with the private variables.

But a counter isn't much good if you can't tell what number it's on right now, so the function `GetValue` returns the value of the private variable.

The body of the page creates the object and puts it in the `Count1` variable. The code then uses `GetValue` to show that the counter starts at zero. Then, `Increment` is called three times and `Decrement` one time, so the final value displayed is 2:

```
Count1 = 0
Count1 = 2
```

Now try adding this line anywhere in the body of your page:

```
<% count1.CounterValue = 5 %>
```

When you try to access the private variable directly, you get an error that looks something like this:

```
Compiler Error Message: BC30390:
'ASP.classes_aspx.Counter.CounterValue' is Private, and is
not accessible in this context.
```

You can include both public and private variables in the same class. Public variables make it easy for those that use your class to set the value directly, if that's what you want. But if you want more control over the way the value is changed, use a private variable and then simply create functions that do the updating and retrieving of the value. For example, you could easily limit this counter so that it can never exceed 100. Simply change the `Increment` subroutine to look like this:

```
Sub Increment
    If CounterValue < 100 Then
        CounterValue = CounterValue + 1
    End If
End Sub
```

Because those who use this class can only change the value through the `Increment` and `Decrement` methods, you know that this small change in the code will do the trick!

OOP folks have a word for the concept of creating private variables and then accessing and manipulating their values through methods. They call it *encapsulation*. It's an important feature of OOP because it helps you maintain control over your data.

Objects Inside of Objects Inside of . . .

I need to tell you about one more little wrinkle that you're likely to encounter. Sometimes, you find objects inside of other objects. For example, suppose you have an object called `Customer`. `Customer` has these properties:

- ✔ `Name`: a string
- ✔ `Address`: a string

And inside `Customer`, you have another object: `Order`, which represents an order made by that customer. `Order` has these properties:

- ✔ `OrderNumber`: an integer
- ✔ `AmountTotal`: a single

Because `Order` is inside `Customer`, you have to mention `Customer` when you access `Order`. You do that with dot notation, too:

```
Customer.Order.OrderNumber = 101
Customer.Order.AmountTotal = 35.75
```

In fact, you can have yet another object inside `Order`. Imagine an `Item` object with `Number` and `Name` properties:

```
Customer.Order.Item.Number = 101
Customer.Order.Item.Name = "Racquetball Racquet"
```

You may have objects inside of objects inside of other objects, as deep as you like. An object inside another object is often called a *nested* or *embedded* object.

Here's how you create an object like this:

```
Dim Customer As CustomerClass
Customer = New CustomerClass
```

Can I do that?

Because I've shown you how to create your own classes and use them to create objects, you may be wondering whether you can create your own objects inside of other objects, and so on. Yes, you can! But I'm not going to show you how here.

You need to know that objects can be inside other objects because you'll use objects like that which are included with the .NET Framework. But you probably won't need to create your own embedded objects until you start creating more complex Web applications.

When you create this type of object, you also *automatically* create the objects inside it. You don't need to instantiate them separately. So, after you instantiate the `Customer`, you can immediately start working with the `Order` object and the `Order.Item` objects inside the `Customer`.

But, Really, So What?

Perhaps you're thinking, "This OOP stuff is interesting and all, but I'm not writing super-complex applications here. I'm not sure I'll need all these extra capabilities. I think I could probably get by just fine with functions and subroutines."

And, at least initially, you're probably right! You probably won't have an immediate need to create lots of classes in your ASP.NET pages.

But you still need to understand what classes and objects are and how to use them. Why? No matter whether you create your own or not, you're going to work with lots of classes and objects.

One of the more important parts of the.NET Framework is the .NET Framework Class Libraries. These libraries provide you with a whole lot of information and functionality that you'd otherwise have to create yourself. They save time and effort and even make lots of things possible that you wouldn't be able to do any other way. (For examples of what you can do with the .NET Framework Class Libraries, see Chapter 16.)

But the class libraries aren't the only thing about the .NET Framework that's object-oriented. In fact, almost everything *in* the Framework works that way. So, as you begin to venture deeper into the capabilities of ASP.NET, the foundation this chapter provides will be very helpful!

In fact, you may want to proceed directly to the next chapter, where I demonstrate numerous interesting objects and the useful capabilities they provide to your ASP.NET pages.

Chapter 7

Cool Stuff You Can Do With ASP.NET Objects

*C*hapter 6 describes what objects are. This chapter helps answer the question, "Why do I care?" You get a taste of how different .NET objects work and, at the same time, discover some practical, commonly used ASP.NET techniques.

ArrayList: The Super, Handy-Dandy, Array-Type Thingy

At the end of Chapter 4, I discuss arrays. Arrays enable you to store several pieces of information under one name. Then, you access those pieces of information using an index number. If you skipped that part or you're a little hazy on the details, go back and understand arrays before you read this section.

During the development of .NET, someone at Microsoft said, "You know, arrays are a nice thing. But wouldn't it be cool if we could create an object that worked like a really smart array? You wouldn't have to worry ahead of time about how many elements the array would have. And it could search itself to find a particular element you're looking for." That's how the `ArrayList` was born.

And that's a good way to think about the ArrayList — as an object that acts like a smart array.

Working over my friends

Here's the example from Chapter 4, reworked to use an ArrayList:

```
<html>
<body>
<%
Dim Friends As ArrayList = New ArrayList
Dim Found As Boolean
Dim FoundIndex As Integer

Friends.Add("Curtis Dicken")
Friends.Add("Dee Townsend")
Friends.Add("Brad Jones")
Friends.Add("Wayne Smith")
Friends.Add("TaKiesha Fuller")
Friends.Add("Mike Lafavers")
Friends.Add("Farion Grove")
Friends.Add("Troy Felton")
Friends.Add("Steve Barron")
Friends.Add("Marc Nelson")

Found = Friends.Contains("Mike Lafavers")
If Found = True Then
    FoundIndex = Friends.IndexOf("Mike Lafavers")
%>
<p>I found Mike Lafavers!</p>
<p>He's at <%=FoundIndex%>!</p>
<% Else %>
<p>I didn't find Mike Lafavers.</p>
<% End If %>
</body>
</html>
```

This code differs quite a bit from the Chapter 4 example. Starting at the top, ArrayList, as I mention earlier in this chapter, is an object. Actually, it's a class from which you can create your own objects:

```
Dim Friends As ArrayList = New ArrayList
```

This line creates the Friends variable, which has an ArrayList type. On the same line, using the New keyword, I create an ArrayList object and assign it to the Friends variable. In short, I create the Friends object using the ArrayList class. (For more on classes and objects, see Chapter 6.)

ArrayList objects have an Add method. Instead of assigning a value to each individual element of the array by number, you simply call Add with whatever you want to add to the array — in this case, a name. I call Add again and again — once for each element:

```
Friends.Add("Curtis Dicken")
Friends.Add("Dee Townsend")
. . .
```

In a short program like the example from Chapter 4, in which I'm adding all the elements to the array in one place, using index numbers to fill in an array isn't a big deal. But in a larger program, you can easily lose track of the last number you filled in. With the ArrayList, the Add method keeps track of it for you and just adds the new element in wherever you left off.

One of the bigger benefits of the ArrayList, however, is that you don't have to use a loop to look at one element after another to find out whether it's in the array:

```
Found = Friends.Contains("Mike Lafavers")
If Found = True Then
    FoundIndex = Friends.IndexOf("Mike Lafavers")
. . .
```

The Contains method takes a value and looks it up in the array to see if it's in there. This method returns True or False. If it returns True, you can use the IndexOf method to get the index number where the value was found. (Finding the index number actually goes a step beyond the Chapter 4 example.)

Tell me more!

What else can you do with an ArrayList? Well, as with arrays, you can get the value of a specific element by using its index number:

```
PickFriend = Friends(2)
```

Keep in mind that an ArrayList is numbered starting at 0, not 1.

You can find out how many elements are in the ArrayList:

```
NumFriends = Friends.Count
```

And because an ArrayList is numbered starting at 0, the last element of the ArrayList is at index number Count - 1. In other words, if Count is 5, you know that you have elements numbered 0 through 4.

You also can easily remove elements from the ArrayList by index number:

```
Friends.RemoveAt(7)
```

This doesn't just make element number 7 blank. It removes that element altogether. You can also remove elements based on their contents:

```
Friends.Remove("Dee Townsend")
```

If you want to remove all the elements, that's easy, too:

```
Friends.Clear
```

You can also change the order of the elements. For example, you can reverse their order (you know, "The last shall be first and the first shall be last . . ."):

```
Friends.Reverse
```

Or, you can sort them:

```
Friends.Sort
```

In addition, if you want to process each element of an ArrayList individually, For Each (described in Chapter 4) works with an ArrayList in exactly the same way it works with an array.

The ArrayList isn't limited to storing strings. You can store virtually anything you like in it, including other objects. And you can even store different types of things in different elements of the same ArrayList — like an integer in one element and a string in another.

You may be thinking, "Gosh, with all the cool stuff you can do with an ArrayList, why would anyone ever use an array?" Well, an array is slightly more efficient and has less overhead. But not enough to really matter. Most people will probably opt for an ArrayList when they need to hold a list of values. The main reason I show you the array in Chapter 4 is because they've been around a long time and you're likely to see them when you work with pages written by others.

There's Nothing Illegal about the HashTable

The .NET Framework offers another interesting object that you can use to hold information. It builds on the concept of the ArrayList, but is used for different things. It's called a HashTable. The HashTable enables you to store elements in a list, like the ArrayList. But when you do, you give them a name. Then, when you want to get your element back out, you can do it by referring to its name, not just a number.

But why *HashTable*?

The term HashTable comes from the way it works, internally. The HashTable stores information according to the name you give it. But, to speed up processing, the name is actually turned into a number, which is called a *hash*.

The hash is then associated with your information. When you come back later to search for your data, the hash speeds up the process of finding exactly what you're looking for.

Hashing out a dictionary with a HashTable

Here's an example that creates a small dictionary with the aid of a HashTable:

```
<%@Page Explicit="True" Language="VB" Debug="True" %>

<html>
<body>
<h1>HashTable ASP.NET Dictionary</h1>
<%
Dim Dict As HashTable = New HashTable

Dict.Add("Static HTML","HTML-only pages that never change.")
Dict.Add("Dynamic Page", _
   "A Web page with smarts that's different all the time.")
Dict.Add("The .NET Framework", _
   "The foundation for a new way of developing software.")
Dict.Add("Automatically Compiled", _
   "Pages run faster and more efficiently than ever before.")
Dict.Add("Visual Basic .NET", _
   "An easy, flexible language for creating ASP.NET pages.")
%>
<b>What is Static HTML?</b><br>
<%=Dict("Static HTML") %><br>
<br>
<b>What is Visual Basic .NET?</b><br>
<%=Dict("Visual Basic .NET") %><br>
</body>
</html>
```

The results look like this:

```
HashTable ASP.NET Dictionary
What is Static HTML?
HTML-only pages that never change.
What is Visual Basic .NET?
An easy, flexible language for creating ASP.NET pages.
```

The first line of code creates a HashTable-type object and stores it in a variable called Dict. Then I use the Add method to add new elements, just as I do with the ArrayList in previous sections of this chapter. The difference is that I pass two values this time, rather than just one. The first is the name I want to give the element (often called the *key*) and the second is the information I want to store in the element (often called the *value*). Because of this, an element for a HashTable is often referred to as a *key/value pair*.

Then when the appropriate question is asked, all I have to do is call up the "definition" by putting the key inside parentheses after Dict:

```
<b>What is Static HTML?</b><br>
<%=Dict("Static HTML") %><br>
```

Directly adding and changing elements

Incidentally, you also can add new elements to the list using syntax like this:

```
Dict("ASP.NET For Dummies") = _
    "Your ticket to the ASP.NET train. All aboard!"
```

If ASP.NET For Dummies had not been defined as the key for an element before now, this line would create a new element with that name and with the value of the string you assign to it.

You can also use this syntax to change an existing element:

```
Dict("The .NET Framework") = "The meaning of life itself."
```

Oh! You mean a Dictionary!

Classic ASP has a structure that enables you to do something very similar to a HashTable — and it's actually called a Dictionary! (So no big surprise where I got the idea for this example, right?) The HashTable is conceptually the same thing and works in much the same way. However, pay attention to the properties and methods — they work a little differently from those of the Dictionary object.

The keys you use in your HashTable *are* case-sensitive. If you save something with the key "Henry" and later try to work with "henry," you won't find it. Or worse, you'll inadvertently create another element with the lowercase name as the key! Be careful.

Tell me more!

As with the ArrayList, you can easily get the number of elements in a HashTable using the Count property:

```
NumEntries = Dict.Count
```

You can also eliminate an entry using Remove:

```
Dict.Remove("Dynamic Page")
```

Or, get rid of all entries with Clear:

```
Dict.Clear
```

You can find out if a HashTable contains a certain key by using the ContainsKey method, which returns True or False:

```
If Dict.ContainsKey("C#") = True Then
. . .
```

You can even find out if a HashTable contains a certain *value* by using the ContainsValue method, which also returns True or False:

```
If Dict.ContainsValue( _
    "HTML-only pages that never change.")= True Then
. . .
```

Finally, like the ArrayList, the HashTable isn't limited to storing strings. You can use almost anything for the key or the value of a HashTable, including other objects. You can also store different types of things in different elements of the same HashTable.

The ArrayList and the HashTable have many similarities but they really fill different roles. If you just want to work with a simple list, or it makes more sense to access your information using index numbers, or you want to be able to easily sort your list, an ArrayList will probably foot the bill. However, if you want to access your information by name, use a HashTable. You'll see both used in a variety of ways throughout the .NET platform.

Using Automatically Created Objects

The `ArrayList` and the `HashTable` are classes from which you can create your own objects that are useful for storing information. The other objects I discuss in this chapter are a little different. They are *automatically* created for you ahead of time by ASP.NET. That means their properties and methods can be put to use right away!

Some objects require that you instantiate them, and some do not. As I've done here, I'll always let you know which is which when I introduce a new object.

The Input and Output Objects: Request and Response

`Request` and `Response` represent information coming *into* the Web server from the browser and information going *out* from the server to the browser. So, from the server's perspective, you could call `Request` the *input* object and you could call `Response` the *output* object. In this section, I present a few of these objects' more important properties and methods and the cool techniques they make possible.

The scribe: Response.Write

Probably the most commonly used method of any object in ASP.NET is the `Response` object's `Write` method. `Response.Write` simply enables you to write text to the page. Of course, you can write text to the page without using `Response.Write`, as the following example from Chapter 4 shows:

```
<%@Page Explicit="True" Language="VB" Debug="True" %>
<html>
<body>
<%
Dim Grade As Integer
Randomize
Grade = Int(Rnd * 100) + 1 ' Random number between 1 and 100
%>
<p>Your grade is <%=Grade%>.</p>
<% If Grade >= 60 Then %>
<p>You passed!</p>
<% Else %>
<p>You failed...</p>
<% End If %>
</body>
</html>
```

Request and Response — I know you!

Classic ASP developers will remember Request and Response as among the more useful ASP Server Objects available in Classic ASP. Most of the properties and methods you use with them in Classic ASP are available in ASP.NET, too. However, ASP.NET gives you much better ways to work with some features — particularly forms. (I discuss the alternative to forms in Part IV.)

Although this example works, you can write this page much more cleanly by using Response.Write:

```
<%@Page Explicit="True" Language="VB" Debug="True" %>
<html>
<body>
<%
Dim Grade As Integer
Randomize
Grade = Int(Rnd * 100) + 1 ' Random number between 1 and 100

Response.Write("<p>Your grade is " & Grade & ".</p>")
If Grade >= 60 Then
    Response.Write("<p>You passed!</p>")
Else
    Response.Write("<p>You failed...</p>")
End If
%>
</body>
</html>
```

Instead of closing the delimiters to switch to HTML again and again, this code uses only one set of delimiters around the whole listing. Any time you want to display something, you use Response.Write. And if you want to display the value of a variable, you just use the concatenation operator & to make it part of the string you send to the Write method. (See Chapter 3 for more on concatenation.)

Although this change cleans up the code a bit and makes it more readable, Response.Write isn't absolutely necessary here. However, it is necessary in functions and subroutines — for example:

```
<%@Page Explicit="True" Language="VB" Debug="True" %>
<html>
<script runat="server">
Sub SayGoodnight(Name As String)
    Response.Write("Goodnight, " & Name)
End Sub
```

```
</script>
<body>
<%
SayGoodnight("Gracie")
%>
</body>
</html>
```

As you might expect, the results of this page are

```
Goodnight, Gracie
```

All functions and subroutines must appear inside the `<script>` tag at the top of your document. You cannot use `<%` and `%>` inside the `<script>` tag because only VB.NET code goes in there. You can't use HTML inside the `<script>` tag, so you don't need to use `<%` and `%>` to distinguish between your code and HTML.

So how do you display some text on the page inside a subroutine or function? That's where `Response.Write` comes in. There's no other way to do it!

Web roulette with Response.Redirect

`Response` has another interesting method called `Redirect`, which enables you to send the user to a different page. This method can be quite handy, as the following example shows:

```
<%
Dim Username As String
...
If Username="Admin" Then
    Response.Redirect("adminhome.aspx")
Else
    Response.Redirect("home.aspx")
End If
%>
```

As you can see, if you want to send the user to another page in the same folder as the current page, simply redirect the user with the page name. However, if you want to send the user to another site, you can use a complete URL:

```
Response.Redirect("http://www.edgequest.com")
```

Here's a fun demonstration of the capabilities that `Redirect` offers. I call it Web Site Roulette. The user clicks a link and is magically taken to a random Web site. Every time, it's a different site.

Web Site Roulette consists of two different pages. The first is a simple HTML page named `roulette.htm`:

```
<%@Page Explicit="True" Language="VB" Debug="True" %>
<html>
<head><title>Web Site Roulette</title></head>
<body>
<h1>Welcome to Web Site Roulette</h1>
<p>Care to take a spin on the wheel? Round and round
she goes! Where she stops - Well, you'll find out...</p>
<p>When you're ready, just click...</p>
<center>
<h3><a href=spin.aspx>SPIN!</a></h3>
</center>
</body>
</html>
```

This page just presents users with a link. The link takes them to `spin.aspx`, where the real work is done:

```
<%@Page Explicit="True" Language="VB" Debug="True" %>
<html>
<head></head>
<body>
<%
Dim Sites(10) As String
Dim Num As Integer
Randomize
Sites(1) = "http://www.microsoft.com"
Sites(2) = "http://www.borland.com"
Sites(3) = "http://www.netscape.com"
Sites(4) = "http://www.sun.com"
Sites(5) = "http://www.ibm.com"
Sites(6) = "http://www.lotus.com"
Sites(7) = "http://www.discovery.com"
Sites(8) = "http://www.comedy.com"
Sites(9) = "http://www.futility.com"
Sites(10) = "http://www.ebay.com"
Num = Int(Rnd * 10) + 1
Response.Redirect (Sites(Num))
%>
</body>
</html>
```

First, I create an array of 10 string variables with the name `Sites`. Then, I fill in each of those variables one at a time with a different URL. (For more information on creating and using arrays, see Chapter 4.)

I generate a random number between 1 and 10 and put it in `Num`. I then call `Response.Redirect` with the array element to which `Num` points.

You'll notice when you try out this example that the spin.aspx page doesn't actually display anything. It doesn't even appear in the Address line of the browser. It just runs this code and immediately sends the user on to the random site. So, from your users' perspective, clicking the link takes them directly to the random site — which is how you want it to look!

This example is both fun and somewhat practical. If you have a Web site dedicated to gardening, gaming, or photography, you can replace the URLs in this example with your own that point to sites on a topic similar to yours. It puts a fun twist on the boring Links section of your site and provides a launching point for your visitors browsing on a topic!

By the way, you can expand the list of sites by simply making the array bigger and filling in more site names. Don't forget to increase the number in the Rnd line, too. You'll probably want to include at least 20 sites, though. Roulette with 10 sites gets boring pretty quickly!

Request.QueryString goes long for the pass

The Response object is the server's output object, writing to a page or sending the user to a different page. The Request object is the server's input object. It gets data from the user.

Here's a really useful technique for using the Request object to pass information from one page to another.

First, imagine you're going to a Web search engine like Yahoo! or Excite. You type in a word to search for — **aardvark,** perhaps — and then click the Find button.

The next page you see has a list of links to all the pages that include your search word. But if you look up at the Address line in your browser, you'll notice that the URL looks something like this:

```
http://www.excite.com/search.gw?search=aardvark
```

It may look a little different or have extra stuff, but I want to draw your attention to the part that begins with the question mark. A common way to pass information from one page to another on the Web is through the URL line itself. After the address, you simply put a question mark and then a "*name=value*" thing. This technique enables you to send named information to a page.

So ya wanna be a gazillionaire — A trivia page

Here's an example:

Create a page called `GazilQues.aspx`. Here's what it should contain:

```
<%@Page Explicit="True" Language="VB" Debug="True" %>
<html>
<body>
<h1>So Ya Wanna Be A Gazillionaire</h1>
For one gazillion dollars, answer this question:<br>
<b>Who was the second man to walk on the moon?</b><br>
<a href="GazilAns.aspx?Answer=Armstrong">
Neil A. Armstrong</a><br>
<a href="GazilAns.aspx?Answer=Collins">
Michael Collins</a><br>
<a href="GazilAns.aspx?Answer=Aldrin">
Edwin E. Aldrin, Jr.</a><br>
<a href="GazilAns.aspx?Answer=Lightyear">
Buzz Lightyear</a><br>
</body>
</html>
```

Actually, this page has no ASP.NET code, so you could just as easily name it with a `.htm` or `.html` extension. But leaving the `.aspx` extension doesn't hurt anything.

It's the big question — your chance to win big on everybody's favorite trivia game show, "So Ya Wanna Be A Gazillionaire." The question is asked, and the user has four options. Each one is a link, but they all link to the same page: `GazilAns.aspx`. The difference is that each link passes a different value for `Answer` after the ? on the URL line. For example, if the user clicks `Edwin E. Aldrin, Jr.`, the URL line changes to look like this:

```
http://localhost/Gazillionaire/GazilAns.aspx?Answer=Aldrin
```

The part before `GazilAns.aspx` may differ depending on how and where you access your page. But you can see that the `Answer` value `Aldrin` appears in the URL line after the ? when opening the new page.

Now create a page called `GazilAns.aspx`. It should look like this:

```
<%@Page Explicit="True" Language="VB" Debug="True" %>
<html>
<body>
<h1>So Ya Wanna Be A Gazillionaire</h1>
The Question Was:<br>
<b>Who was the second man to walk on the moon?</b><br>
<br>
```

```
Your answer was:<br>
<%=Request.QueryString("Answer")%><br>
<br>
<%
Dim Chosen As String
Chosen = Request.QueryString("Answer")
Select Case Chosen
Case "Armstrong"
    Response.Write("No, sorry! Neil Armstrong was actually ")
    Response.Write("the <i>first</i> man to walk on the ")
    Response.Write("moon.")
Case "Collins"
    Response.Write("No, sorry! Michael Collins never ")
    Response.Write("actually made it to the moon's surface.")
Case "Aldrin"
    Response.Write("Yes! You're right! Edwin Aldrin, Jr. ")
    Response.Write("was the second man to walk on the moon.")
Case "Lightyear"
    Response.Write("Nope. You've been watching way too ")
    Response.Write("many Disney movies.")
End Select
%>
</body>
</html>
```

You retrieve the value from the URL line by using the QueryString property of the Request object. Inside the parentheses after QueryString, you put the name that you've given the information. QueryString retrieves the value from the URL line and enables you to store the information in a string variable. So, here's how you display the value from the URL line:

```
<%=Request.QueryString("Answer")%><br>
```

A Select Case statement then uses this value to decide how to respond. A different response is provided for each possible answer. Response.Write lines are used to put the text on the page. (For information on Select Case, see Chapter 4.)

Passing multiple variables

The example in the preceding section passes hard-coded information to the receiving page, based on which link the user clicks. You can also pass information held in variables.

Here's another example. Create the following page and save it as Sender.aspx:

```
<%@Page Explicit="True" Language="VB" Debug="True" %>
<html>
<body>
<%
Dim Die1, Die2 As Integer
Randomize
Die1 = Int(Rnd * 6) + 1
Die2 = Int(Rnd * 6) + 1
%>
Click
<a href="Receiver.aspx?First=<%=Die1%>&Second=<%=Die2%>">
Here</a> To See The Result Of Your Roll!
</body>
</html>
```

This page creates two variables and puts a different random number (between 1 and 6) in each of them. Then, when the user clicks the link, the values of these two variables are placed inside the value of href. For example, if the numbers generated were 2 and 5, the URL in the Address line of the browser after the user clicked this link would look like this:

```
http://localhost/dice/Receiver.aspx?First=2&Second=5
```

Again, the part before Receiver.aspx in the URL may be different for you. But notice that you now have two pieces of information after the ?, each with a different name and separated from each other with an &. You can actually string together as many of these *name=value* items as you like, separating each with an &.

This information is then received in Receiver.aspx. Create a new file with that name and these contents:

```
<%@Page Explicit="True" Language="VB" Debug="True" %>
<html>
<body>
<%
Dim FirstDie, SecondDie As Integer

FirstDie = Request.QueryString("First")
SecondDie = Request.QueryString("Second")

Response.Write("You rolled a " & FirstDie & _
    ", and a " & SecondDie & ".<br>")
If FirstDie = 6 And SecondDie = 6 Then
    Response.Write("Boxcars!<br>")
ElseIf FirstDie = 1 And SecondDie = 1 Then
    Response.Write("Snake eyes!<br>")
ElseIf (FirstDie + SecondDie = 7) Or _
    (FirstDie + SecondDie = 11) Then
        Response.Write("7/11 - A Winner!<br>")
```

```
End If
%>
</body>
</html>
```

Here, `FirstDie` and `SecondDie` get the values returned from `QueryString`. Notice that both pieces of data are available separately, by simply including the name given to the data as a string inside parentheses after `QueryString`.

`Response.Write` is used to display the two variables. Notice that the line-continuation character allows the string to spill over into a second line. Finally, an `If...Then...ElseIf` statement identifies boxcars, snake eyes, and a winner with either 7 or 11. (For more information on the line-continuation character or `If...Then...ElseIf`, see Chapter 4.)

Request.Browser: Forms? Tables? KitchenSink?

The `Request` object contains an interesting object called `Browser`. `Request.Browser` enables you to get lots of useful information about the user's browser. Each bit of information is conveniently stored in `Browser` properties. Specifically, these properties provide two different types of information:

- The browser's capabilities
- The browser's identity and the platform on which it runs

Each property holds a value of either True or False to indicate whether the browser has a particular capability. For example, you can check the `Tables` property to find out if the user's browser supports tables. After performing that test, the following code uses the `<pre>` tag to format some information if the user's browser doesn't support tables:

```
<% If Request.Browser.Tables = True Then %>
<table>
<tr><td>aaa</td><td>bbb</td></tr>
<tr><td>ccc</td><td>ddd</td></tr>
<tr><td>eee</td><td>fff</td></tr>
</table>
<% Else %>
<pre>
aaa    bbb
ccc    ddd
eee    fff
</pre>
<% End If %>
```

Table 7-1 lists the more common browser capability properties.

Table 7-1	Common Browser Capability Properties
Property	*Indicates Whether the Browser Supports . . .*
Tables	HTML tables
Frames	HTML frames
JavaScript	JavaScript
VBScript	VBScript
ActiveXControls	ActiveX controls
Cookies	Cookies
JavaApplets	Java applets
BackgroundSounds	Background sounds
CDF	Channel Definition Format (CDF) for webcasting

Table 7-2 lists the more commonly used properties to identity the browser and the platform on which it runs.

Table 7-2	Common Browser Identity Properties
Property	*What It Identifies*
Browser	The browser string (if any) that was transmitted in the User-Agent HTTP header
Type	The name and major version number of the browser
Version	The version number of the client browser
Beta	Whether this is a beta release of the client browser (true/false)
EcmaScriptVersion	The version number of ECMA script (JavaScript) that the client browser supports
AOL	Whether this is an America Online (AOL) browser (true/false)
Platform	The name of the platform that the client uses
Crawler	Whether the client browser is a Web crawler search engine (true/false)

(continued)

Table 7-2 *(continued)*	
Property	*What It Identifies*
Win16	Whether the browser is running on a Win16-based machine, like Windows 3.1 (true/false)
Win32	Whether the browser is running on a Win32-based machine, like Windows 95/98/ME/NT/2000/XP (true/false)

Just one more small request

I want to point out one more highlight before leaving the topic of the Request and Response objects. The Request object has several interesting properties that you may find useful:

- ✔ **Url:** The URL that the user entered to get to this page.
- ✔ **UrlReferrer:** The URL where the user was before coming to this page. You can use this property to find out what other pages link to yours.
- ✔ **UserAgent:** The name and version of the browser from the HTTP headers.
- ✔ **UserHostName:** The domain name of the client.
- ✔ **UserHostAddress:** The IP address of the client.

How would you use this information? Well, sometimes people are less likely to try to cheat you if they know you have a way to track them down. Try adding these lines to the bottom of your shopping cart page:

```
<p>Credit card fraud is a Federal Offense.
Do not use someone else's credit card.
Your IP address <%=Request.UserHostAddress%>
has been recorded in our records.</p>
```

Application and Session: More Variable Scope Options

The Application and Session objects work similarly, and you use them for similar tasks. The Application object holds information about the ASP.NET application. The Session object keeps track of each person who accesses the application, individually.

The application versus the session

To explain the difference between the `Application` and `Session` objects, here's an example. Imagine your Web server has a really cool real estate ASP.NET application that enables users to look at a variety of homes, pick one, and then calculate what their mortgage payment would be if they bought it. Only one copy of this application exists on the Web server. The application starts up the first time someone accesses a page for that application. It doesn't end until the last person has left the Web application or the Web server is shut down. That's the `Application` object's domain: the entire application for its entire life.

The session is much different. Suppose Sparky logs on to your real estate application and begins looking through the homes. Soon after, Judd pulls up a page and begins looking at houses, too. Now, two different people are running the same application. You don't have two different *applications,* but you do have two different *sessions.* Each time a new person accesses your ASP.NET application, a new session is created. If Sparky gives up for the night and comes back tomorrow, he will be in a different session from the one he was in tonight.

Variable scope review

A variable's *scope* determines where you can access a variable and how long the variable will live. An ASP.NET page can contain three different levels of scope:

- **Body variables:** Declared in the body of the page. They can be accessed in the body of the page, but nowhere else.

- **Local variables:** Declared inside a function or subroutine. They can be accessed only from within that function or subroutine and cease to exist when it finishes executing.

- **Global variables:** Declared inside the `<script>` tag but outside any function or subroutine. They can be accessed inside functions or subroutines and in the body of the page.

For more information on variable scope, see Chapter 5.

More old friends — Session and Application

ASP.NET's `Session` and `Application` objects work pretty much just as they do in Classic ASP. Feel free to skim or skip the next few sections.

It's a bird. It's a plane. No, it's a super-global Session variable!

After you've experimented with ASP.NET pages for a while, you'll find yourself wishing for a *super-global* variable — a variable that keeps its value from one *page* to the next.

What you really want is a Session variable:

```
Session("HouseCost") = 175000
```

This code creates a new variable called HouseCost, if it didn't already exist before, and assigns it the value 175000. (If the variable already exists, this code just changes its value.) This variable is a session-level variable that can be accessed from any page as long as the current user continues to use this application.

You access a Session variable in the same way:

```
If Session("HouseCost") > 150000 Then
```

Unlike variables declared with Dim, Session variables do not have a specified data type. They get their data type from the information you store in them.

Because you don't actually declare Session variables (you just begin using them), the chance exists that you'll misspell a variable name and it won't get caught. ASP.NET will just assume that you're trying to create a new variable and it will do it. So watch out for typos!

Even-more-super Application variables

As you may expect, application-level variables also exist. You create them and assign values to them just as you do with Session variables:

```
Application("NumberOfHits") = 0
```

But don't forget that an application is universal. Only one application exists, no matter how many people use it. So, whenever you change an Application variable, be careful that you are the only one changing it at that time. You do that by using the Application object's Lock and Unlock methods. Instead of just setting a value, as I do in the preceding code, I should do this:

```
Application.Lock
Application("NumberOfHits") = 0
Application.Unlock
```

While the `Application` object is locked, no other sessions can change it. Of course, you should not keep it locked any longer than the millisecond or two you take to make your change.

You don't need to use the `Lock` and `Unlock` methods when you simply want to access an `Application` variable's value:

```
If Application("NumberOfHits") > 1000 Then
```

What's the difference?

Here's the big difference between session-level variables and application-level variables: If five people are using your real estate Web application at the same time, five copies of the `HouseCost` session-level variable are present — one for each session. Only one copy of the `NumberOfHits` variable exists. If you truly want to create a super-global variable to share information from one page to another, you definitely want to use the session-level variables.

Typically, application-level variables are used much less frequently. But they are great for keeping track of the number of hits a page has taken or other application-level statistics. You also can use them to share information among several sessions.

For a real-world example of using an application-level variable to share information between sessions, see Chapter 20's Café Chat Room application. In this application, several people take part in a common conversation. The key to sharing the same conversation among many different participants is an application-level variable that is displayed, and redisplayed as it is updated, in the browsers of all participants.

Session variables — No longer evil

`Session` variables had a bad name in Classic ASP primarily for two reasons. First, they didn't work in Web Farms, and second, they required that the user have cookies enabled to work.

Both of these problems are solved now. For more information on how they are solved, see Chapter 17.

How does the Web server know what a session is?

The World Wide Web uses HTTP as its protocol language for communication. Unfortunately, HTTP is what techie-types call a *stateless* protocol, which means that, unlike other networks, you don't log on and log off machines in order to use them. When you ask for a page, that is an independent request. The server sends you the page and then forgets about you. If you click a link to go to another page on that server, the request is sent, and the server sends that page to you — without any realization at all that you are the same person who asked for a page a minute ago.

So, if this is true, how can you talk about a session? Well, ASP.NET has several different methods that it can use to keep track of sessions. By

default, it uses cookies to keep track of sessions by uniquely identifying each person when that user first makes a request. Then, after that user makes another request in the near future, the server recognizes the user and accepts this new request as part of the same session. After a request, the server waits up to 20 minutes for a new request. If a new request doesn't happen in that time, the server assumes that the user has gone to some other site or gotten off the Internet entirely, and it considers the session ended.

If many of your users' browsers don't support cookies, or cookie support is turned off, you can change the ASP.NET configuration to track users without the use of cookies.

Do Application and Session objects work like a HashTable?

If you read the section titled "There's Nothing Illegal about the HashTable," earlier in this chapter, you may be thinking that Session and Application variables work a lot like the elements in a HashTable. And you're right; they do. In fact, both the Session and Application objects have a Count property, an Add method, a Remove method, and a Clear method that all work just as they do in HashTable objects.

However, unlike a HashTable, the Session and Application objects don't have a ContainsKey method or a ContainsValue method. Another distinction to keep in mind is that a HashTable is case-sensitive while Session and Application variables are not.

Part IV
Creating Interactive Web Applications

In this part . . .

After you have the Visual Basic .NET language under your belt, you're ready to go interactive! In this part of the book, you discover how to create pages for filling out forms, taking part in surveys, calculating mortgage payments, and much more. In other words, this is the part where your applications come to life and really start doing something for the people who visit your site.

In addition, you find out how to help your users discover mistakes they've made when filling out a form — forgetting to fill in a required textbox or accidentally typing in a value that can't possibly be right. ASP.NET provides an innovative approach to this common task.

Chapter 8

Interfacing With Your Users

- -

In This Chapter

▶ Discovering .NET Web Forms and how they work

▶ Exploring server control events and properties

▶ Figuring out how to work with all the different kinds of properties

- -

*A*re you ready to get *interactive?* In this chapter, you find out how to create pages that not only display information for the user to see, but also ask for input and respond intelligently. Discover how your pages can make the leap from boring documents to living applications!

HTML Forms? Forget It . . .

If you've done much work creating Web pages in the past, you may be familiar with HTML forms. HTML forms are a set of tags that you use to make things like textboxes and radio buttons appear on the page so the user can respond to questions or provide input.

If you have worked with HTML forms before, I have a small favor to ask of you: Please, right here and now, forget everything you know about them. Why? Because ASP.NET Web Forms work very differently, and if you try to compare them to HTML forms, you'll only get confused.

Forget Request.Form, too!

In Classic ASP, you access the information posted back from a form using the Request object. Technically, you could still use that technique, but Web Forms provide a much better approach to interacting with your users. However, it's also a very different approach. Carefully follow the example in this chapter to see how it works.

Examining Web Forms and Server Controls

Controls — for example, textboxes, checkboxes, and buttons — are familiar to anyone who has used Windows or Web pages. They enable users to interact with applications. So, understanding how to create and use controls is the first step in making your pages interactive.

When Microsoft's developers began thinking about how to create the best environment for interactive Web pages, they realized that the code you write in ASP.NET runs on the server. So, it makes sense that the controls you put on your page should run on the server, too. That way, you can easily access and manipulate them in your code. And if the controls and the code both reside on the server, you can respond more easily when things happen, like when the user clicks a button.

That notion led to the development of .NET *Web Forms*. A Web Form is just a page that uses .NET *server controls*. I show you all about how server controls work in the coming sections.

A simple form

Here's an example of a Web Form that uses .NET server controls. Create a page called age.aspx and enter these lines:

```
<%@Page Explicit="True" Language="VB" Debug="True" %>
<html>
<body>
<h1>If You Were A Dog</h1>
<form runat="server">
How old are you?<br>
<asp:textbox id="Age" runat="server"/>
<asp:button text="OK" runat="server"/>
</form>
</body>
</html>
```

Figure 8-1 shows how this page looks in the browser.

The <form> tag surrounds all the server controls that a user will use to enter information. Standard HTML tags can appear inside the <form> tag, too. The <form> tag has a single attribute: runat="server". This indicates that the form is a Web Form, not an HTML form, and it is to be processed on the server.

What's a />?

You may have noticed that the `<asp:textbox>` tag and the other server control tags on the page end with a `/>`. This syntax is relatively new to HTML. It basically means that you want to bundle the opening tag and the closing tag into one tidy unit. So, if you were to see `<head></head>`, you could express it this way instead: `<head/>`. Both mean the same thing.

So, when you see `<asp:textbox . . . />`, it's the same as `<asp:textbox . . . ></asp:textbox>`, with nothing in-between.

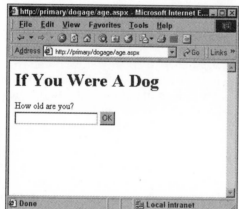

Figure 8-1:
The "If You Were A Dog" page.

The page has some text asking users for their age, followed by a line that creates a textbox server control:

```
<asp:textbox id="Age" runat="server"/>
```

Although this looks like a normal HTML tag, two important clues tell you that it isn't:

- ✔ The tag name has the prefix `asp:`, which identifies the textbox as an ASP.NET tag.
- ✔ Just as it does in the `<form>` tag, the attribute `runat="server"` tells you that the tag will be evaluated on the server before it is sent to the browser.

You'll see the `asp:` prefix and the `runat="server"` attribute on all ASP.NET server controls.

The id attribute gives this textbox a name that you can use to refer to it in code (which I demonstrate in the section "Capturing events and changing properties," later in this chapter).

Next in the listing is another server control — a button:

```
<asp:button text="OK" runat="server"/>
```

The text attribute determines what text appears on the face of the button.

However, if you click the button in your browser, nothing happens. I show you how to fix that situation in the next section.

Capturing events and changing properties

The preceding sections show you how to create ASP.NET Web Forms and how to use server controls such as the textbox and the button. But a form that doesn't *do* anything isn't a very interesting form. So, I want to show you one more important feature: responding to server control *events*.

An event is something that occurs in your application. Usually, the events that you care about are triggered by the user. For example, when the user clicks a button, that kicks off an event. You can *capture* that event and do something when it happens. To show you how it's done, I've added a few things to the "If You Were a Dog" example that I introduce in previous sections of this chapter:

```
<%@Page Explicit="True" Language="VB" Debug="True" %>
<html>
<script runat="server">
Sub OKButton_Click(Sender As Object, E As EventArgs)
    Dim UserAge, DogAge As Integer
    UserAge = Age.Text
    DogAge = UserAge / 7
    Message.Text="If you were a dog, you'd be " & _
        DogAge & " years old."
End Sub
</script>
<body>
<h1>If You Were A Dog</h1>
<form runat="server">
How old are you?<br>
<asp:textbox id="Age" runat="server"/>
<asp:button text="OK" onclick="OKButton_Click"
runat="server"/><br>
<asp:label id="Message" runat="server"/>
</form>
</body>
</html>
```

Going behind the scenes with server controls

Perhaps you're thinking, "If the server controls run on the server, why do they show up in my browser?" Good question.

The server controls *do* run on the server. And that enables you to access and work with them in your ASP.NET code (as I show you in this chapter). That's very handy. But when the server creates the page that's sent to the browser, you want these server controls to show up on your page as real controls that the user can interact with. To make this happen, each server control uses HTML tags to paint a picture of itself in the user's browser. This all

happens automatically. The result is that the server control appears on the page just as you'd expect it to look.

If you've worked with HTML forms before and want to see exactly how this works, choose View⇨Source from the menus in your browser while looking at the "If You Were A Dog" page. You'll see <input> tags for the textbox and button. You'll also see another hidden input tag called __VIEWSTATE, which ASP.NET uses internally to keep track of information from one round-trip to the server to the next.

I've highlighted the three things that I've added to this listing:

- A <script> tag and a subroutine within it.
- A new control: a label with its id set to Message.
- A new attribute on the button called onclick.

I'll start with the new attribute on the button:

```
<asp:button text="OK" onclick="OKButton_Click"
runat="server"/><br>
```

The onclick attribute captures the event that happens when the user clicks this button. How? By specifying the name of a subroutine to execute when the event happens. So, in this case, when the user clicks the OK button, the OKButton_Click subroutine is called, and you can write code there that will respond appropriately.

What does "respond appropriately" mean in this case?

```
Sub OKButton_Click(Sender As Object, E As EventArgs)
    Dim UserAge, DogAge As Integer
    UserAge = Age.Text
    DogAge = UserAge / 7
    Message.Text="If you were a dog, you'd be " & _
        DogAge & " years old."
End Sub
```

This subroutine accepts two arguments: Sender and E. All subroutines that respond to events receive these arguments. You have to specify them here because that's what the event requires. But you don't have to use them. For now, you can ignore them.

First, I create a couple of integer variables. Then, I assign a value to one of them. The value is Age.Text:

```
UserAge = Age.Text
```

As you might expect, Age is an object, and Text is a property of the Age object. But what does Age refer to? Remember your textbox?

```
<asp:textbox id="Age" runat="server"/>
```

Its id is set to Age. That enables you to refer to it as an object from your ASP.NET code. When you work with server controls, the server creates the objects for you automatically so that you can immediately access the control's properties.

In this case, the Age textbox's Text property holds the information in the textbox. The text in the textbox is then placed in the UserAge variable.

DogAge is then calculated by dividing UserAge by 7.

Finally, the result is displayed:

```
Message.Text="If you were a dog, you'd be " & _
    DogAge & " years old."
```

This time, I refer to another object: Message. Message is another server control. It's the new label control that I added to this listing:

```
<asp:label id="Message" runat="server"/>
```

A label control is a lot like a textbox, except it's designed only for showing text. You can't edit the text in a label. In this case, I use it to display the result of the calculation. I simply assign a value, using & to stick the strings together with the variable DogAge.

If You Were a Dog: In action

If you haven't already, try out the "If You Were a Dog" page. It's not all that informative, but it is vaguely amusing.

Notice a couple of things as you try out the page. When you click the button, you may notice the page flash a bit before you see the label filled in with its message. Why does this happen? Well, the subroutine that executes when you click that button is written in ASP.NET code, so it runs on the server. When you click the button, the page automatically goes back to the server, executes the subroutine, and sends the resulting page back. You may think that's a lot of trouble to go through, but it usually happens so fast you barely notice it.

Also, after you fill in the textbox and click the button, and after the page returns from the server, you'll notice that the textbox still contains the value you entered. That may seem like perfectly logical behavior, but if you've worked with HTML forms in the past, you may know that HTML forms don't work that way by default. Fortunately, Web Forms do. Unless you specifically change the text in a textbox, it remains there no matter how many trips you make to the server and back.

Manipulating Server Control Properties

The example in the preceding section shows how you can assign a value to a property of a server control to change how the server control looks on the page. In that case, it was pretty simple. You assign a string to the Text property of a label, and the label suddenly appears on the page with the new text in it.

A capital idea

If you're one of those detail-oriented types, you may have noticed that the capitalization of stuff in my HTML and my code sometimes seems inconsistent.

First, you should know that the way you choose to capitalize stuff in either HTML or in ASP.NET code doesn't really matter. It will work either way. That being said, of course, you should be consistent.

Throughout this book, I've chosen to make all HTML and server control tags lowercase. However, in the VB.NET code, I always capitalize keywords. And if a keyword or variable name consists of multiple words, I capitalize each word — for example, DogAge.

To make matters more confusing, you can use the same properties in the tag and in your VB.NET code. And because of the style I use, I'll capitalize one and use lowercase for the other. Further, because the name of the control exists primarily to be used in ASP.NET code, I've chosen to capitalize the value I assign to the ID attribute in the server tag — for example:

```
<asp:textbox id="Age"
    runat="server"/>
```

In the same way, I capitalize the value assigned to the onclick and similar attributes because they refer to the names of subroutines in the code portion.

No system is perfect, but I've chosen to go with this style throughout the book. Pick your own style and stick with it.

Properties and methods are the primary ways you work with server controls on your page. So, understanding which properties and methods are available for each control helps you understand what you can do with the controls. I spend the next few chapters helping you do just that.

But before I dive into each control and its members, you should know a few things about properties and giving them values. Not all of them work as simply as the label's Text property. But after you get the hang of these few variations, you'll be able to work with any property on any control without trouble!

Don't skip these sections; otherwise, you may be baffled by the different ways properties are handled in subsequent chapters.

Changing properties in code and in the tag

To assign a value to a property from ASP.NET code, you simply refer to the server control object by its name (specified in the id attribute of the server control tag):

```
Message.Text = "Hello There!"
```

You can also specify a value for a server control's property in one other place: in the tag itself. For example, if you want the Message label to start out holding the text "I'll calculate your age in dog-years", just change the server control tag to look like this:

```
<asp:label id="Message" runat="server"
text="I'll calculate your age in dog-years" />
```

You can specify almost any property of a server control either way. Put it in the tag if you want it to come up that way first on the page. Change the property in code if you want to manipulate it based on user input.

Using enumeration properties to assign values

When you're working with the tag, you can almost always assign a string value to a property that will be interpreted correctly. For example, to set the color of a label's text to red, you change the tag to look like this:

```
<asp:label id="Message" runat="server" forecolor="Red"
text="I'm so embarassed!"/><br>
```

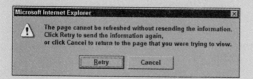

A common error when you click Refresh

In Chapter 1, when I show you how to create and test ASP.NET pages, I explain that you can change your code in Notepad and then click Refresh in your browser to see the result. If you use that technique with the "If You Were a Dog" page (and many other pages that I show you in subsequent chapters), you may get an error.

Here's how this page works: If you enter an age and click the button, the page returns to the server and executes the subroutine. The resulting page, with the label filled in, comes back to the browser. At this point, if you switch over to your editor and make a change in the page and then come back and click the Refresh button in the browser, you'll likely see an error message that looks like the example in the accompanying figure.

Here's what this message is trying to tell you: The last time this page returned to the server, it was not getting a fresh new page. Instead, it was responding to you clicking the button and executing a subroutine which then made changes to this existing page. So, when you click Refresh, the browser thinks you want to do *that* process over again. The message is asking you to confirm that. This is *not* what you want — you want to get a fresh page and start over.

There are two ways you can avoid this error message when you are modifying and testing your pages.

- ✔ Click the Back button until you get to a blank page — that is, a page before you entered any text and clicked the button. Then click Refresh on that page.

- ✔ Click in the Address line, add a 1 (or any character) to the end of the URL, and click Enter. You get the `Page cannot be found` error. Then take off the character and press Enter again. Now you have a fresh copy of your page. (It's goofy, but it works!)

So, your natural inclination would be to change the property in code using a line like this:

```
' Sorry - this doesn't work!
Message.ForeColor = "Red"
```

Unfortunately, this doesn't work. Instead, you have to assign a special value that represents the color red to the `ForeColor` property when you are setting it from code.

However, you don't have to remember some complex number that represents the color red every time you want to set a color. Instead, the .NET Framework provides objects with a special kind of property called an *enumeration*. Enumerations are properties that hold a specific value that you'll commonly need to use. The values for colors, for instance, are stored in an object called `Drawing.Color`. So, if you want to set the foreground color of Message to red, you do it this way:

```
Message.ForeColor = Drawing.Color.Red
```

Of course, the `Drawing.Color` object has values for Blue, Green, and many, many other colors you might need. (For more information, see Chapter 10.)

I refer to objects that have enumeration properties as *enumeration objects*. Enumeration objects are everywhere in the .NET Framework. As I show you different properties that use enumeration values in the coming chapters, I always provide the name of the enumeration object and a list of its common enumeration properties for you to use.

Using enumeration object methods

Some enumeration objects, like `Drawing.Color`, also offer *methods* to help in assigning a value to a property — for example:

```
Message.ForeColor = Drawing.Color.FromARGB(255,255,255)
```

`FromARGB` is a method that enables you to specify a color by indicating the amount of red, green, and blue you want mixed in, each on a scale of 0 to 255. For more information on `FromARGB`, see Chapter 10.

So, enumeration objects can have specific enumeration property values, like `Drawing.Color.Red`, *and* they sometimes provide methods for generating values, like `Drawing.Color.FromARGB`.

Working with sub-object properties

Some server controls have properties that are actually objects themselves. In Chapter 6, I describe how you access an object inside of another object: You simply use dot notation. For example, to set a label's font to bold, you use the `Bold` property of the `Font` object that's inside a label server control. If the label control was named `MyLabel`, your code would look like this:

```
MyLabel.Font.Bold = True
```

But it works a little differently for server control tags. Here's an example of setting the font to bold in the tag itself:

```
<asp:label id="MyLabel" runat="server"
font-bold="true" Text="I'm FLASHY!"/><br>
```

Here, you use the sub-object name and its property name together, separated by a *dash*. This example demonstrates how you handle all sub-object properties in server control tags.

Chapter 9

Turn the Page

In This Chapter

▶ Discovering the Page object

▶ Using the Page_Load event to initialize controls

▶ Understanding server round-trips and the problems they can cause

▶ Figuring out ViewState

*I*n this chapter, I introduce you to a couple of common problems and confusing situations that you can get yourself into with Web Forms. Then, I show you the slick features ASP.NET offers to handle those situations. It all starts with the Page object.

Page Me!

The Page object isn't just another control. Instead, it represents the whole Web page. The Page object — like any object — has its own properties and methods. It also has an event or two that you'll find helpful. The following sections demonstrate how the Page object helps you solve a common problem that you're likely to encounter.

The problem: Initializing with a function

Typically, if you want to create a control that has specific property values when it's first displayed, you set each property's value in the server control tag. For example, if you want users to fill in a Country textbox, you may want to give that textbox a default value of USA. That's easy:

```
<asp:textbox id="Country" runat="server"
text="USA"/>
```

When the page is displayed, this textbox appears with USA already in it. Users can then leave it alone or change it if they like.

But suppose you're creating a page on which people can register the software they just bought from the company you work for. The registration page asks all the familiar stuff — name, e-mail address, product purchased, and so on. But your problem comes when asking for the purchase date. Because most people register their software right away (if they register it at all), using today's date as the default for this textbox makes sense. Then, even if the purchase date was yesterday or the day before, users can easily change the value in the textbox. But how do you use today's date as the default value? You might try something like this:

```
<!-- This doesn't work! -->
<asp:textbox id="DatePurchased" runat="server"
text=<%=Today%>/>
```

That looks reasonable enough. When you want to use variable or function values in HTML, you do it that way, right?

If you try this approach, you get an error message that looks like this:

```
Server tags cannot contain <% ... %> constructs.
```

Why not? Well, remember, server control tags are *not* HTML tags. You know that because of the `runat="server"` part. They are evaluated and created on the server long before the `<%...%>` code on the page is evaluated. So that doesn't work.

The solution: The Page_Load event

The problem I describe in the preceding section has a solution, and it lies in the `Page` object. The `Page` object has an event called `Page_Load`. `Page_Load` is the *first* event triggered when a page is retrieved and it's triggered *every* time the page is loaded.

This example demonstrates how you can use `Page_Load` to fix the problem I present in the preceding section:

```
<%@Page Explicit="True" Language="VB" Debug="True" %>
<html>
<script runat="server">
Sub Page_Load(Sender As Object, E As EventArgs)
DatePurchased.Text = Today
End Sub
</script>
<body>
<h1>Software Registration Form</h1>
<form runat="server">
Name:<br><asp:textbox id="Name" runat="server"/><br>
Email:<br><asp:textbox id="Email" runat="server"/><br>
```

```
Product:<br><asp:textbox id="Product" runat="server"/><br>
Date Purchased:<br>
<asp:textbox id="DatePurchased" runat="server"/><br>
<asp:button text="OK" runat="server"/>
</form>
</body>
</html>
```

This code produces a form that looks like Figure 9-1.

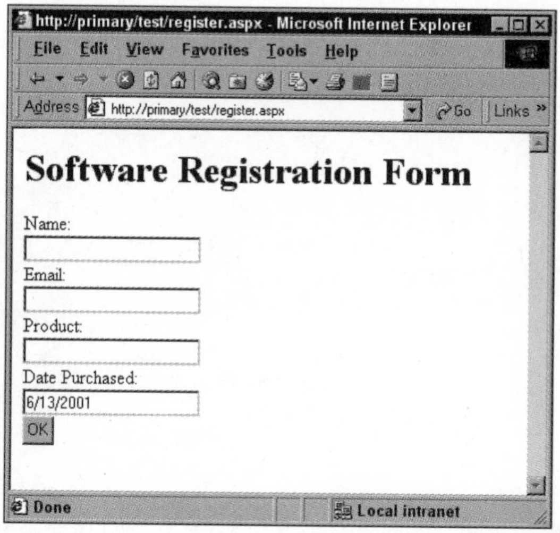

Figure 9-1:
The
Software
Registration
Form with
date
defaulting to
today.

The Page_Load event is similar to the button's onclick event. It is triggered at a particular time and enables you to write a subroutine that will execute in response to it. And, like the onclick event, it accepts the Sender and E as arguments. (For more information on the button's onclick event , see Chapter 8.)

However, the onclick event and Page_Load differ in a couple of ways:

✔ Page_Load is not triggered directly by something the user does. The system triggers this event when it loads the page to be processed. (Yeah, yeah, technically, you could say that the user requested the page and thus caused the system to process the page, but I did say *directly*.)

✔ You can give the subroutine triggered from a button's onclick event any name you want. You just have to specify that name as the value for the asp:button onclick attribute. Page_Load is not specified in any tag's attribute. It must always have the name Page_Load and is automatically triggered (if you've written a subroutine with that name) when the page is loaded.

The Page_Load event is a perfect place to initialize textbox values that you couldn't initialize in the tag itself — as in this case. It's also a good place to do any general preparation or startup stuff you want done before the rest of the page executes. You'll find that Page_Load is a handy spot for lots of things.

Page_Load: First time or every time?

The example that I present in the preceding section has a small problem. Change the example to look like this listing, adding the parts in bold:

```
<%@Page Explicit="True" Language="VB" Debug="True" %>
<html>
<script runat="server">
Sub Page_Load(Sender As Object, E As EventArgs)
DatePurchased.Text = Today
End Sub

Sub OK_Click(Sender As Object, E As EventArgs)
Header.Text="You Entered:"
LabelName.Text = Name.Text
LabelEmail.Text = Email.Text
LabelProduct.Text = Product.Text
LabelDatePurchased.Text = DatePurchased.Text
End Sub
</script>
<body>
<h1>Software Registration Form</h1>
<form runat="server">
Name:<br><asp:textbox id="Name" runat="server"/><br>
Email:<br><asp:textbox id="Email" runat="server"/><br>
Product:<br><asp:textbox id="Product" runat="server"/><br>
Date Purchased:<br>
<asp:textbox id="DatePurchased" runat="server"/><br>
<asp:button text="OK" runat="server"
onclick="OK_Click" /><br>
<asp:label id="Header" runat="server" /><br>
<asp:label id="LabelName" runat="server"/><br>
<asp:label id="LabelEmail" runat="server"/><br>
<asp:label id="LabelProduct" runat="server"/><br>
<asp:label id="LabelDatePurchased" runat="server"/><br>
</form>
</body>
</html>
```

When you try out the page, fill in all the information, but change the date. Now click the OK button.

You should notice that all the information is displayed below the OK button with one small error: The date you entered is changed *back* to the current date. In fact, if you look back up at the textboxes, the value has been changed there, too! What's going on?

Well, when you click the OK button, the page is actually "loaded" again on the server. And because of that, the Page_Load event is the first thing that happens. So, regardless of what you type into the DatePurchased textbox, the current date always overwrites it.

What you *really* want to do is set DatePurchased to Today only the *first* time the page is loaded. Fortunately, you can easily determine whether this is the first time the page is loaded.

Change the Page_Load subroutine to look like this:

```
Sub Page_Load(Sender As Object, E As EventArgs)
If IsPostBack=False Then
    DatePurchased.Text = Today
End If
End Sub
```

This time, the page should work as you expect it to, retaining the value in the date when you click OK.

IsPostBack works like a predefined ASP.NET variable that holds a Boolean value (either true or false). The first time a page is loaded, IsPostBack is false. Every time the page *returns* to the server to do something, like to execute the OK_Click subroutine, ASP.NET automatically sets IsPostBack to true. So, you can use this value to find out if this is the first time the page was loaded or if this is a post-back.

In this case, I check to see if IsPostBack is false — that is, if this is the first time the page has been loaded. If it is, I initialize the textbox. Later, when the OK button is clicked, IsPostBack will be true, and the initialization line won't execute again.

Here's another way to do the same thing:

```
If Not IsPostBack Then
```

Because IsPostBack is a Boolean variable, you can use it directly in an If...Then statement without the =True part, if you like. But in this case, the Not reverses the Boolean value, so the statements inside the If...Then are only executed if IsPostBack is false. So, this works exactly like the previous code.

It's a common approach, and a very good idea, to include all your preparation and initialization code inside an If statement that checks for IsPostBack=False (or Not IsPostBack) in the Page_Load event.

Server Round-Trips Make Your Page's Head Spin

In this section, I want to clear up one more interesting little gotcha that all this going back and forth between the browser and the Web server can cause. And, in the process, I introduce you to a handy feature of ASP.NET.

A puzzling example: The no-count counter

To demonstrate the problem, I've created an example that initializes a variable called Counter to 1 and displays it on the page with a label control. Then, each time you click a button, the counter is increased by one and then displayed. At least, that's the way it's supposed to work:

```
<%@Page Explicit="True" Language="VB" Debug="True" %>
<html>
<script runat="server">
Dim Counter As Integer

Sub Page_Load(Sender As Object, E As EventArgs)
If Not IsPostBack Then
    Counter = 1
    ShowCounter.Text = Counter
End If
End Sub

Sub PushMe_Click(Sender As Object, E As EventArgs)
Counter = Counter + 1
ShowCounter.Text = Counter
End Sub
</script>
<body>
<form runat="server">
Counter: <asp:label id="ShowCounter" runat="server" /><br>
<asp:button id="PushMeButton" text="Push Me"
runat="server" onclick="PushMe_Click"/><br>
</form>
</body>
</html>
```

Here's what you see when you show this page in your browser:

```
Counter: 1
```

Under this label, there's a button labeled Push Me. Push the button. Nothing happens. Push it again. Still nothing. What happened? Why doesn't the counter's value increase by 1 each time?

Examining the page

The body of the page includes a label and a button — nothing special.

At the top of the page, Counter is declared as a global variable — it's declared inside the <script> tag but outside any specific subroutine or function (see Chapter 5 for more information on global, local, and body variables):

```
<script runat="server">
Dim Counter As Integer
. . .
```

Now, according to what I say in Chapter 5, a global variable should be available to be used anywhere on the page — in a subroutine or function inside the <script> section or in the body of the page.

So, in the Page_Load event, I take the opportunity to give it value:

```
Sub Page_Load(Sender As Object, E As EventArgs)
If Not IsPostBack Then
    Counter = 1
    ShowCounter.Text = Counter
End If
End Sub
```

I only want to do this the first time the page is loaded, so I enclose it inside an If Not IsPostBack Then statement (see the preceding section). I initialize the Counter to 1 and then I display the value of Counter by putting it in the ShowCounter label.

Now the page appears in the browser for the first time. The user sees it and pushes the button. The button is associated with the PushMe_Click subroutine. So the page returns to the server to execute it:

```
Sub PushMe_Click(Sender As Object, E As EventArgs)
Counter = Counter + 1
ShowCounter.Text = Counter
End Sub
```

So what's wrong?

The answer to the mystery

Global variables *are* accessible from anywhere on the page. I didn't lie to you. However, global variables do *not* remember their value from one round-trip to the server to the next.

When the page is first requested, the value for `Counter` is set in the `Page_Load` event and displayed. That all happens in the *first* trip to the server. Clicking the button causes the page to go *back* to the server a second time. This time, the global variable is essentially *created anew* and has a value of 0.

So when the `PushMe_Click` subroutine adds 1 to `Counter`, its new value is 1! This value is then displayed in the label. Likewise, every time the user clicks the button, the variable is re-created with the value 0, its value is increased to 1, and it's displayed.

ViewState to the rescue

Your Web page contains a hidden field called `ViewState`. ASP.NET uses `ViewState` to store all the information about the server controls on the page — not only their contents, but also whether they are enabled, what color they are, and so on. Then, when ASP.NET is ready to create the page again on a future round-trip to the server, it has the information it needs. You can think of `ViewState` as the scrap paper on which ASP.NET writes down everything it needs to remember about this page.

That's a very nice feature. And it all happens automatically. But, wouldn't it be nice if you could tap into that feature somehow to store the value of global variables you want to remember? Well, the good folks at Microsoft thought so, too.

In this listing, I fix the problem by using `ViewState`:

```
<%@Page Explicit="True" Language="VB" Debug="True" %>
<html>
<script runat="server">
Dim Counter As Integer

Sub Page_Load(Sender As Object, E As EventArgs)
If Not IsPostBack Then
    Counter = 1
    ShowCounter.Text = Counter
    ViewState("Counter") = Counter
End If
End Sub

Sub PushMe_Click(Sender As Object, E As EventArgs)
Counter = ViewState("Counter")
Counter = Counter + 1
ShowCounter.Text = Counter
ViewState("Counter") = Counter
End Sub
</script>
<body>
<form runat="server">
```

```
Counter: <asp:label id="ShowCounter" runat="server" /><br>
<asp:button id="PushMeButton" text="Push Me"
runat="server" onclick="PushMe_Click"/><br>
</form>
</body>
</html>
```

I've bolded the lines that are new. When you try this page, it should work as you'd expect.

To get ASP.NET to store your values in the ViewState hidden field, you create ViewState variables. This works just like it does for the Session and Application variables I describe in Chapter 7. You create a new ViewState variable by simply choosing a name, putting it in quotes inside parentheses, and then assigning a value to it.

You can see this at the end of the Page_Load event. I store the global variable in the ViewState with the name Counter:

```
ViewState("Counter") = Counter
```

(The ViewState variable name doesn't have to match your global variable name, but if it does, it can help you keep things straight!) Then when you need it, you simply get it out, as I do first-thing in the PushMe_Click subroutine:

```
Counter = ViewState("Counter")
```

If I had other event subroutines on the page where I wanted to use the Counter variable, I'd have to include this line at the top of each of them, too.

Finally, because I changed the value of the Counter global variable in the PushMe_Click subroutine, I need to store it back into the ViewState at the end of the subroutine so that it is remembered next time around:

```
ViewState("Counter") = Counter
```

As you can see, this solves the problem. The only catch is that you have to put the ViewState values back into their associated global variables at the top of any event subroutine where you want to use them. And if you change the global variable, you must be sure to put the value back into the ViewState variable.

An easier way . . .

The approach to this problem described in the previous section works perfectly well. But I began thinking, if you have quite a few event subroutines in which you use global variables, you're going to have to retrieve the global variables out of `ViewState` at the beginning of each subroutine and then put them all back in at the end of each subroutine. All this shuffling of information can become annoying! Wouldn't it be nice if you had one place where you could put all the global variables into `ViewState` and one place where you could get them all back out of `ViewState`? You do:

```
<%@Page Explicit="True" Language="VB" Debug="True" %>
<html>
<script runat="server">
Dim Counter As Integer
Dim StringVar As String
Dim SingleVar As Single

Sub Page_Load(Sender As Object, E As EventArgs)
If Not IsPostBack Then
    Counter = 1
    StringVar = "Hello"
    SingleVar = 3.5
    ShowCounter.Text = Counter
    ShowStringVar.Text = StringVar
    ShowSingleVar.Text = SingleVar
Else
    Counter = ViewState("Counter")
    StringVar = ViewState("StringVar")
    SingleVar = ViewState("SingleVar")
End If
End Sub

Sub Page_PreRender(Sender As Object, E As EventArgs)
ViewState("Counter") = Counter
ViewState("StringVar") = StringVar
ViewState("SingleVar") = SingleVar
End Sub

Sub PushMe_Click(Sender As Object, E As EventArgs)
Counter = Counter + 1
StringVar = StringVar & "!"
SingleVar = SingleVar + 0.1
ShowCounter.Text = Counter
ShowStringVar.Text = StringVar
ShowSingleVar.Text = SingleVar
End Sub
</script>
<body>
<form runat="server">
Counter: <asp:label id="ShowCounter" runat="server" /><br>
StringVar: <asp:label id="ShowStringVar"
runat="server" /><br>
SingleVar: <asp:label id="ShowSingleVar"
runat="server" /><br>
```

```
<asp:button id="PushMeButton" text="Push Me"
runat="server" onclick="PushMe_Click"/><br>
</form>
</body>
</html>
```

This is essentially the same page as I use in the previous examples, except I've added two global variables: StringVar and SingleVar. I've also added labels to display their values and have changed their values in a noticeable way in the PushMe_Click subroutine. I added them to show that this solution can work for a whole group of global variables. When you try out the page, you'll see that all the values are updated each time you click the button.

To describe how this page works, I'll walk through the lifetime of the page, starting at the beginning. When the page is first requested, the following process is kicked off:

1. The Page_Load event is triggered and IsPostBack is false. This causes the code inside the If Not IsPostBack Then statement to execute, initializing the global variables.

2. Just before the page is sent to the browser, the Page_PreRender event is triggered. I haven't described this event before, but it's an event associated with the page that happens *after* all the other server control events are done and *before* the page is sent off to the browser. What a perfect opportunity to save off all the global variables into ViewState!

3. The page is created and sent out to the browser. The user clicks the button.

4. The Page_Load event is triggered, and IsPostBack is true. This causes the code inside the Else part of the If statement to execute. Here, all the information in ViewState is pulled out and put into the appropriate global variables.

5. The PushMe_Click event happens. Here, I can use, display, and even change the value of global variables without worrying about them being preserved. That's true for all the other events that you'd put on a page, too. After this structure is in place, the events can simply assume that the globals will be available anytime, anywhere.

6. The Page_PreRender event happens just before the page is created and sent back to the browser. Any changes made in the global variables are stored back safe in ViewState.

7. The page is created and sent out to the browser. If the user clicks the button again, the process continues with Step 4 again.

Doing it this way gets the global variables out once — before any event occurs — and puts them away once — after all other events are done. If you add a new global variable to the page, you have to remember to add entries in the Page_Load and Page_PreRender events for it to ensure that the global is remembered.

Chapter 10

Basic Server Controls: Labels, Textboxes, and Buttons

. . . .

In This Chapter

▶ Creating and manipulating the label server control

▶ Working with textboxes and their properties

▶ Pushing buttons

. . . .

*I*n Chapter 8, you get a feel for how Web Forms and server controls can work together. Now, I want to go through each of the important server controls individually so I can show you all the cool stuff that's built in!

But trust me — I won't give you a regurgitation of the documentation. Chapters 10–12 offer a quick survey, with liberal examples, showing all the important stuff and none of the boring stuff. Nevertheless, if you're in a hurry, you can skim through this information and come back to it later as you need the specific information provided.

Don't Label Me!

First up is the humble label, one of the simpler server controls. It does nothing but display text. And, unlike the textbox, the user can't mess with the text in the label.

But that doesn't mean the label is boring — far from it! In this section, I explore some of the more interesting properties you can manipulate. But before I dive into the specifics, Table 10-1 summarizes them all. The table may not make much sense until you've read through the descriptions in the coming sections. But after you do, it can serve as a quick reference when you need the information again in the future.

Table 10-1	Important Label Control Properties		
Property	*What It Specifies*	*How You Set It*	*Where to Go for More*
Text	The string that appears in the label	string	"Capturing events and changing properties" in Chapter 8
ForeColor, BackColor, BorderColor	The text color, background color, and border color of the control	Drawing. Color enumeration properties (Red, Green, Blue, and so on) or FromARGB function	"A splash of color" and "A border dispute," later in this chapter
BorderStyle	The look and color of the border surrounding the control	BorderStyle enumeration properties (Solid, Dashed, Dotted, Double, and so on)	"A border dispute," later in this chapter
Font.Bold, Font. Underline, Font. Italic	Whether each of these states is on or off for the text	true or false. Default: false	"The font of youth" and "Here comes crazy label!," later in this chapter
Font.Name	The name of the typeface	string	"The font of youth" and "Here comes crazy label!," later in this chapter
Font.Size	Size of the text in the control	FontUnit enumeration properties (Medium, Small, Large, and so on) or Point method	"The font of youth" and "Here comes crazy label!," later in this chapter
Height, Width	Size of the control itself	Unit enumeration object, Pixel or Point method	"Sizing up your label with Height and Width," later in this chapter

Property	What It Specifies	How You Set It	Where to Go for More
ToolTip	Text that appears in a yellow pop-up window when the user hovers the mouse pointer over the control	string	"ToolTip: Don't run with scissors!," later in this chapter
Visible, Enabled	Whether the control is visible and whether it's usable	true or false. Default: true	"Enabled and Visible," later in this chapter

A splash of color

The label has two important color properties. In fact, these same properties are available on most controls and they work the same way there as they do here:

- ✔ ForeColor: Holds the color of the text.
- ✔ BackColor: Holds the color of the background.

Setting colors in the server control tag

Here's an example that shows how you set a label's text and background colors:

```
<%@Page Explicit="True" Language="VB" Debug="True" %>
<html>
<body>
<form runat="server">
<asp:label id="FlashyLabel" runat="server" forecolor="Red"
backcolor="Yellow" text="I'm FLASHY!"/><br>
</form>
</body>
</html>
```

In case you're wondering, the capitalization doesn't matter. For consistency, I use lowercase for all my HTML and server control tags and attributes. ASP.NET doesn't care either way.

When you try out this page, you see the words I'm FLASHY! in the upper-left corner of your browser window — red text on a yellow background.

Setting colors in code with enumeration properties

So, based on your experience so far, setting the `ForeColor` and `BackColor` from code should be a piece of cake, right? Wrong:

```
' Sorry - this doesn't work!
FlashyLabel.ForeColor = "Red"
FlashyLabel.BackColor = "Yellow"
```

Unfortunately, this doesn't work. Instead, you have to use enumeration properties. (For more information on how enumeration properties work, see Chapter 8.)

The values for colors are stored in an object called `Drawing.Color`. So, here's how you set the foreground color of `FlashyLabel` to red:

```
FlashyLabel.ForeColor = Drawing.Color.Red
```

Here's an example of a page with a label that starts off in one color scheme and changes to another when you click the button:

```
<%@Page Explicit="True" Language="VB" Debug="True" %>
<html>
<script runat="server">
Sub ChangeButton_Click(Sender As Object, E As EventArgs)
    FlashyLabel.ForeColor = Drawing.Color.Blue
    FlashyLabel.BackColor = Drawing.Color.Green
End Sub
</script>
<body>
<form runat="server">
<asp:label id=" FlashyLabel" runat="server" ForeColor="Red"
BackColor="Yellow" BorderColor="Blue"
Text="I'm FLASHY!"/><br>
<asp:button text="Change!" onclick="ChangeButton_Click"
runat="server"/>
</form>
</body>
</html>
```

The red on yellow text turns to blue on green when you click the button.

Any time you need to specify a color in your code, you'll probably use the `Drawing.Color` object's enumerated properties. Table 10-2 lists some of the color properties available in that object. Because that object has well over a hundred color properties available, I don't list them all, but I do list the common ones. The words in parentheses after some colors mean that you can prefix those words on the color's name to give it a different nuance. So, Gray (Dark, Light, Dim) means that Gray, DarkGray, LightGray, and DimGray are all options.

Table 10-2	The Drawing.Color Object's Common Enumeration Color Properties	
Red (Dark, Indian, Orange, PaleViolet)	Green (Light, Dark, DarkOlive, Forest, Lawn, Lime, Pale, Yellow	Black
Blue (Light, Dark, Medium, Alice, Cornflower, Dodger, Midnight, Powder, Royal)	SeaGreen (Light, Dark, Medium)	White (Floral, Ghost, Navajo)
SkyBlue (Deep, Light)	SpringGreen (Medium)	Gray (Light, Dark, Dim)
SlateBlue (Dark, Medium)	Cyan (Light, Dark)	SlateGray (Dark, Light)
SteelBlue (Light)	Salmon (Light, Dark)	Silver
Yellow (Light, Green, LightGoldenrod)	Pink (Light, Deep, Hot)	Brown (Rosey, Saddle, Sandy)
	Purple (Medium)	Beige
	Violet (Blue, Dark)	Tan

Setting colors in code with FromARGB

The `Drawing.Color` object provides another way for you to specify what color you want: the `FromARGB` method.

`FromARGB` works like you would if you were mixing a palette of red, green, and blue paints together — the higher the number (up to 255), the more paint you use. A little red and no green or blue (100,0,0) makes a dark red or maroon. No red but lots of blue and green (0,200,200) makes cyan. They don't mix exactly like paints do, though. For example, to get white, you mix a lot of all three colors together (255,255,255). Likewise, none of anything (0,0,0) makes black. This example shows how to change a label's text color to gray:

```
' Give FlashyLabel's text a gray color
FlashyLabel.ForeColor = Drawing.Color.FromARGB(128, 128, 128)
```

A border dispute

Like the color properties, the border properties are not specific to the label. These properties are available on most of the server controls:

- ✔ `BorderStyle`: Style of border
- ✔ `BorderColor`: Color of the border

`BorderColor` works just like the other color properties that I describe in the preceding section.

`BorderStyle` has its own set of enumerated properties. To make this one easy to remember, the object holding the enumerated properties is called `BorderStyle`. So, if you want a red on yellow label with a green dotted border, you can do it this way in the tag:

```
<asp:label id="FlashyLabel" runat="server" ForeColor="Red"
BackColor="Yellow" BorderColor="Green" BorderStyle = "Dotted"
Text="I'm FLASHY!"/><br>
```

Or, you can do it this way in code:

```
FlashyLabel.ForeColor = Drawing.Color.Red
FlashyLabel.BackColor = Drawing.Color.Yellow
FlashyLabel.BorderColor = Drawing.Color.Green
FlashyLabel.BorderStyle = BorderStyle.Dotted
```

`BorderStyle` offers lots of fun possibilities:

- Solid
- Dashed
- Dotted
- Double
- None
- NotSet

You can even give your page a more 3D look with these options for `BorderStyle`:

- Inset: Inset border, sunken control
- Outset: Outset border, raised control
- Groove: Grooved, sunken border
- Ridge: Ridged, raised border

The font of youth

If you've used a word processor, you know what a *font* is: It's the typeface of your text. It determines whether your text looks simple and readable or extravagant and outlandish. The `Font` object is built into the label control (and pretty much every other control that can display text).

You can use the properties of the Font object to determine exactly what the text in the label will look like. Here's a list of the important Font properties:

- ✔ Name: The name of the typeface you want. Common typefaces are Arial, Times New Roman, and Courier New.

- ✔ Size: The size of the text.

- ✔ Bold, Italic, Underline: True/false settings indicating whether you want those styles added to the text.

To access the property of a sub-object from a server control tag, you use a dash between the sub-object name and the property within the sub-object. (For more information on setting sub-object properties, see Chapter 8.) Here's an example:

```
<asp:label id="FlashyLabel" runat="server"
font-name="Arial" font-size="30pt" font-bold="true"
Text="I'm FLASHY!"/><br>
```

This technique works whenever you're assigning a value to the property of a sub-object in a server control tag.

To assign these values in code, Bold, Underline, Italic, and Name work as you'd expect them to:

```
FlashyLabel.Font.Bold = True
FlashyLabel.Font.Underline = True
FlashyLabel.Font.Italic = True
FlashyLabel.Font.Name = "Arial"
```

But assigning the Font object's Size property is a little trickier. You use an enumeration object called FontUnit. Just as when you are assigning colors, you have two different options: enumeration properties or a method.

```
FlashyLabel.Font.Size = FontUnit.Large
```

Options for the enumerated properties are: XXSmall, XSmall, Smaller, Small, Medium, Large, Larger, XLarge, XXLarge. You also can use these values inside quotes when specifying the size in the server control tag:

```
<asp:label id="FlashyLabel" runat="server"
font-name="Arial" font-size="Smaller" font-bold="true"
Text="I'm FLASHY!"/><br>
```

The other option for specifying the size in code is to use the Point method:

```
FlashyLabel.Font.Size = FontUnit.Point(12)
```

This example sets the text in the label to a size of 12 points.

Here comes crazy label!

Here's an example that picks a random font and a random size, randomly turns the Bold property on or off, and then displays the result every time you click the button:

```
<%@Page Explicit="True" Language="VB" Debug="True" %>
<html>
<script runat="server">
Sub ChangeButton_Click(Sender As Object, E As EventArgs)
Dim Fonts(5) As String
Dim RndFont, RndSize, RndBold, RndItalic As Integer
Randomize
Fonts(1) = "Arial"
Fonts(2) = "Times New Roman"
Fonts(3) = "Courier New"
Fonts(4) = "Broadway"
Fonts(5) = "Calligrapher"
RndFont = Int(Rnd * 5) + 1
RndSize = Int(Rnd * 70) + 1
RndBold = Int(Rnd * 2) + 1
CrazyLabel.Font.Name = Fonts(RndFont)
CrazyLabel.Font.Size = FontUnit.Point(RndSize)
If RndBold = 1 Then
    CrazyLabel.Font.Bold = True
End If
End Sub
</script>
<body>
<form runat="server">
<asp:label id="CrazyLabel" runat="server"
text="Crazy Label"/><br>
<asp:button onclick="ChangeButton_Click" text="Change!"
runat="server" />
</form>
</body>
</html>
```

This example uses a technique similar to the one I use in Chapter 7 to pick a random font (see "Web roulette with Response.Redirect"). This example creates an array of five elements and chooses a different one with the RndFont variable each time the button is clicked. A font point size between 1 and 70 is applied, and the font is made bold about 50 percent of the time.

This is a fun way to play with all the different options available on the label. You could add underline and italics in the same way that I've done bold. You could even generate three random numbers between 0 and 255 and feed them to the FromARGB method to set it to a random color.

Sizing up your label with Height and Width

Height and Width set the size of the label. You don't usually have to mess with these directly because when you set the size of your label's font to something large, the size of the label expands to fit it.

But if you ever do need to resize the label, you should know that you set both Height and Width using an enumeration object method. The object's name is Unit. The methods you can use are Pixel, to give it a size in pixels, or Point, to give it a size in points:

```
MyLabel.Height = Unit.Pixel(50)
MyLabel.Width = Unit.Pixel(100)
```

These lines change the size of the label to 50 x 100 pixels.

ToolTip: Don't run with scissors!

A ToolTip is a little yellow box that appears with a helpful description in it when your mouse pointer hovers over something on the screen for a second or two. You usually see ToolTips used with toolbar buttons, but you can use them with nearly any control — even a label:

```
<asp:label id="FlashyLabel" runat="server"
tooltip="This is one flashy label, no doubt!"
Text="I'm FLASHY!"/><br>
```

Now when you hover over the label, the little yellow ToolTip box appears with your text in it. Simple, and potentially quite informative. For an example of using ToolTips with textboxes, see "TextBox's TextChanged event and AutoPostBack property," later in this chapter.

Enabled and Visible

Enabled and Visible are simple *Boolean* values — they take either true or false. But which value they have has a big impact on your control.

Visible is true by default. When you set it to false, the control seems to disappear off the page. The user can't see or interact with the control when it is not visible. You can set it back to visible by assigning true to the property.

Enabled determines whether the control can be used or not. It is true by default, but when you set it to false, the control is visible, but dead. The effect is much clearer on a textbox: The user simply can't enter any text. But for a label, the effect is subtler: Any text inside the label simply turns gray. If you use a label to prompt the user to enter information in a nearby textbox, setting the label's Enabled property to false at the same time you set the textbox's Enabled property to false gives users an extra visual clue that they can't use the textbox right now (both the textbox and its label are grayed out).

Shadowboxing? No, Textboxing!

The textbox is probably the most commonly used user interface control. It enables users to enter small amounts of text, like their first name. Or large amounts of text, like a description of the car they're trying to sell.

In this section, you discover the more important textbox properties and how to use them in your own Web applications.

For completeness, I want to mention that all the label-related properties that I describe in the previous sections — for example, to manipulate the color, border, font, and so on — are available on the textbox as well. And they work in just the same way. So, if you want information on those properties, read the previous sections in this chapter. I only cover them here if they work differently, or you use them differently with a textbox.

Table 10-3 lists all the important properties that I describe in the next few sections. Like Table 10-1, which lists important properties for labels, this table should prove a good reference after you understand how the properties work.

Table 10-3	The Key Textbox Server Control Properties		
Property	*What It Specifies*	*How You Set It*	*Where to Go for More*
Text	The text in the textbox. Use to set a default value or get a value the user entered.	string	"Capturing events and changing properties," in Chapter 8
Enabled	When set to false, turns off textbox functionality. Any text in the textbox turns gray, and no additional text can be entered.	true or false. Default: true	"TextBox's TextChanged event and AutoPostBack property," later in this chapter
ToolTip	A string that's displayed in a tiny yellow box when the user's mouse pointer hovers over the textbox	string	"TextBox's TextChanged event and AutoPostBack property," later in this chapter

Property	What It Specifies	How You Set It	Where to Go for More
ReadOnly	Disallow user entry or modification of text	true or false. Default: false	"He's only half illiterate — He's ReadOnly," later in this chapter
TabIndex	Where this control should fall in the tab order, as the user tabs through the controls on a page	integer	"Put TabIndex A in SlotIndex B," later in this chapter
TextMode	Which type of textbox you want	TextBoxMode enumeration values (SingleLine, Password, MultiLine). Default: SingleLine	"The many faces of TextMode," "Using a password textbox to create a login page," and "Multiple line textboxes," later in this chapter
MaxLength	The maximum number of characters that can be entered into this textbox	integer. Default: 0 (meaning unlimited)	"SingleLine size matters with MaxLength and Columns," later in this chapter
Columns, Rows	The physical width and height in characters of the textbox	integer	"SingleLine size matters with MaxLength and Columns" and "Multiple line textboxes," later in this chapter
AutoPostBack	Whether the page should return to the server when the user modifies the textbox value and then presses Tab or clicks away.	true or false. Default: false	"TextBox's TextChanged event and AutoPostBack property," later in this chapter
ForeColor, BackColor, BorderColor, BorderStyle, Font, Height, Width, Visible			*See Table 10-1 in the section "Don't Label Me!," earlier in this chapter*

He's only half illiterate — He's ReadOnly

By assigning a value of either true or false to ReadOnly, you indicate whether the user can edit the textbox. By default, ReadOnly is false.

If you find yourself using ReadOnly in the server control tag, ask yourself whether you really want a label.

If you want the textbox to be ReadOnly at some times and not at others, think about using the Enabled property instead. It grays out the control so the user knows the textbox is unavailable. ReadOnly does not.

Put TabIndex A in SlotIndex B

If you have a form that includes lots of controls, users can click each one in turn to get around, if they like. But most users prefer to use the Tab key to jump from one control to the next if they already have their fingers on the keyboard.

Unfortunately, the computer has no way of knowing which control should come next in the list each time the user presses the Tab key. That's where TabIndex comes in.

You can set TabIndex to any integer value. The value for any individual control isn't so important. What's important is where that value falls in the list of TabIndex values for all the other controls on the page. When the user presses the Tab key, the cursor jumps to the control with the next highest TabIndex. So, if you have three controls — A, B, and C — that have TabIndex values of 5, 10, and 1 respectively, the cursor will start out on C, then jump to A when the user presses Tab, and then on to B.

The many faces of TextMode

The textbox is a flexible control. TextMode has three different possible values that enable you to create three very different kinds of textboxes.

TextMode uses an enumeration object named TextBoxMode. It has three enumeration properties:

- ✔ SingleLine: The default value, creates a textbox designed to get a single word or a single line of text.
- ✔ Password: A special kind of single line textbox, this one causes the characters to come up looking like asterisks. This keeps people from reading passwords over the shoulder of someone entering them.
- ✔ MultiLine: A textbox for entering multiple lines of text, like a memo field.

In the next three sections, I show examples and point out important properties to keep in mind with these three different kinds of textboxes.

SingleLine size matters with MaxLength and Columns

If you're working with a `SingleLine` textbox (the default), a couple of properties are important for sizing: `MaxLength` and `Columns`.

By setting the `MaxLength` property to an integer value, you limit the number of characters that users can enter. If you don't set it (or you set it to zero), users can enter any number of characters in the textbox. If you set this property, you usually do it in the control tag:

```
<asp:textbox id="UserName" runat="server"
maxlength="8"/><br>
```

`Columns`, likewise, can be set to any integer. This value determines how long the textbox is — that is, how much space it takes up on the page.

So, if you set `Columns` to 20 and `Maxlength` to 40, what happens? Try it out!

```
<%@Page Explicit="True" Language="VB" Debug="True" %>
<html>
<body>
<form runat="server">
<asp:textbox id="Name" runat="server"
columns="20" maxlength="40" />
</form>
</body>
</html>
```

When you type in the textbox, it begins to scroll sideways until you get to the maximum length.

Now try reversing it: Give `Columns` a value of 40 and `Maxlength` a value of 20. Although the textbox takes up lots of room, you can only use about half of it to enter text!

Using a password textbox to create a login page

Here's an example that provides a very simple login page:

```
<%@Page Explicit="True" Language="VB" Debug="True" %>
<html>
<script runat="server">
Sub OKButton_Click(Sender As Object, E As EventArgs)
If UserID.Text = "king" And Password.Text="kong" Then
    Message.Text = "Welcome, your majesty."
Else
    Message.Text = "Sorry, you're not allowed!"
End If
End Sub
</script>
<body>
<form runat="server">
<h1>Please Log In</h1>
User ID:<br>
<asp:textbox id="UserID" runat="server" /><br>
Password:<br>
<asp:textbox id="Password" runat="server"
textmode="Password"/><br>
<asp:button text="OK"
onclick="OKButton_Click" runat="server"/><br>
<asp:label id="Message" runat="server"/>
</form>
</body>
</html>
```

When you try this example and type a user ID and password and then click
OK, you may see a dialog box that says Do you want Windows to remember
this password, so that you don't have to type it again the
next time you visit this page? This functionality is built into Internet
Explorer to help you avoid having to remember dozens of passwords for
different sites. Click No.

When you type in a user ID, this control works as any textbox would. When
you type in the password, though, you'll notice the * characters that come
up instead of the letters you type. Click OK when you're done.

When the page is processed and the label is filled in, the User ID textbox still
has the User ID you entered, but the password textbox doesn't contain the
password you entered. That's how a password textbox works. You don't want
to leave old passwords sitting around in textboxes!

Multiple line textboxes

The third option for TextMode is MultiLine, which enables you to create a
memo-like text field for entering several lines of information all at once. Give
it a try:

```
<%@Page Explicit="True" Language="VB" Debug="True" %>
<html>
<body>
<form runat="server">
<asp:textbox id="Memo" runat="server"
textmode="multiline" /><br>
</form>
</body>
</html>
```

This page produces a two-line textbox with a scrollbar along the right-hand side. Try typing some text. When you get to the end of a line, the textbox automatically wraps words down to the next line. If you type more than two lines, it begins scrolling up.

Just as with the SingleLine textbox, you can use the Columns property to set the width. You also can use a Rows property to set the height. Change the textbox line in the preceding code to look like this:

```
<asp:textbox id="Memo" runat="server"
textmode="multiline" columns="40" rows="10" /><br>
```

This makes the memo box much bigger.

TextBox's TextChanged event and AutoPostBack property

In Chapter 8, I demonstrate a way to capture the button's click event so you can write a subroutine that will react intelligently. The textbox also has an event that you can capture. It's called TextChanged.

The TextChanged event happens when the user changes the text in the textbox and then presses Tab or uses the mouse to click elsewhere.

Here's an example that demonstrates using the TextChanged event to automatically enable or disable other textboxes, as appropriate:

```
<%@Page Explicit="True" Language="VB" Debug="True" %>
<html>
<script runat="server">
Sub HaveCell_TextChanged(Sender As Object, E As EventArgs)
If HaveCell.Text <> "yes" Then
    LabelCellPhone.Enabled = False
    CellPhone.Enabled = False
    CellPhone.ToolTip = "No Cell Phone"
```

```
Else
    LabelCellPhone.Enabled = True
    CellPhone.Enabled = True
    CellPhone.ToolTip = "Please enter your cell phone number"
End If
End Sub
</script>
<body>
<h1>Add Phonebook Entry</h1>
<form runat="server">
<asp:label id="LabelName" text="Name"
runat="server"/><br>
<asp:textbox id="Name" runat="server"
tooltip="Please enter your name"
tabindex=10/><br>

<asp:label id="LabelHomePhone" text="Home Phone"
runat="server"/><br>
<asp:textbox id="HomePhone" runat="server"
tooltip="Please enter your home phone number"
tabindex=20/><br>

<asp:label id="LabelHaveCell"
text="Do you have a cell phone?"
runat="server"/><br>
<asp:textbox id="HaveCell" runat="server"
tooltip="Do you have a cell phone? Answer yes or no."
ontextchanged="HaveCell_TextChanged"
autopostback="true" tabindex=30/><br>

<asp:label id="LabelCellPhone" text="Cell Phone"
runat="server"/><br>
<asp:textbox id="CellPhone" runat="server"
tooltip="Please enter your cell phone number"
tabindex=40/><br>

</form>
</body>
</html>
```

When you try out this page, it will look much like Figure 10-1.

Before you type anything, allow your mouse pointer to hover over each of the textboxes. You should see the text specified for tooltip for each one. These handy ToolTips give the user more information about what to enter than you've provided on the page.

Next, begin entering a name and home phone for someone. When you get to the question about a cell phone, type **no** and then press Tab or click in another textbox. The page will return to the server. Because of the value specified in ontextchanged in the HaveCell textbox, the server executes the `HaveCell_TextChanged` subroutine. In doing so, it notices what you've entered for the cell phone question and therefore disables the cell phone textbox. It even changes the cell phone textbox's ToolTip.

If you try typing something else in the `HaveCell` textbox, you'll notice that it goes back to the server each time you move away. This happens because you set the `autopostback` property of the `HaveCell` textbox to true. If you didn't set this property to true, the page would not return to the server when you tab away and it would never have the opportunity to check to see if it should trigger the `ontextchanged` event.

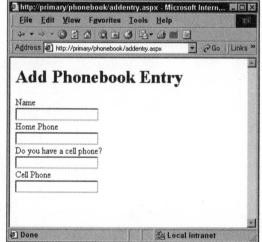

Figure 10-1:
The Add Phonebook Entry page.

So, whenever you want to capture the `ontextchanged` event, you must set the `autopostback` property to true; otherwise, the server will never have the chance to see if the event should be triggered.

Of course, the only way to get the `CellPhone` textbox enabled again is by typing **yes** in the `HaveCell` textbox and the pressing the Tab key.

You may have noticed that the code in the subroutine disables *both* the textbox and the label. I do this so the label will appear grayed out and offer a visual cue to the users, indicating that they can't use the associated textbox.

Finally, I set the `tabindex` property for each textbox. Is that necessary? In this page, probably not. If you don't include `tabindex`, the page will try to guess what order it should go in, generally moving left to right and down the page. You only need to set the `tabindex` if you want to change how it works normally. You probably also noticed that the values assigned to the `tabindexes` are numbered by tens. Why? Simple. That leaves room to add new controls in the middle, if necessary, in later updates to this form.

Button, Button — Who's Got the Button?

The button is a very simple control. Its primary purpose in life is to kick off a process or make something happen. Table 10-4 summarizes the more common properties for button controls.

Table 10-4	The Key Button Server Control Properties		
Property	*What It Specifies*	*How You Set It*	*Where to Go for More*
Text	The text that appears on the button	string	"Capturing events and changing properties," in Chapter 8
Enabled	When set to false, turns off button. Any text on button turns gray, and the onclick event is not triggered.	true or false. Default: true	"TextBox's TextChanged event and AutoPostBack property," earlier in this chapter
Visible	When set to false, causes button to disappear from the page completely.	true or false. Default: true	"Enabled and Visible," earlier in this chapter
ToolTip	A string that's displayed in a tiny yellow box when the user's mouse pointer hovers over the button	string	"TextBox's TextChanged event and AutoPostBack property," earlier in this chapter
ForeColor, BackColor, BorderColor, BorderStyle, Height, Width, Font			See Table 10-1 in "Don't Label Me!," earlier in this chapter

All the properties that I describe for the label (see previous sections in this chapter) also apply to the button. Only a few are different enough to discuss here:

✔ Height and Width: When using the label, you don't usually care about directly specifying the Height and Width properties because the label automatically adjusts to fit the size of the text it holds. But buttons stand out more, and giving them a consistent size, shape, and placement is often important to creating a clean, well-organized page. You'll most likely use the Unit.Pixel method to set a button's Height and Width.

✔ ToolTip: Although you almost never use a ToolTip on a label, you will very often use them for buttons. If you have a button with only a graphic (as on a button bar) or with only one or two words on it, the ToolTip is a good place to provide some additional information about what the button does.

✔ Text: This property contains the text that appears on the button. Make the text clear, concise, and consistent. Go with the Windows standards of using OK and Cancel wherever appropriate, because people are used to seeing and responding to that.

✔ Font: The Font object is used to change the text that appears on the button. Typically, you'll choose a font and size and use them consistently in all your buttons.

✔ Enabled and Visible: These properties are used often with buttons. If a particular command is not available for some reason, you simply disable the associated button. Disabling a button is better than making it invisible. Seeing buttons appear and disappear can be confusing to the user.

Of course, the most important thing about a button is its onclick event:

```
<asp:button onclick="OK_Click"
text="OK" runat="server" />
```

It is customary to name the subroutine that's executed based on the button's ID and the event, separated by an underscore. Although this is a good idea (to help keep your subroutines straight), it isn't required. Whatever you put inside the quotes assigned to onclick will be the subroutine name it looks for.

For examples using the button server control, see "Capturing events and changing properties," in Chapter 8. Also see "A splash of color," "Here comes crazy label!," "Using a password textbox to create a login page," and "TextBox's TextChanged event and AutoPostBack property," earlier in this chapter.

Chapter 11

Making a List Control (And Checking It Twice)

. . . .

In This Chapter

▶ Playing with checkboxes

▶ Tuning in radio buttons

▶ Sorting out listboxes

▶ Dissecting drop-down lists

. . . .

*I*f necessary, you could get by with the labels, textboxes, and buttons that I describe in Chapter 10. But you'd have a tough time creating a really interesting or exciting user interface. Fortunately, those controls are only the beginning of your many options. In this chapter, I add several new options to your toy box: checkboxes, radio buttons, listboxes, and drop-down lists.

Checking for Checkboxes

Checkboxes provide an easy way for a user to answer a yes/no or true/false question. They also can give users a list of possible options and enable them to choose all that apply.

A CheckBoxList example: Know Your Primes

You can present checkboxes to the user with the CheckBoxList server control. Here's an example that demonstrates how this control works:

```
<%@Page Explicit="True" Language="VB" Debug="True" %>
<html>
<script runat="server">
Sub OK_Click(Sender As Object, E As EventArgs)
Dim ItemNum As Integer
Chose.Text = "You chose "
For ItemNum=0 To Primes.Items.Count - 1
    If Primes.Items(ItemNum).Selected = True Then
        Chose.Text = Chose.Text & _
            Primes.Items(ItemNum).Text & " "
    End If
Next
End Sub
</script>
<body>
<h1>Know Your Primes</h1>
Do you know what a prime number is? Simple!
It's any number that can't be divided by another
number (besides 1 and itself). For example, 4 is
not a prime number because you can divide it by
2. But 7 is prime because it can only be divided by 1
and 7.<br><br>
<form runat="server">
So which of the following numbers are prime
numbers?<br>
<asp:checkboxlist id="Primes" runat="server">
    <asp:listitem>2</asp:listitem>
    <asp:listitem>5</asp:listitem>
    <asp:listitem>18</asp:listitem>
    <asp:listitem>27</asp:listitem>
    <asp:listitem>149</asp:listitem>
</asp:checkboxlist>
<br>
<asp:button id="OKButton" text="OK" runat="server"
onclick="OK_Click" /><br>
<asp:label id="Chose" runat="server" /><br>
</form>
</body>
</html>
```

When you try out this page, your browser will look a lot like Figure 11-1.

Try clicking a few of the checkboxes and then click the OK button. You'll see the label at the bottom of the page display a line that looks like this:

```
You chose 5 18 27
```

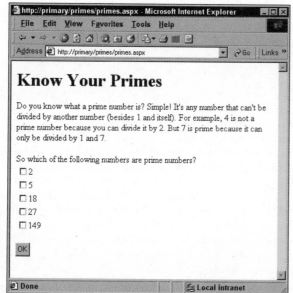

Figure 11-1:
The Know
Your Primes
page.

This server control tag looks a little different from a `<asp:textbox>` or `<asp:label>`:

```
<asp:checkboxlist id="Primes" runat="server">
    <asp:listitem>2</asp:listitem>
    <asp:listitem>5</asp:listitem>
    <asp:listitem>18</asp:listitem>
    <asp:listitem>27</asp:listitem>
    <asp:listitem>149</asp:listitem>
</asp:checkboxlist>
```

The `<asp:checkboxlist>` tag has an `id` and the ever-present `runat="server"`, but it also has another set of tags inside it: `<asp:listitem>`. The `<asp:checkboxlist>` tag represents the whole list, while the `<asp:listitem>` tags represent individual checkboxes within the list. Inside each `<asp:listitem>` tag is the text that will label the checkbox. In this case, a number appears next to each checkbox, but you could just as easily use text, including text with HTML tags.

Now take a look at the code in the `OK_Click` subroutine:

```
Sub OK_Click(Sender As Object, E As EventArgs)
Dim ItemNum As Integer
Chose.Text = "You chose "
```

```
For ItemNum=0 To Primes.Items.Count - 1
    If Primes.Items(ItemNum).Selected = True Then
        Chose.Text = Chose.Text & _
            Primes.Items(ItemNum).Text & " "
    End If
Next
End Sub
```

I refer to the list of checkboxes as one control, named `Primes`. `Primes` is a
`CheckBoxList` and it contains an object called `Items`. `Items` is actually a *collection*. A collection is simply an object that contains several other objects,
which you can access by number, like an array. The collection object also
typically has a few properties, including one called `Count`, which tells you
how *many* objects are in the collection. So, in this case, I check to see how
many objects are in the collection and then I loop through each object.

There's just one catch: The items in a collection are numbered starting with
0. So, if `Primes.Items.Count` holds a value of 5, the items in that collection
are numbered 0 through 4. That's why the loop goes from 0 to
`Primes.Items.Count - 1`.

Inside the loop, there's an `If...Then` statement:

```
If Primes.Items(ItemNum).Selected = True Then
    Chose.Text = Chose.Text & _
        Primes.Items(ItemNum).Text & " "
End If
```

Each time through the loop, this statement checks the `Selected` property of
the current item in the list. This property is true or false, indicating whether
the checkbox for that item is checked. If it is checked, the `Text` property of
this item (the number, in this case) is added to end of the `Chose.Text` string
with a space following it.

A prime example

That example in the preceding section may demonstrate how to use checkboxes, but it does not tell users whether they were right or not! So, to provide a more complete example and to give you some tips on how to use
control properties to interact with your users, here's a more complete Know
Your Primes example.

Add the highlighted code to the `OK_Click` subroutine:

```
. . .
    End If
Next
If (Primes.Items(0).Selected = True) And _
```

```
    (Primes.Items(1).Selected = True) And _
    (Primes.Items(2).Selected = False) And _
    (Primes.Items(3).Selected = False) And _
    (Primes.Items(4).Selected = True) Then
        RightOrWrong.Text = "You are exactly right!"
        OKButton.Enabled = False
Else
    RightOrWrong.Text = "Nope. You got one or more wrong."
    OKButton.Text = "Try Again!"
End If
End Sub
</script>
```

And add the highlighted label to the end of the page:

```
. . .
<asp:label id="Chose" runat="server" /><br>
<asp:label id="RightOrWrong" runat="server" /><br>
</form>
</body>
</html>
```

Now try it out. You'll see something that looks like this:

```
You chose 5 18 27
Nope. You got one or more wrong.
```

You'll also notice that the OK button's text changed! Instead of OK, it now says Try Again! That prompts users to go ahead and change the checkboxes and click the button again and again until they get it right:

```
You chose 2 5 149
You are exactly right!
```

And to ensure that users don't *continue* clicking the button after they get it right, the button is disabled.

Changing the Text and the Enabled properties of buttons on your page can help users understand their options as well as which options are available or not at different times.

Common CheckBoxList members

The CheckBoxList represents the whole group of checkboxes. When you set properties for this object, they typically affect the list or all the individual checkboxes. The CheckBoxList has a collection property called Items, which enables you to access all the individual checkboxes. You can check or set the properties of individual checkboxes through this collection.

Table 11-1 shows the common properties for `CheckBoxList`.

Table 11-1	The Key CheckBoxList Server Control Properties		
Property	**What It Specifies**	**How You Set It**	**Where to Go for More**
`Items(x). Selected`	Whether or not the checkbox with the index of x is selected	true or false. Default: false	"A CheckBoxList example: Know Your Primes" and "A prime example," earlier in this chapter
`Items(x).Text`	The text that labels the check box with the index of x	string	"A CheckBoxList example: Know Your Primes" and "A prime example," earlier in this chapter
`TextAlign`	Whether the text labeling the checkbox appears to the right or to the left of the checkbox itself	`TextAlign` enumeration values (Right and Left). Default: Right	"TextAlign," later in this chapter
`RepeatColumns`	Number of columns used to display the list of checkboxes	integer	"Repeat after me . . . ," later in this chapter
`RepeatDirection`	Whether the check boxes are listed across the page (horizontal) or down the page	`RepeatDirection` enumeration values (Horizontal, Vertical). Default: Vertical (vertical)	"Repeat after me . . . ," later in this chapter
`RepeatLayout`	Whether an HTML table is used to organize the checkboxes into neat rows and columns	`RepeatLayout` enumeration values (Table, Flow). Default: Table	"Repeat after me . . . ," later in this chapter
`CellPadding, CellSpacing`	How far apart the checkboxes are from each other	integer	"CellPadding and CellSpacing," later in this chapter

Property	What It Specifies	How You Set It	Where to Go for More
AutoPostBack	Whether the page should return to the server when the user changes one of the checkboxes	true or false. Default: false	"AutoPostBack and Selected IndexChanged," later in this chapter
Enabled, Visible, ToolTip, ForeColor, BackColor, BorderColor, BorderStyle, Font, Height, Width, Visible			See Table 10-1 in Chapter 10

TextAlign

TextAlign determines whether the text appears on the right or left side of the checkbox. The one you choose simply depends on the layout of your page and what you think looks best. Figure 11-2 shows two short lists: The first is Right aligned (the default) and the second is Left aligned. Remember that Right and Left refer to the *text*, not the checkbox.

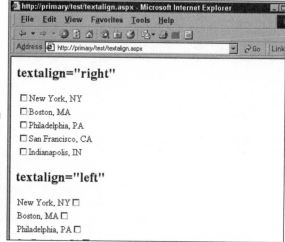

Figure 11-2: Right-aligned (the default) and left-aligned CheckBox Lists.

Repeat after me . . .

The `RepeatColumns`, `RepeatDirection`, and `RepeatLayout` properties give you some flexibility and options when deciding how your checkbox list should look.

`RepeatColumns` determines how many columns you want to use for organizing the checkboxes. ASP.NET does the math to figure out how many items should be in each column to balance it out. Here's an example:

```
<asp:checkboxlist id="States" runat="server"
repeatcolumns="3">
    <asp:listitem>1. Honda Accord</asp:listitem>
    <asp:listitem>2. Honda Civic</asp:listitem>
    <asp:listitem>3. Toyota RAV4</asp:listitem>
    <asp:listitem>4. BMW 3-Series</asp:listitem>
    <asp:listitem>5. Volkswagen Jetta</asp:listitem>
    <asp:listitem>6. Ford Escape</asp:listitem>
    <asp:listitem>7. Toyota Camry</asp:listitem>
</asp:checkboxlist>
```

Figure 11-3 shows the result.

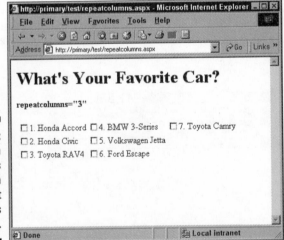

Figure 11-3:
Seven checkboxes in a list with Repeat Columns set to 3.

`RepeatDirection` determines whether the checkboxes are organized horizontally or vertically within the columns you create. The default is vertical. That's what you see in Figure 11-3. Figure 11-4 shows how the page differs if you add `repeatdirection="horizontal"` to the `<asp:checkboxlist>` tag.

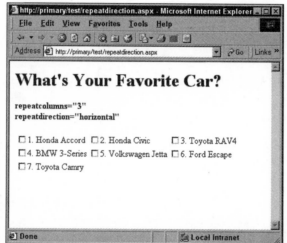

By default, an HTML table is used to organize your checkboxes into neat rows and columns. That's why the checkboxes in Figures 11-3 and 11-4 look so tidy. However, you can turn this off, if you want. That's what the RepeatLayout property does. You can set it to one of two values: table (the default) or flow. Figure 11-5 shows what setting repeatlayout to "flow" does to the appearance.

CellPadding and CellSpacing

CheckBoxList organizes the individual checkboxes into an invisible HTML table to help lay them out appropriately. HTML tables have two attributes that control how the content in them is spaced out: CellPadding and CellSpacing. These attributes appear as properties on the CheckBoxList. They work like this: Each cell in a table is a box that contains one checkbox and its associated text. CellPadding determines how big that box is and thus how much space exists around the checkbox and text. CellSpacing, on the other hand, determines how far apart each box is from the other boxes (or cells) in the table.

Because you can't actually see the table when using the CheckBoxList, CellPadding and CellSpacing both end up having the net effect of simply moving your checkboxes further away from each other.

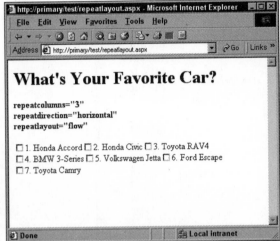

Figure 11-5:
Same
checkboxes
with Repeat
Layout set
to Flow.

AutoPostBack and SelectedIndexChanged

If you want to do something immediately when the user changes a checkbox in the list, use the AutoPostBack property and the SelectedIndexChanged event. As with the textbox, if AutoPostBack gets set to true, the page returns to the server every time the user makes a change to any of the checkboxes in the list. This gives the server a chance to catch the SelectedIndexChanged event and then execute the subroutine you specify. Here's an example:

```
<asp:checkboxlist id="FavoriteFoods"
onselectedindexchanged="Favorite_Change"
autopostback="true" runat="server">
    <asp:listitem>T-Bone Steak</asp:listitem>
    <asp:listitem>Mashed Potatoes</asp:listitem>
    <asp:listitem>Broccoli</asp:listitem>
</asp:checkboxlist>
```

These foods appear as a list of checkboxes. Whenever the user clicks one on or off, the page returns to the server (because autopostback is set to true). When this happens, the server sees that a value has been set for onselected indexchanged and then executes the Favorite_Change subroutine. For a complete example demonstrating the corresponding properties for a textbox (which work exactly the same way), see the section "Textbox's TextChanged event and AutoPostBack property," in Chapter 10.

The CheckBox control

CheckBoxList is a great option if you want to ask users several yes/no or true/false questions. But in some cases, you have only one question. Or, you have several, but you want to control the formatting and HTML that appears between them. In those cases, using the individual CheckBox server control is usually easier. Here's an example:

```
<%@Page Explicit="True" Language="VB" Debug="True" %>
<html>
<script runat="server">
Sub OK_Click(Sender As Object, E As EventArgs)
If Hollywood.Checked=True and Music.Checked=True Then
    Feedback.Text = "You subscribed to both. Thanks!"
ElseIf Hollywood.Checked=True Then
    Feedback.Text = _
        "You subscribed to Hollywood Gossip. Thanks!"
ElseIf Music.Checked=True Then
    Feedback.Text = "You subscribed to Music Gossip. Thanks!"
Else
    Feedback.Text = "You didn't subscribe to either!"
End If
End Sub
</script>
<body>
<h1>Sign Up For Our Electronic Newsletters</h1>
Are you sad because you don't receive enough junk in your
email box? Let us help. Sign up for our electronic
newsletters and you'll get a full Inbox every day!<br><br>
<form runat="server">
<h2>Hollywood Gossip</h2>
Get all the dirt on all your favorite actors and
actresses.<br>
<asp:checkbox id="Hollywood" runat="server"
text="Sign Me Up For Hollywood Gossip!"/><br>
<h2>Music Gossip</h2>
Get all the dirt on all your favorite musicians.<br>
<asp:checkbox id="Music" runat="server"
text="Sign Me Up For Music Gossip!"/><br><br>
<asp:button id="OKButton" text="OK" runat="server"
onclick="OK_Click" /><br><br>
<asp:label id="Feedback" runat="server" /><br>
</form>
</body>
</html>
```

You can see the result in Figure 11-6.

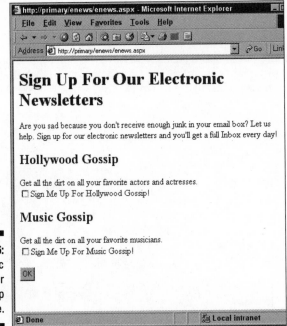

Figure 11-6:
Electronic
Newsletter
Signup
page.

The CheckBox is a pretty simple control. When you create it, you assign the text property, which becomes the label for the checkbox. Then, you simply look at the Checked property to find out what the user chose.

Common CheckBox members

In this section, I highlight the important CheckBox control properties, methods, and events. Table 11-2 summarizes the important CheckBox properties.

Table 11-2	The Key CheckBox Server Control Properties		
Property	**What It Specifies**	**How You Set It**	**Where to Go for More**
Text	The text that appears as a label for the checkbox	string	"The CheckBox control," earlier in this chapter
Checked	Whether a check-mark appears in the checkbox	true or false. Default: false	"The CheckBox control," earlier in this chapter

Property	What It Specifies	How You Set It	Where to Go for More
TextAlign	Whether the text labeling the checkbox appears to the right or to the left of the checkbox	TextAlign enumeration values (Right and Left). Default: Right	"TextAlign," earlier in this chapter
AutoPostBack	Whether the page should return to the server when the user changes the checkbox	true or false. Default: false	"AutoPostBack and CheckChanged," later in this chapter
Enabled, Visible, Tool Tip, ForeColor, BackColor, BorderColor, BorderStyle, Font, Height, Width, Visible			See Table 10-1 in Chapter 10

AutoPostBack and CheckChanged

AutoPostBack works for an individual checkbox the same way it does for the CheckBoxList. If AutoPostBack is set to true, then whenever the checkbox is changed, the page returns to the server to see if it needs to execute any events. The event name to capture for a CheckBox differs from the one for the CheckBoxList, however. In this example, the Agree_Change subroutine is executed whenever the checkbox is changed:

```
<asp:checkboxlist id="Agree"
Text="I agree to the terms stated above."
oncheckchanged="Agree_Change"
autopostback="true" runat="server"/>
```

Checked or Selected?

You may have noticed an inconsistency between CheckBoxList and the CheckBox control. If you want to see if an item in a CheckBoxList has a checkmark beside it, you use the Selected property:

```
If Primes.Items(ItemNum).Selected = True Then
```

But if you want to find out whether a CheckBox has a checkmark beside it, you use the Checked property:

```
If Hollywood.Checked=True and Music.Checked=True Then
```

Why? I don't know. But it is important to remember!

This is also true of the `RadioButtonList` and `RadioButton` **server controls.**

Radio for Help on Radio Buttons

Radio buttons are very similar to checkboxes. The only difference is that users may choose only one out of a list of a radio buttons. This characteristic makes them ideal for multiple-choice questions.

A RadioButtonList example: More gazillionaire trivia

In Chapter 7, I show you an example of using HTML links and the `QueryString` to create a trivia question page and another page that tells you whether you got the question right. In this section, I show you how to use the `RadioButtonList` to do the same thing in one simple page:

```
<%@Page Explicit="True" Language="VB" Debug="True" %>
<html>
<script runat="server">
Sub OK_Click(Sender As Object, E As EventArgs)
If Deadly.SelectedItem.Text = "Cowardice" Then
    Message.Text = "You're right! You really know your sins!"
    OKButton.Enabled = False
Else
    Message.Text = "No, sorry. " & Deadly.SelectedItem.Text &
    " is one of the Seven Deadly Sins."
    OKButton.Text = "Try Again!"
End If
End Sub
</script>
<body>
<h1>So Ya Wanna Be A Gazillionaire</h1>
For one gazillion dollars, answer this question:<br><br>
<b>Which of the following is <i>not</i> one of the
Seven Deadly Sins?</b><br>
<form runat="server">
<asp:radiobuttonlist id="Deadly"
repeatcolumns="2" runat="server">
    <asp:listitem selected="true">Gluttony</asp:listitem>
    <asp:listitem>Greed</asp:listitem>
    <asp:listitem>Envy</asp:listitem>
    <asp:listitem>Cowardice</asp:listitem>
    <asp:listitem>Anger</asp:listitem>
</asp:radiobuttonlist><br>
```

```
<asp:button id="OKButton" text="OK" runat="server"
onclick="OK_Click" /><br><br>
<asp:label id="Message" runat="server" /><br>
</form>
</body>
</html>
```

You can see the result in Figure 11-7.

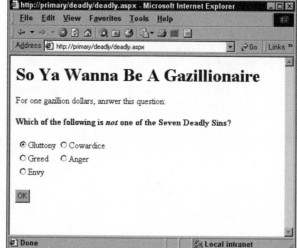

Figure 11-7:
Gazillionaire
trivia
question #2:
Know Your
Deadly Sins!

The `<asp:radiobuttonlist>` tag looks and works almost exactly like the `<asp:checkboxlist>` tag. The specific items are listed within the `<asp:radiobuttonlist>` tag using `<asp:listitem>`. The text in each list item is used to label each radio button.

In the first list item in this example, notice that `selected` is set to `"true"`. That's how you specify a default selected value for a list of radio buttons.

Always have a default radio button selected in a `RadioButtonList`. Otherwise, you run the risk that the user won't pick *any* of the possibilities and then you'll have to check for that possibility separately. If you start with a default, the user either has to stay with the default or choose a different option. After one of the radio buttons is selected, there's no way to unselect it without selecting another one.

Also, in this example, I use `repeatcolumns` to organize the radio buttons into two columns.

When the user chooses an option and clicks the button, the `OK_Clicked` subroutine is executed:

```
Sub OK_Click(Sender As Object, E As EventArgs)
If Deadly.SelectedItem.Text = "Cowardice" Then
    Message.Text="You're right! You really know your sins!"
    OKButton.Enabled=False
Else
    Message.Text="No, sorry. " & Deadly.SelectedItem.Text & _
        " is one of the Seven Deadly Sins."
    OKButton.Text="Try Again!"
End If
End Sub
```

Deadly is the name that was given to the RadioButtonList. SelectedItem
is a property that holds the currently selected item in the list. So, I simply
check the Text property of that item and see if it's the right one. If so, I con-
gratulate the user and disable the button.

If not, I apologize and inform the user that the selected option is, in fact, a
deadly sin. I do this by using the & concatenation operator to add the Text
property of the radio button item chosen. Then, I change the OK button's
text to "Try Again!"

A RadioButton example: Notification options

In much the same way as you can create individual checkboxes using the
CheckBox server control, you can create individual radio buttons using the
RadioButton server control. Here's an example:

```
<%@Page Explicit="True" Language="VB" Debug="True" %>
<html>
<script runat="server">
Dim UserEmail As String = "bradjones@edgequest.com"
Dim UserMail As String = "613 S. Grove St., Marion, IN"

Sub OK_Click(Sender As Object, E As EventArgs)
If Mail.Checked=True Then
    Feedback.Text = "You'll be notified by mail."
Else
    Feedback.Text = "You'll be the first to know via email!"
End If
End Sub
</script>
<body>
<h1>Notification Options</h1>
Please tell us how you'd prefer to be notified of updates
to our software:<br><br>
```

```
<form runat="server">
<asp:radiobutton id="Mail" runat="server"
text="Mail, Delivered To:" groupname="notification"/><br>
<b><%=UserMail%></b><br><br>
<asp:radiobutton id="Email" runat="server"
text="Email, Delivered To:" groupname="notification"/><br>
<b><%=UserEmail%></b><br><br>
<asp:button id="OKButton" text="OK" runat="server"
onclick="OK_Click" /><br><br>
<asp:label id="Feedback" runat="server" /><br>
</form>
</body>
</html>
```

In this page, information from variables is used within the radio button list. This isn't possible with the RadioButtonList control. Using individual RadioButton controls provides for more flexible formatting.

But you still need to have the radio buttons work together. That is, when one in the list is selected, you want all the rest to be unselected. You accomplish this with the groupname property. By setting it to be the same for both radio buttons, ASP.NET knows that you want them to work together as a group. You can include several groups of radio buttons on a page, as long as each group has a unique name.

Common RadioButtonList and RadioButton members

For a list of common properties used with RadioButtonList and RadioButton, see "Common CheckBoxList members" and "Common CheckBox members," earlier in this chapter. All the properties and events work the same and have the same names.

Only two properties exist that you're likely to use with a RadioButtonList that you wouldn't likely use with a CheckBoxList:

- SelectedIndex: A number indicating which radio button in the Items list is selected.
- SelectedItem: The actual radio button item that's selected.

These properties provide the most convenient way to determine which option the user chose. For a complete example of using a RadioButtonList and the SelectedItem property, see the section "A RadioButtonList example: More gazillionaire trivia," earlier in this chapter.

And there's only one property you're likely to use with `RadioButton` that you don't use with `CheckBox`: `GroupName`. The `GroupName` property determines the other radio buttons on the page with which this one should work. For an example of `GroupName` in action, see "A RadioButton example: Notification options," earlier in this chapter.

Your Kiss Is On My ListBox!

Similar to a list of checkboxes or radio buttons, a listbox enables the user to pick one or more options from a long list. But because a listbox can scroll its list of options, you can put many more possibilities in the list without taking up most of a page.

A ListBox example: The Personalize Your PC page

In this example, you provide your users with a listbox full of options they can add on to the new PC they're buying from you. The page then adds up the price and provides the user with a total.

```
<%@Page Explicit="True" Language="VB" Debug="True" %>
<html>
<script runat="server">
Sub OK_Click(Sender As Object, E As EventArgs)
Dim Total, ItemIndex As Integer
Message.Text = "You chose:<br>"
Total = 1000
For ItemIndex = 0 To PCOptions.Items.Count -1
    If PCOptions.Items(ItemIndex).Selected = True Then
        Message.Text = Message.Text & _
            PCOptions.Items(ItemIndex).Text & "<br>"
        Total = Total + PCOptions.Items(ItemIndex).Value
    End If
Next
Message.Text = Message.Text & "Your total is $" & Total
End Sub
</script>
<body>
<h1>Personalize Your PC</h1>
Thanks for deciding to purchase our choice,
one-of-a-kind Generic PC for a base price of only
$1000. Now you can pick from the following options
you'd like to add.<br>
<form runat="server">
```

```
<asp:listbox id="PCOptions" selectionmode="multiple"
runat="server">
   <asp:listitem value="100">
   CD-ROM Drive - $100</asp:listitem>
   <asp:listitem value="200">
   19 Inch Monitor - $200</asp:listitem>
   <asp:listitem value="150">
   Ink Jet Printer - $150</asp:listitem>
   <asp:listitem value="50">
   Joystick - $50</asp:listitem>
   <asp:listitem value="100">
   128MB More RAM - $100</asp:listitem>
</asp:listbox><br><br>
<asp:button id="OKButton" text="OK" runat="server"
onclick="OK_Click" /><br><br>
<asp:label id="Message" runat="server" /><br>
</form>
</body>
</html>
```

This page ends up looking like Figure 11-8.

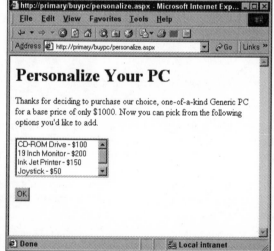

Figure 11-8:
The
Personalize
Your PC
page.

The format of the `<asp:listbox>` tag is similar to the `<asp:checkboxlist>` and `<asp:radiobuttonlist>` tags discussed earlier in this chapter. The outer tag surrounds several `<asp:listitem>` tags that include, as their text, the text that will appear on each line within the listbox.

Several new attributes inside the tag deserve attention. First, in the `<asp:listbox>` tag, notice that I set `selectionmode` to `multiple`. This setting enables users to choose multiple items in the listbox by holding down the Shift or Control keys as they click. You need to include this setting because the default value for `selectionmode` is `single`.

The `<asp:listitem>` tags also contain something new: `value`. The `value` attribute enables you to specify some information about each line that you want to keep, but don't necessarily want to display as part of the line in the listbox. You don't have to use `value` at all, but it is handy in cases like this. If I didn't have the value, I'd have to keep a separate list of the prices in an array or try to grab the last few characters of each string and figure it out from there.

When the user selects a few of the options and clicks OK, the `OK_Click` subroutine is executed:

```
Sub OK_Click(Sender As Object, E As EventArgs)
Dim Total, ItemIndex As Integer
Message.Text = "You chose:<br>"
Total = 1000
For ItemIndex = 0 To PCOptions.Items.Count -1
    If PCOptions.Items(ItemIndex).Selected = True Then
        Message.Text = Message.Text & _
            PCOptions.Items(ItemIndex).Text & "<br>"
        Total = Total + PCOptions.Items(ItemIndex).Value
    End If
Next
Message.Text = Message.Text & "Your total is $" & Total
End Sub
```

The loop goes through all the items in the listbox. (For more information on walking through a collection of items with a `For...Next` loop, see the section "A CheckBoxList example: Know Your Primes," earlier in this in chapter.)

If the current item is selected, the label `Message` has this item's name appended to it, followed by a `<br>` tag. In addition, the value of this item is added to the total.

Finally, after the loop ends, the `Message` label gets one more string added to the end: a total for the items selected, as the following example shows:

```
You chose:
CD-ROM Drive - $100
Ink Jet Printer - $150
Your total is $1250
```

Common ListBox members

Table 11-3 lists the important ListBox properties.

Table 11-3	The Key ListBox Server Control Properties		
Property	*What It Specifies*	*How You Set It*	*Where to Go for More*
Items(x). Selected	Whether the listbox item with the index of *x* is selected	true or false. Default: false	"A ListBox example: The Personalize Your PC page," earlier in this chapter
Items(x).Text	The line of text in the listbox for the item with the index of *x*	string	"A ListBox example: The Personalize Your PC page," earlier in this chapter
Items(x).Value	The value associated with the item in the listbox with the index of *x*	string	"A ListBox example: The Personalize Your PC page," earlier in this chapter
SelectionMode	Whether the user can select only one item or multiple items in the listbox	ListSelection Mode enumeration value (Multiple, Single). Default: Single	"A ListBox example: The Personalize Your PC page," earlier in this chapter
Rows	The height of the listbox in rows	integer. Default: 4	"An Add/ Remove/Clear example: The Grocery List page," later in this chapter
SelectedIndex	The index number of the currently selected item in the listbox	integer and	"SelectedIndex and SelectedItem," later in this chapter

(continued)

Table 11-3 *(continued)*

Property	What It Specifies	How You Set It	Where to Go for More
SelectedItem	The `ListItem` object of the currently selected item in the listbox	`ListItem` object	"SelectedIndex and SelectedItem" and "An Add/Remove/Clear example: The Grocery List page," later in this chapter
AutoPostBack	Whether the page should return to the server when the user changes the selected item(s)	true or false. Default: false	"AutoPostBack and Selected IndexChanged," later in this chapter
ForeColor, BackColor, BorderColor, BorderStyle, Font, Height, Width, Visible			See Table 10-1 in Chapter 10

Rows

The `Rows` property determines how many items appear in your `ListBox` at once. If the `ListBox` contains more than that number of items, the scrollbar enables you to see the rest.

The `ListBox` doesn't have a `Columns` property. By default, the `ListBox` makes itself wide enough to display the text of its longest item.

SelectedIndex and SelectedItem

As with radio buttons, the `SelectedIndex` and `SelectedItem` properties are quite handy for listboxes in which users can select only one item. `SelectedIndex` gives you the index number of that property, while `SelectedItem` actually returns the `ListItem` object itself.

AutoPostBack and SelectedIndexChanged

As with checkboxes and radio buttons, the listbox has an `AutoPostBack` property which, when set to true, causes the browser to return to the server every time the user changes the items selected. If your page specifies a `Selected IndexChanged` event for the `ListBox` control, the event is then executed.

Although this option is available, users don't usually expect to kick off a process by simply changing their selection in a listbox. Unless you have a very specific need, you should probably avoid using this event.

Common ListBox.Items members

The `ListBox` includes a collection called `Items`, which holds all the items in the `ListBox`. Table 11-3 includes some of the properties associated with *individual* items. However, numerous methods are associated with the *entire list*. You can use these methods to add items to the list, remove items from the list, clear the list entirely, and even search the list. Table 11-4 summarizes these methods.

Table 11-4	The Key ListBox.Items Methods	
Method	*What It Does*	*Where to Go for More*
`Items.Add(string1)`	Adds a row to the end of the list using *string1* as its text	"Items.Add and Items.Insert" and "An Add/Remove/Clear example: The Grocery List page," later in this chapter
`Items.Insert (integer1,string1)`	Adds a row at *integer1* index location in the list using *string1* as its text	"Items.Add and Items.Insert," later in this chapter
`Items.Remove (string1)`	Removes item from the list that has the text *string1*	"Items.Remove and Items.RemoveAt" and "An Add/Remove/Clear example: The Grocery List page," later in this chapter
`Items.RemoveAt (integer1)`	Removes item from the list that has the index *integer1*	"Items.Remove and Items.RemoveAt," later in this chapter
`Items.Clear()`	Removes all items from the list	"Items.Clear" and "An Add/Remove/Clear example: The Grocery List page," later in this chapter

(continued)

Table 11-4 *(continued)*

Method	What It Does	Where to Go for More
`Items.FindByText (string1)`	Finds the item in the list with text that matches *string1*	" The item sleuths: Items.FindByText and Items.FindByValue" and "Searching the grocery list with FindByText," later in this chapter
`Items.FindByValue (string1)`	Finds the item in the list with the value that matches *string1*	" The item sleuths: Items.FindByText and Items.FindByValue," later in this chapter

Items.Add and Items.Insert

When you want to add a new item to a listbox, you have a couple of different options, depending on whether you care about where the new item is placed in the list.

If you don't care, or you want the item placed at the bottom of the list, you can use `Items.Add`:

```
FavoriteFruit.Items.Add("Apple")
```

If you want the new item added at a specific index, you can use `Items.Insert`, as shown in the following example:

```
FavoriteFruit.Items.Insert(2, "Apple")
```

Before this line is executed, your list may look like this:

```
Pear
Grape
Lime
```

Here's what the list looks like after the line with `Items.Insert` is executed:

```
Pear
Apple
Grape
Lime
```

Items.Remove and Items.RemoveAt

To take items out of the list, use one of the Remove functions: Items.Remove and Items.RemoveAt. The only difference between the two is how you indicate which item you want to remove. With Items.Remove, you pass a string that matches the text of the one you want to remove — for example:

```
FavoriteFruit.Items.Remove("Grape")
```

There's another way you can indicate which item to get rid of with the Remove method: Send the ListItem object itself. Here's a common example:

```
FavoriteFruit.Items.Remove(FavoriteFruit.SelectedItem)
```

This line grabs the currently selected item object and sends it to the Remove function.

The Items.RemoveAt method requires you to send the index number of the item you want to remove. For example, assume you have the following list:

```
Pear
Apple
Grape
Lime
```

You'd use this line to remove Grape:

```
FavoriteFruit.Items.RemoveAt(2)
```

The index to a collection always begins counting with zero.

Items.Clear

The Items.Clear method is probably the simplest of them all. You don't pass any arguments. It simply removes all the items in the list at once:

```
FavoriteFruit.Items.Clear
```

The item sleuths: Items.FindByText and Items.FindByValue

If you're looking for a particular item in the list, you can always use a For...Next loop to go through all the items and compare Items(x).Text to whatever you're looking for. But there's a faster and easier way: Items.FindByText. Here's an example:

```
FoundItem = FavoriteFruit.Items.FindByText("Lime")
```

The Items.FindByText doesn't return the index of the item found. It returns the item *itself*. So, before you can receive the item back into a variable, you have to declare the variable to hold an object of type ListItem, as the following example shows:

```
Dim FoundItem As ListItem
FoundItem = FavoriteFruit.Items.FindByText("Lime")
If IsNothing(FoundItem) Then
    Response.Write("I found this item: " & FoundItem.Text)
End If
```

This code declares the variable, receives the object back, and displays it. There's just one gotcha. What if the item *isn't* found? Well, in that case, FoundItem will contain *nothing*. If you declare an integer, its initial value is set to 0. If you declare a variable to hold an object, like ListItem, what does it contain? Nothing. VB.NET's built-in IsNothing function enables you to check whether an object variable holds an object. If not, IsNothing returns true. In this example, you need to check that. If you try to display FoundItem.Text, and FoundItem contains nothing, you'll get an error.

The Items.FindByValue method works exactly like the Items.FindByText except, as you might expect, it looks through all the Items(x).Value properties for the string you pass. For more information on the Value property of the ListBox, see "A ListBox example: The Personalize Your PC page," earlier in this chapter.

An Add/Remove/Clear example: The Grocery List page

To demonstrate some of the important Items methods, I've created an example page that enables you to enter your grocery list:

```
<%@Page Explicit="True" Language="VB" Debug="True" %>
<html>
<script runat="server">
Sub Add_Click(Sender As Object, E As EventArgs)
GroceryList.Items.Add(AddText.Text)
End Sub
Sub Remove_Click(Sender As Object, E As EventArgs)
GroceryList.Items.Remove(GroceryList.SelectedItem)
End Sub
Sub Clear_Click(Sender As Object, E As EventArgs)
GroceryList.Items.Clear
End Sub
```

```
</script>
<body>
<h1>Your Online Grocery List</h1>
Welcome to your very own online grocery list.
I've included some items for you to get started. Feel
free to add and remove items as you see fit. Clear
erases the whole list, so be careful with that button!<br>
<form runat="server">
<asp:listbox id="GroceryList" rows="3" runat="server">
    <asp:listitem>5 Apples</asp:listitem>
    <asp:listitem>Orange Juice</asp:listitem>
    <asp:listitem>2 Gal. Milk</asp:listitem>
    <asp:listitem>2 Loaf Bread</asp:listitem>
    <asp:listitem>Potato Chips</asp:listitem>
</asp:listbox><br><br>
<asp:textbox id="AddText" runat="server" />
<asp:button id="AddButton" text="Add" runat="server"
onclick="Add_Click" /><br>
<asp:button id="RemoveButton" text="Remove" runat="server"
onclick="Remove_Click" />
<asp:button id="ClearButton" text="Clear" runat="server"
onclick="Clear_Click" /><br><br>
<asp:label id="Message" runat="server" /><br>
</form>
</body>
</html>
```

The result looks like Figure 11-9.

Figure 11-9:
The Grocery
List page.

Just type something in the textbox and click the Add button. The new item should be added to the bottom of the list. (You may have to scroll down to see it.) Then, click an item that you want to get rid of and click Remove. Or just click Clear to remove all the items.

Each button has its own subroutine, which is called when you click the button. When you click the Add button, for instance, the Add_Click subroutine is executed:

```
Sub Add_Click(Sender As Object, E As EventArgs)
GroceryList.Items.Add(AddText.Text)
End Sub
```

This subroutine simply takes the text and uses it as the argument for the Add function.

The Remove button calls the Remove_Click subroutine:

```
Sub Remove_Click(Sender As Object, E As EventArgs)
GroceryList.Items.Remove(GroceryList.SelectedItem)
End Sub
```

Here, the SelectedItem property is used to get the currently selected item and send it to the Remove method. The item is deleted.

Finally, the Clear button calls the Clear_Click subroutine:

```
Sub Clear_Click(Sender As Object, E As EventArgs)
GroceryList.Items.Clear
End Sub
```

Calling the Clear method removes all the items from the listbox.

Searching the grocery list with FindByText

You can enhance the Grocery List page with a Find capability by using the FindByText method.

Add these lines to the bottom of the page, just before </form>:

```
<asp:textbox id="FindText" runat="server" />
<asp:button id="FindButton" text="Find" runat="server"
onclick="Find_Click" /><br><br>
<asp:label id="FindMessage" runat="server" /><br>
```

This code creates the textbox, Find button, and label for displaying the results of the find.

Now add this subroutine in the `<script>` tag at the top of the page to respond to the `FindButton` click event:

```
Sub Find_Click(Sender As Object, E As EventArgs)
Dim FoundItem As ListItem
FoundItem = GroceryList.Items.FindByText(FindText.Text)
If Not IsNothing(FoundItem) Then
    FindMessage.Text = "Yes! Found it: " & FoundItem.Text
Else
    FindMessage.Text = "Nope! Sorry, didn't find it."
End If
End Sub
```

The `Items.FindByText` method is sent the text in the `FindText` textbox. If the item is found, it's returned into the `FoundItem` variable. Using the `IsNothing` function, the `If...Then` statement checks whether `FoundItem` contains an object. If it does, the `FoundItem` object's text is displayed.

Dropping in on the DropDownList

The drop-down list is a hybrid beast that looks like a textbox with a button beside it. When you click the button, you see something that looks like a list-box. But, when you're designing your user interface, the drop-down list works more like a set of radio buttons: It enables a user to pick one option from a list.

With a drop-down list, however, the option you choose remains clearly visible, but the other options don't appear on the screen unless you click the button. In this way, a drop-down list saves space and enables you to create a nicer looking page.

It's a listbox! No, it's a button!

Typically, the drop-down list is used on Web pages for two different purposes. Like a listbox or a list of radio buttons, it can simply enable the user to pick an option. Then, later, when a button is pushed, the chosen option can be noted, displayed, or stored.

But Web applications also have another common use for the drop-down list: kicking off an action, much like a button does. But instead of simply kicking off one predefined action, the drop-down list enables you to choose one of several actions.

A DropDownList example: Site navigation

The drop-down list is often used as a navigational tool, listing the popular destinations of your Web site. When users choose a destination from the drop-down list, they are immediately whisked away to that page.

As with the TextBox, CheckBoxList, RadioButtonList, and ListBox, the DropDownList has an AutoPostBack property. This property, in coordination with the SelectedIndexChanged event, provides the key to making this example work:

```
<%@Page Explicit="True" Language="VB" Debug="True" %>
<html>
<script runat="server">
Sub JumpTo_Change(Sender As Object, E As EventArgs)
Response.Redirect(JumpTo.SelectedItem.Text & ".aspx")
End Sub
</script>
<body>
<h1>Jump Page</h1>
<form runat="server">
Jump To:<br>
<asp:dropdownlist id="JumpTo" runat="server"
onselectedindexchanged="JumpTo_Change" autopostback="true">
    <asp:listitem></asp:listitem>
    <asp:listitem>News</asp:listitem>
    <asp:listitem>Articles</asp:listitem>
    <asp:listitem>Links</asp:listitem>
</asp:dropdownlist><br>
</form>
</body>
</html>
```

The page contains an <asp:dropdownlist> server control named JumpTo. The autopostback property is set to true, and onselectedindexchanged is set to the name of the subroutine that's at the top of the listing, inside the <script> tag.

If no list item is selected, the first one is selected by default. But notice here that the first item doesn't contain any text. Consequently, nothing is displayed in the box by default. This is important because the SelectedIndex Changed event only gets triggered if the selection *changes*. So, you need to start with a blank default.

Then, when the user chooses one of the other options, AutoPostBack causes the page to return to the server, and the JumpTo_Change subroutine is executed. That subroutine has only one line: a Response.Redirect that gets the text of the currently selected item and then appends ".aspx" to the end. So, if the user chooses News, the page attempts to redirect to News.aspx, and so on.

Providing a DropDownList to navigate your site or kick off one of multiple possible actions is very handy for your users.

Common DropDownList members

All the members of the ListBox and the ListBox.Items are available and work in the same way for the DropDownList. You need to be aware of only a few differences:

- DropDownList has no SelectionMode property. By its nature, a DropDownList allows the user to pick one and only one option. If the user needs to pick more than one option, use a ListBox or a CheckBoxList.

- DropDownList has no Columns or Rows properties. The control is automatically sized as needed.

- As demonstrated in the preceding section, the AutoPostBack property and the SelectedIndexChanged event are much more useful with the DropDownList than they are with the ListBox.

Chapter 12

Even More User Interface Goodies

*P*revious chapters in this part of the book explore all the common user interface elements that you can use to create interactive pages. In this chapter, I introduce three additional user interface topics.

First, I briefly discuss four additional controls that don't fit neatly anywhere else. They give you more flexibility by providing additional options when designing your pages.

I also introduce you to two very rich controls that provide a flexible calendar and a simple-to-use but full-featured banner ad rotator.

Finally, I explain how you can easily combine several controls together with your own functionality to create your own user control.

A Few Image, Link, and Button Controls

In this section, I describe some simple but interesting controls that provide a few more options when you're creating your own pages.

Your image consultant

If you've worked with HTML for long, you're familiar with the tag that's used to display pictures on a Web page. Here's an example:

```
<img src="stoplight.jpg" alt="Always Obey Stoplights!"
align="left">
```

The <img> tag displays the image specified by the src attribute and aligns the image with the other text on the page as specified by its align attribute. The alt attribute provides text that's displayed instead of the image in browsers that don't support images, or have them turned off.

Of course, you can use the <img> tag in the body of your ASP.NET pages, just as you can any HTML tag. But suppose you want to change the picture that's displayed with an <img> tag from your ASP.NET code? That would take some work.

But it's easy if you use the Image server control instead. Suppose you have two images: one of a stoplight that's green and another of a stoplight that's red. You want to display one of the images and switch to the other every time the user clicks a button. Piece of cake!

```
<%@Page Explicit="True" Language="VB" Debug="True" %>
<html>
<script runat="server">
Sub Switch_Click(Sender As Object, E As EventArgs)
If Stoplight.ImageURL="stoplightgo.bmp" Then
    Stoplight.ImageURL="stoplightstop.bmp"
Else
    Stoplight.ImageURL="stoplightgo.bmp"
End If
End Sub
</script>
<body>
<form runat="server">
<asp:image id="Stoplight" runat="server"
imageurl="stoplightgo.bmp"
alternatetext="Always Obey Stoplights!"
imagealign="top" /><br><br>
<asp:button id="Switch" text="Switch" runat="server"
onclick="Switch_Click"/>
</form>
</body>
</html>
```

The beautifully rendered bitmaps created by my art department (uh, that's me) and used on this page can be found on the CD-ROM in the back of this book.

This code produces a very simple page with the image and a button, as shown in Figure 12-1. Try clicking the button a few times. The image should switch back and forth.

The <asp:image> tag creates the server control. The imageurl attribute contains the path and filename of the image, and the alternatetext attribute displays the text that appears in browsers that don't support images. And finally, `imagealign` determines how the image appears alongside the rest of the text on the page.

You see the real benefit of using this control over the HTML `<img>` tag in the code at the top of the page in the `Switch_Click` subroutine. An `If...Then` statement checks for the current value of the `ImageURL` property and then switches it to the other one. You simply assign a new value to the `ImageURL` property, and the new image appears.

Click me — I'm beautiful: ImageButton

In some cases, it makes more sense for the user to click an image, rather than a button, to kick off some action. For example, if you show a picture of your family, you may enable users to click each person in turn within the image and see the name and other important information about that person.

You can't capture the click event for an `Image` server control. But another server control does provide a click event: the `ImageButton`. In fact, it not only informs you when the user clicks the image, it also tells you the precise location within the image where the user clicked!

Here's an example that extends the page from the previous section. You no longer need a button; you click directly on the stoplight image. And the image doesn't simply go back and forth between red and green anymore, either. If you click the top of the image, it turns red; if you click the bottom of the image, it turns green.

```
<%@Page Explicit="True" Language="VB" Debug="True" %>
<html>
<script runat="server">
Sub Stoplight_Click(Sender As Object, _
    E As ImageClickEventArgs)
If E.Y < 32 Then
    Stoplight.ImageURL="stoplightstop.bmp"
Else
    Stoplight.ImageURL="stoplightgo.bmp"
End If
End Sub
</script>
<body>
<form runat="server">
<asp:imagebutton id="Stoplight" runat="server"
imageurl="stoplightgo.bmp"
alternatetext="Always Obey Stoplights!"
imagealign="top"
onclick="Stoplight_Click" /><br><br>
</form>
</body>
</html>
```

As shown in Figure 12-2, the result is a page that contains only the image. If you click the top part of the image, the red light bitmap is displayed. And if you click the bottom part of the image, the green light bitmap appears.

The `<asp:image>` tag is replaced with the `<asp:imagebutton>` tag. All the attributes are the same, with the addition of `onclick`. This event triggers the `Stoplight_Click` subroutine at the top of the page.

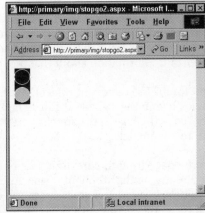

Figure 12-2:
The stoplight page, revision 2.0.

You may have noticed that this event's second argument is a bit different from normal. Usually, you'd expect to see this: E As EventArgs. Because this event provides specific information through this argument, you must use ImageClickEventArgs as the type for E instead.

How does this event use the E argument? Well, two important pieces of information are passed as properties of E: the X and Y coordinates of the mouse pointer when the user clicked. If you think of the image as a tiny grid of dots, E.X identifies how many dots from the left the user clicked. E.Y indicates how many dots from the top the user clicked.

In this page, I only care about how far from the top the user clicked. Because 32 is roughly between the two circles, I check to see if the user clicked above or below that line. If above, I use the red light image; if below, I use the green light image.

How did I figure out that 32 was the magic number? I just created a page that displayed E.Y in a label every time I clicked on the image. That way, I could find a number that was in the middle. That's usually the easiest approach if you want to use techniques like this in your own pages.

A button disguised as a link: LinkButton

Usually, when users click a link, they expect to be whisked away to another page. But in some cases, you'd like a link to do what a button normally does: return to the server and execute code you've written to respond to the event. That's what the LinkButton does.

Think of the LinkButton as a normal button dressed up to look like a link. In this example, users type their name and then click a link. Instead of sending users to another page, as they might expect, this page executes a subroutine and uses a label to respond to the users:

```
<%@Page Explicit="True" Language="VB" Debug="True" %>
<html>
<script runat="server">
Sub NormalLink_Click(Sender As Object, E As EventArgs)
Message.Text = "Fooled you, " & Name.Text & _
    "! Thought you were going somewhere, didn't you?"
End Sub
</script>
<body>
<form runat="server">
Enter Your Name:<br>
<asp:textbox id="Name" runat="server" /><br><br>
```

```
Then click on the link below:<br>
<asp:linkbutton id="NormalLink" runat="server"
onclick="NormalLink_Click">
This looks like a normal link
</asp:linkbutton><br><br>
<asp:label id="Message" runat="server" />
</form>
</body>
</html>
```

After you type your name and click the link, the page looks something like Figure 12-3.

Figure 12-3:
Looks like a link, acts like a button: the LinkButton.

The `<asp:linkbutton>` tag doesn't have any unusual attributes. The text that appears as a link is the text between the open and close tag. The `onclick` attribute sends you to the `NormalLink_Click` subroutine. There, the label's text is filled in, making use of the name the user entered.

The hysterical HyperLink

Just like a normal HTML `<a>` tag, a `HyperLink` enables you to display some text that users can click to go to another page. However, because `HyperLink` is a server control, you also can access and manipulate it from code just as you do with the `Image` server control (see "Click me — I'm beautiful: ImageButton," earlier in this chapter).

For example, in your code, you can dynamically change the target of a
`HyperLink`.

In Chapter 7, I demonstrate a couple of pages that together create Web
Roulette. The first page simply provides users with a link. When users click
the link, Web Roulette sends them to a second page that picks a Web site at
random from an array and then uses `Response.Redirect` to send them to
the randomly selected site.

By using the `HyperLink` server control, you can do the same thing with only
one page. It looks like this:

```
<%@Page Explicit="True" Language="VB" Debug="True" %>
<html>
<script runat="server">
Sub Page_Load(Sender As Object, E As EventArgs)
Dim Sites(10) As String
Dim Num As Integer
Randomize
Sites(1) = "http://www.microsoft.com"
Sites(2) = "http://www.borland.com"
Sites(3) = "http://www.netscape.com"
Sites(4) = "http://www.sun.com"
Sites(5) = "http://www.ibm.com"
Sites(6) = "http://www.lotus.com"
Sites(7) = "http://www.discovery.com"
Sites(8) = "http://www.comedy.com"
Sites(9) = "http://www.futility.com"
Sites(10) = "http://www.ebay.com"
Num = Int(Rnd * 10) + 1
RouletteLink.NavigateURL = Sites(Num)
End Sub
</script>
<body>
<h1>Welcome to Web Site Roulette</h1>
<p>Care to take a spin on the wheel? Round and round
she goes! Where she stops - Well, you'll find out...</p>
<p>When you're ready, just click...</p>
<form runat="server">
<asp:hyperlink id="RouletteLink" runat="server" >
<center><h3>SPIN!</h3></center>
</asp:hyperlink>
</form>
</body>
</html>
```

The page looks like Figure 12-4. Click the link. Go back. Click Refresh. Then
click the link again. Keep it up. You should go to a different place each time.

Figure 12-4:
Web
Roulette,
revision 2.0.

Although this page and the one in Chapter 7 look similar to the user, they work very differently. The one in Chapter 7 decides which page to go to after the user clicks. This page decides when the page is first loaded. In fact, in Internet Explorer, you can make your pointer hover over the link and look down at the browser status bar and see where the link will take you. Each time you click Refresh, that changes.

Why? Well, the `<asp:hyperlink>` control appears in the body with only `id` and `runat` attributes. The important attribute — `NavigateURL`, which identifies the destination Web site — isn't filled in until the code in the `Page_Load` event is executed (when the page is requested). This code picks a random element from the array and assigns that to `NavigateURL`, thus sending the user to a different spot every time the page is refreshed and the link is clicked.

Marking Time with the Calendar Control

All the server controls that I show you in previous pages of this book are used to create relatively standard user interface elements that are pretty familiar to you. But Microsoft didn't stop there. Just to show what's possible with server controls, Microsoft created a couple of *rich* user interface controls. *Rich* in this context means that they have lots of built-in functionality and they provide a broad range of properties, events, and methods that enable you to customize how they work.

The first of these rich server controls that I describe is the `Calendar`. By including just a single tag and setting a couple of attributes, you can create a fully functional monthly calendar that users can easily navigate.

A Calendar example: Unborn Baby Age Calculator

To demonstrate the `Calendar` server control (and because my wife is about 37 weeks pregnant with our first child as I write!), I have created the Unborn Baby Age Calculator:

```
<%@Page Explicit="True" Language="VB" Debug="True" %>
<html>
<script runat="server">
Sub DateSelected(Sender As Object, E As EventArgs)
Dim WeeksUntilDue,WeeksOld As Integer
TodayDate.Text = "Today's Date: <b>" & Today & "</b>"
DueDate.Text = _
    "Due Date: <b>" & BabyAgeCalendar.SelectedDate & "</b>"
WeeksUntilDue = _
    DateDiff("w",Today,BabyAgeCalendar.SelectedDate)
If WeeksUntilDue > 40 Then
    Message.Text = "<i>If that's your due date, " & _
        "then you haven't conceived yet!</i>"
ElseIf WeeksUntilDue < -5
    Message.Text = "<i>You really should have " & _
        "delivered this child by now!</i>"
Else
    WeeksOld = 40 - WeeksUntilDue
    Message.Text = _
        "Your baby is <b>" & WeeksOld & "</b> weeks old"
End If
End Sub
</script>
<body>
<h1>Unborn Baby Age Calculator</h1>
<p>So you're expecting! Congratulations! Find out how many
weeks old the baby forming inside you is right now. Just
click on your due date!</p>
<form runat="server">
<center>
<asp:calendar id="BabyAgeCalendar" runat="server"
onselectionchanged="DateSelected"/><br>
</center>
<asp:label id="TodayDate" runat="server" /><br>
<asp:label id="DueDate" runat="server" /><br>
<asp:label id="Message" runat="server" /><br>
</form>
</body>
</html>
```

If you are pregnant (or know someone who is), just click the little arrows in the upper-left and upper-right corners of the calendar to navigate to the right month and year. Then click the due date and find out exactly how many weeks old the little one is, as shown in Figure 12-5.

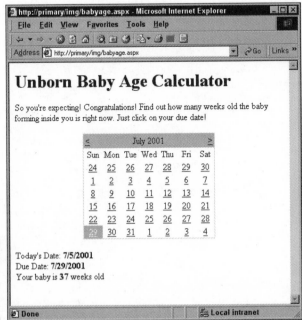

Figure 12-5:
Unborn
Baby Age
Calculator.

This control is amazingly cool and functional, and getting it to work takes incredibly little effort. As you can see, the `<asp:calendar>` tag requires only an `id` and a `runat` attribute. And, if you want to capture the user's click as an event, you need `onselectionchanged`.

After the user clicks a date, the `DateSelected` subroutine is executed. The `SelectedDate` property returns the date the user clicked. This, along with today's date, is displayed in the appropriate labels.

After that comes the real calculation:

```
WeeksUntilDue = _
    DateDiff("w",Today,BabyAgeCalendar.SelectedDate)
```

`DateDiff` is a built-in VB.NET function. It accepts two dates and returns the number of days, weeks, months, or years between the dates. Because I included a `"w"` as the first argument, it gives me the difference in weeks.

The only other little bit of information you need to know is that the average pregnancy goes about 40 weeks. So, subtracting WeeksUntilDue from 40 gives you the age of the child!

Common Calendar members

The Calendar example in the preceding section looks simple but works quite well. However, if you couldn't change its look and feel, it might look out of place on some sites. Fortunately, the folks at Microsoft made this control very customizable. They did this by providing a whole host of properties and methods.

I don't have the space to introduce and explain each of those properties here. You can look them up for yourself as you need them. But I do point out a few highlights.

Global Calendar properties

You can change the look of the whole calendar by setting a couple of properties. FirstDayOfWeek, for example, enables you to determine which day of the week shows up in the first column of the calendar. ShowGridLines determines whether lines appear separating the days. (This property is false, by default.)

Parts is parts — The pieces of a calendar

But most of the changes you can make to the calendar involve the individual sections of the control:

- ✔ **Title:** The part at the top that contains the month and year. Title includes the Next/Prev Month arrows described in the next bullet.
- ✔ **Next/Prev Month:** The little arrows on either side of the month/year that enable you to navigate to the next and previous month.
- ✔ **Day Header:** The first row of column headers, with the day names.
- ✔ **Days:** All the individual days listed on the calendar.
- ✔ **Weekend Days:** The days on the calendar that represent Saturday and Sunday.
- ✔ **Selected Days:** The day or days that have been selected by the user.

You can turn the display of some of these parts on or off using these calendar properties: ShowTitle, ShowNextPrevMonth, and ShowDayHeader. You can change the formatting of some of these parts by changing these properties: TitleFormat, NextPrevFormat, and DayNameFormat.

In addition, numerous sub-objects inside the calendar represent the style of these different parts of the calendar control. By manipulating the properties of these sub-objects, you describe how you want that part to look. These are some of the important style sub-objects: `TitleStyle`, `NextPrevStyle`, `DayHeaderStyle`, `DayStyle`, `WeekendDayStyle`, and `SelectedDayStyle`.

How do these sub-objects work? Well, you'll find various style properties for nearly any visible server control. Examples include: `ForeColor`, `BackColor`, `BorderStyle`, `BorderWidth`, and the `Font` object with all its properties. They are available for the calendar control itself, and when you set them, the settings affect the whole control.

But each of these style objects also has *its own set* of those same properties. If you set them, you affect just *that part* of the calendar control.

For example, change the calendar control in the Unborn Baby Age Calculator example from earlier in this chapter to look like this:

```
<asp:calendar id="BabyAgeCalendar" runat="server"
showgridlines="true" backcolor="skyblue"
titlestyle-backcolor="yellow"
dayheaderstyle-backcolor="red"
onselectionchanged="DateSelected"/>
```

Notice that `backcolor` for the calendar control itself is set to `skyblue`. That affects the whole calendar. But the `titlestyle` sub-object's `backcolor` is set to `yellow`, and the `dayheaderstyle` sub-object's `backcolor` is set to `red`. So when you see the calendar, everything is blue but the title and day headers. Figure 12-6 shows the new calendar, but doesn't quite capture all the subtle hues described.

Sub-object syntax

When you refer to the properties of sub-objects in the `<asp:calendar>` tag, you use the sub-object name, then a dash, and then the property name. I describe this syntax in Chapter 8, but because you may not have run into it very often, I mention it again here.

Of course, if you're referring to the sub-object property in code, you use dot notation and enumeration properties (also covered in Chapter 8), as in the following example:

```
BabyAgeCalendar.TitleStyle.BackColor = Drawing.Color.Yellow
```

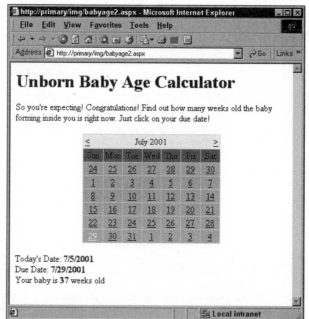

Figure 12-6:
The colorful
Unborn
Baby Age
Calculator.

The Calendar has lots of sub-objects, each with numerous properties. If you're setting several properties on several sub-objects, you might find it easier to use this alternate syntax:

```
<asp:calendar id="BabyAgeCalendar" runat="server"
showgridlines="true" backcolor="skyblue"
onselectionchanged="DateSelected">

<titlestyle backcolor="yellow"
forecolor="blue" font-bold="true" />

<dayheaderstyle backcolor="red"
forecolor="yellow" font-italic="true"/>

</asp:calendar>
```

Here, instead of immediately closing the <asp:calendar> tag, I've put additional tags inside it. These additional tags *are* the sub-objects. Then, within each sub-object's tags, you can set *its* individual properties. If the sub-object itself has a sub-object, as in the case of font, you can use the dash notation: font-bold="true".

Calendar events

Finally, in addition to the `SelectionChanged` event that I use in the Unborn Baby Age example, there's one more event you might find useful: `VisibleMonthChanged`. It happens, as you might expect, when the user clicks the next or previous links to change the displayed month.

Rotating Banner Ads Made Easy

Another very useful server control that Microsoft includes with the .NET Framework is the `AdRotator`. This control, as you might have guessed, enables you to display banner ads on your site and easily control their rotation and frequency of appearance.

An AdRotator example

Adding the `AdRotator` to your page is pretty simple. Here's a page with the `AdRotator` centered at the top. (Don't try this example yet. To make it work, you need the advertisement file that I describe in the next section.)

```
<%@Page Explicit="True" Language="VB" Debug="True" %>
<html>
<body>
<form runat="server">
<center>
<asp:adrotator id="HeaderAd"  runat="server"
advertisementfile="adlist.xml"/>
</center>
<h1>Really Important News</h1>
<p>Blah blah blah. Blah blah blah blah blah blah. Blah blah
blah blah blah. Blah blah blah. Blah blah blah blah blah
blah. Blah blah blah blah blah.</p>
</form>
</body>
</html>
```

You can see the result in Figure 12-7.

The XML AdvertisementFile

The `AdRotator` server control is pretty simple because another file actually holds all the important information that the control needs to work. The `advertisementfile` property points to that file. In my `AdRotator` example, it points to a file named `adlist.xml`.

This file, you notice, has the extension .xml. It's an XML file. XML is a way of formatting information in data files to make it easy to read and easy to access. XML looks a lot like HTML in that it has named tags that surround text. There are two primary differences:

✔ XML files aren't typically used to display information in a browser. Instead, they are used to store and transmit information.

✔ Different XML files have their own set of tag names and rules about how the different tags work together.

For example, the AdRotator control works with an XML file that looks something like this:

```
<Advertisements>
<Ad>
  <ImageUrl>widgets.jpg</ImageUrl>
  <NavigateUrl>http://www.edgequest.com/widgets</NavigateUrl>
  <AlternateText>Buy Widgets!</AlternateText>
  <Impressions>25</Impressions>
</Ad>
<Ad>
  <ImageUrl>books.jpg</ImageUrl>
  <NavigateUrl>http://www.edgequest.com/books</NavigateUrl>
  <AlternateText>Books For Sale!</AlternateText>
  <Impressions>75</Impressions>
</Ad>
</Advertisements>
```

Try out the example page presented in the preceding section with this XML file as its `adlist.xml`. You can create your own image files or you can use the ones from the CD-ROM in the back of the book.

You should note several important things about this file:

- ✔ It's just a text file that can be created in Notepad, just as you would an HTML file. Be sure you save it with the `.xml` extension.

- ✔ You can have as many `<Ad>` tags, one after the other, inside the `<Advertisement>` tag as you like. You can have one only `<Advertisement>` tag in a file, and it must surround everything else in the file.

- ✔ Every open tag must have a corresponding close tag.

- ✔ Unlike HTML, the upper- or lowercase letters used in the names of the tags *are important*. The tags should always appear exactly as you see them here.

- ✔ The tags inside the `<Ad>` tag can appear in any order.

Each `<Ad>` tag surrounds a single advertisement that you want to display. You can specify several tags for each ad. Each of these tags is optional, but you'll likely always want to specify a few of them:

- ✔ `<ImageUrl>`: The name of the image file to display.

- ✔ `<NavigateUrl>`: The URL where users should be sent if they click on the ad.

- ✔ `<AlternateText>`: The text that should appear in place of the graphic in browsers that don't support graphics or have graphics turned off. (Also, the text that appears as a ToolTip in Internet Explorer when your mouse pointer hovers over an image.)

- ✔ `<Impressions>`: A number indicating how often you want this ad to appear as opposed to all the other ads in this file.

How it works

The process works like this: When the `AdRotator` control is first processed on the page, it goes out to the specified XML file and reads in the information. It notes how many ads are in the file. It then chooses one of the ads to display at random. But they don't all have an even chance. Their chances are weighted based on the number for each ad in the `<Impressions>` tag. The higher the number, the more likely that particular ad is to come up. You can put any number you like in the `<Impressions>` tag for each ad.

One strategy is to coordinate all the numbers so they add up to 100. Then, each number represents the percentage of time that ad will appear. You aren't constrained to this approach, but it is one way to help keep things clear!

Other possibilities

In the preceding sections, I present a simple example of using the AdRotator. It's capable of much more.

For example, you can choose ads for a given page more specifically by setting a keywordfilter attribute that is then matched to one or more keywords in the <Keyword> tag in the XML file. This is handy if you want to display more targeted ads based on the users' interests or based on search words they enter.

When users click the banner, you can choose to launch a new page or send the resulting page to a specific frame of a frameset. All this is possible with the target attribute.

Or, if you want to control more precisely where and how the ads are displayed, you can specify a value for onadcreated to capture the AdCreated event. There, through the arguments the event subroutine receives, you can control virtually every aspect of the process of picking and displaying the ad.

For more information on these and other features, see the.NET Framework online help.

Do It Yourself: User Controls

Microsoft has obviously provided a bunch of interesting server controls to make designing the user interface of your Web applications a fruitful task.

You mean like #include?

In Classic ASP, the best way to share subroutines or HTML across several pages is to use the #include directive. Although this option is still available, user controls offer a much better approach. When using #include, you have to make sure that you don't declare variables or use subroutine or function names that might conflict with names on a page. And often, using #include several times on a page with the same file causes problems. All these troubles vanish if you use user controls.

But wouldn't it be nice if you could package up parts of your page and reuse those parts in other pages, as if they were a new server control? That's exactly what user controls enable you to do.

Creating a reusable page header

When you design a Web site, you may want to create a banner that goes across the top of virtually every page on your site. This page header prominently displays the name of your site at the left and perhaps provides some commonly accessed links along the right.

You could simply create the header and then copy and paste the HTML into each page where it's needed. That works and doesn't require too much effort. But suppose you change your color scheme. Or, you change the name or location of one of those pages listed among the banner's links. Now you have to revisit every page with a banner and change it. A major pain!

There's a better way! You can create a user control that contains the header and then drop that user control on each page where it should appear. In the future, when you change the user control, all the pages that use are automatically updated.

Here's an example of just such a header created as a user control:

Enter the following code into a file and save the file with the name `Header.ascx`. Notice the extension: `.ascx`. It's different from a typical page. (You won't be able to see the results of this page until you create a page that uses this control, which I show you how to do in the next section of this chapter.)

```
<%@ Control Explicit="True" Language="VB" Debug="True" %>
<table width="100%" cellpadding="10" bgcolor="blue"><tr><td>
<asp:label id="HeaderLabel" runat="server"
backcolor="blue" forecolor="yellow"
font-size="18 pt" font-name="Arial" font-bold="true"
text="EdgeQuest"/></td>
<td align="right" ><b>
<asp:hyperlink id="HomeLink" runat="server"
navigateurl="home.htm">
<font color="yellow">Home</font>
</asp:hyperlink> *
<asp:hyperlink id="NewsLink" runat="server"
navigateurl="news.htm">
<font color="yellow">News</font>
</asp:hyperlink> *
<asp:hyperlink id="ArticlesLink" runat="server"
navigateurl="articles.htm">
<font color="yellow">Articles</font>
</asp:hyperlink> *
```

```
<asp:hyperlink id="LinksLink" runat="server"
navigateurl="links.htm">
<font color="yellow">Links</font>
</asp:hyperlink>
</b></tr></table>
```

This is a user control. It looks and works very much like a normal ASP.NET page: HTML and server controls are mixed freely throughout the page. Specifically, this control has five server controls: a label for the site name and four hyperlink controls to provide quick access to key areas on the site. These server controls are organized into an HTML table to format them and add a bit of color.

You can even have a `<script runat="server">` section in a user control, if you like. However, a user control differs from a normal ASP.NET page in a few important ways:

- ✔ The name of the file has an extension of `.ascx` rather than `.aspx`. That ensures that no one will try to retrieve the user object page directly.

- ✔ The `@ Page` directive at the top is replaced with the `@ Control` directive. The attributes you specify within the directive are largely the same.

- ✔ There are *no* `<html>`, `<body>`, or `<form>` tags. Never use these tags in a user control.

That's all there is to creating a user control!

Using the page header

You can make use of a user control in any ASP.NET page. Here's a very simple page that makes use of the header you created in the preceding section:

```
<%@ Page Explicit="True" Language="VB" Debug="True" %>
<%@ Register TagPrefix="ASPFD" TagName="Header"
Src="header.ascx" %>
<html>
<body>
<form runat="server">
<aspfd:header runat="server"/>
<h1>Really Important News</h1>
<p>Blah blah blah. Blah blah blah blah blah blah. Blah blah
blah blah blah. Blah blah blah. Blah blah blah blah blah
blah. Blah blah blah blah blah.</p>
</form>
</body>
</html>
```

The user control provides a header for the page, as you can see in Figure 12-8.

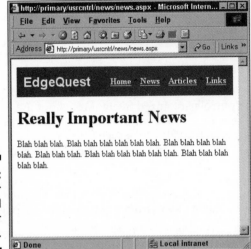

Figure 12-8:
The user
control
header
on a page.

The first thing you notice is the @ Register directive, which appears right below the @ Page directive. You must include an @ Register directive line for *each different type* of user control you use on this page.

The @ Register directive provides two important bits of information: the *name* (including prefix) you want the control to have in this page and the *file* where the user control can be found.

On this page, I've given the control a prefix of ASPFD (an abbreviation for the title of this book) and a name of Header. You can pick any prefix and name you want. It is common to make the prefix the name of your company or your department and use the same prefix for all user controls you develop.

If the user control's .ascx file is in a different folder, you can specify a path in the Src attribute, along with the filename. In this case, the file is in the same folder as the page that uses it.

Finally, after the user control is registered, you can use it one or more times anywhere in the page, just as you would a server control:

```
<aspfd:header runat="server"/>
```

You can add an id if you need to refer to the control from code. If you don't need to refer to the control from code, an id isn't necessary.

Rolling your own dice

As useful as the techniques in the previous couple of sections are, user controls can do much more than simply package controls and HTML to be dropped on a page. They can help make your pages come to life!

Here's an example: Suppose you were creating one or more Web games that used standard dice. Wouldn't it be nice to have a die user control that you could just drop into a page whenever you needed one?

I thought so. So I created this one, which I called `die.ascx`:

```
<%@ Control Explicit="True" Language="VB" Debug="True" %>
<script runat="server">
Public Showing As Integer

Private Sub ClearDie
UpLeft.Text = " "
UpMid.Text = " "
UpRight.Text = " "
MidLeft.Text = " "
MidMid.Text = " "
MidRight.Text = " "
LowLeft.Text = " "
LowMid.Text = " "
LowRight.Text = " "
End Sub

Sub Roll
Showing = Int(Rnd * 6) + 1
ClearDie
Select Case Showing
Case 1
   MidMid.Text = "O"
Case 2
   UpLeft.Text = "O"
   LowRight.Text = "O"
Case 3
   UpLeft.Text = "O"
   MidMid.Text = "O"
   LowRight.Text = "O"
Case 4
   UpLeft.Text = "O"
   LowRight.Text = "O"
   UpRight.Text = "O"
   LowLeft.Text = "O"
Case 5
   UpLeft.Text = "O"
   LowRight.Text = "O"
```

```
      UpRight.Text = "0"
      LowLeft.Text = "0"
      MidMid.Text = "0"
Case 6
      UpLeft.Text = "0"
      MidLeft.Text = "0"
      LowLeft.Text = "0"
      UpRight.Text = "0"
      MidRight.Text = "0"
      LowRight.Text = "0"
End Select
End Sub

</script>
<table width="75" height="75" border="1"
cellspacing="0"><tr><td>
<table width="100%"><tr>
<td align="center">
<asp:label id="UpLeft" runat="server" /></td>
<td align="center">
<asp:label id="UpMid" runat="server" /></td>
<td align="center">
<asp:label id="UpRight" runat="server" /></td>
</tr><tr>
<td align="center">
<asp:label id="MidLeft" runat="server" /></td>
<td align="center">
<asp:label id="MidMid" runat="server" /></td>
<td align="center">
<asp:label id="MidRight" runat="server" /></td>
</tr><tr>
<td align="center">
<asp:label id="LowLeft" runat="server" /></td>
<td align="center">
<asp:label id="LowMid" runat="server" /></td>
<td align="center">
<asp:label id="LowRight" runat="server" /></td>
</tr></table></tr></td></table>
```

Unlike the previous example, this one does include a `<script runat="server">` section. But before I get to that, take a look at the table in the bottom part of the page. Actually, there are two tables. The first is just a one-cell table that has a one-pixel border and a set height and width. This defines the box within which I create a die.

Inside the box is another table. This one has no border and is designed to fill the space inside the outer table. The inner table has three rows and three columns for a total of nine cells. Inside each cell is a label with a name appropriate to its location: UpLeft, MidRight, LowRight, and so on. Think of it like a tic-tac-toe board. I place dots in these labels as appropriate to mimic the way a die looks for each roll.

Now look back up in that `<script>` section. There's a subroutine called `Roll` which, appropriately enough, rolls this die. It does that by picking a random number between 1 and 6. That's the easy part. The tougher part is showing the result.

First, I call the `ClearDie` subroutine. This subroutine simply goes through all the labels and puts an ` ` or *non-breaking space* inside each one. This is a character that you can use in HTML to force a space to appear in a location. HTML typically ignores regular spaces, but this kind of space is not ignored.

Notice that the `ClearDie` subroutine is labeled as `Private`. This means that only other subroutines *in this user control* can call it. It can't be called from the page that uses this user control. On the other hand, `Roll` is not labeled `Private` and it is available to be called from the page.

After the die is empty, I can use a `Case` statement to fill in the appropriate dots for each possible outcome:

```
Select Case Showing
Case 1
    MidMid.Text = "O"
Case 2
    UpLeft.Text = "O"
    LowRight.Text = "O"
. . .
Case 6
    UpLeft.Text = "O"
    MidLeft.Text = "O"
    LowLeft.Text = "O"
    UpRight.Text = "O"
    MidRight.Text = "O"
    LowRight.Text = "O"
End Select
```

I use a capital *O* to create the dots. You can change it to *, +, or whatever you prefer.

And that's all there is to the die user control. It's completely self-contained: a random number generator and an intuitive way to display the results.

Yacht. See?

Now you can create a page that puts the die user control to work. One of the more popular dice games in the U.S. is called Yacht (commercially sold as Yahtzee®). Although creating a full-blown Yacht game would take more time and space than I can offer to the project in these pages, I can create a miniature version that uses only three dice and has only one goal: to get three of a kind with three dice!

```
<%@Page Explicit="True" Language="VB" Debug="True" %>
<%@ Register TagPrefix="ASPFD" TagName="Die"
Src="die.ascx" %>
<html>
<script runat="server">
Sub Roll_Click(Sender As Object, E As EventArgs)
Dim HowMany(6) As Integer
Dim Pips As Integer
Message.Text = ""
Die1.Roll
Die2.Roll
Die3.Roll
If Die1.Showing = Die2.Showing And _
    Die2.Showing = Die3.Showing Then
        Message.Text = _
            "You WIN! You got three of a kind with " & _
            Die1.Showing
End If
End Sub
</script>
<body>
<form runat="server">
<h1>Mini-Yacht</h1>
<table><tr>
<td><aspfd:die id="Die1" runat="server" /></td>
<td><aspfd:die id="Die2" runat="server" /></td>
<td><aspfd:die id="Die3" runat="server" /></td>
</tr></table><br>
<asp:button runat="server" text="Roll!"
onclick="Roll_Click" /><br><br>
<asp:label id="Message" runat="server" />
</form>
</body>
</html>
```

I placed three die user controls on this page. And to get them to line up nicely beside each other, I use a simple one-row, three-column table (with no border). Initially, the dice appear as blank boxes. But when you click the Roll! button, the boxes are filled with the values rolled, as shown in Figure 12-9.

Clicking the button causes the Roll_Click subroutine to be executed.

The Roll method of each die is called. Then, the Showing property is used to see the value showing on each die. I didn't really mention the Showing property before, but if you look at the code for the user control, you'll see it up at the top of the <script> section:

```
. . .
<script runat="server">
Public Showing As Integer
```

```
Private Sub ClearDie
UpLeft.Text = " "
UpMid.Text = " "
. . .
```

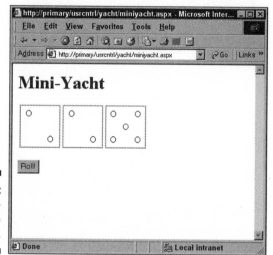

Because this variable is identified as `Public`, it effectively becomes a property of this user control. This enables the page that uses the control to access its value. Each die uses this variable to hold the random number generated:

```
Sub Roll
Showing = Int(Rnd * 6) + 1
ClearDie
Select Case Showing
```

If all three dice show the same number, the user wins and is informed using the Message label:

```
If Die1.Showing = Die2.Showing And _
    Die2.Showing = Die3.Showing Then
        Message.Text = _
            "You WIN! You got three of a kind with " & _
            Die1.Showing
End If
```

Otherwise, the user can keep clicking the button until the dice show a winning combination. Sometimes, that takes a lot of clicks.

Chapter 13

Getting It Right: Validating User Input

In This Chapter

▶ Exploring validation

▶ Making sure they filled it in

▶ Using comparisons to validate a value

▶ Checking for values within a range

▶ Comparing client validation and server validation

"To err is human . . ." If that's true, then users are the most human people I've ever met. – An anonymous ASP developer

L et's face it — everyone makes mistakes! That's why validation is so important. *Validation* is the process of making sure that users type the correct information into a form.

Of course, if you ask for a name, and the user types `Elmer Fudd`, your page can't figure out whether the user is yanking your chain.

But if your page asks for a phone number, and the user types in only three digits, or nothing at all, your page *can* catch that error and ask the user to complete the information. So, validation is really about just trying to get the best information you can before you accept it.

Validation — The Old Way

In the days before ASP.NET, people developing Web applications, and those developing almost any other type of application, wrote their own code to do all the validation they needed. If you were to write a page that worked that way in ASP.NET, it might look something like this:

```
<%@Page Explicit="True" Language="VB" Debug="True" %>
<html>
<head/>
<script runat="server">
Sub CreateButton_Click(Sender As Object, E As EventArgs)
Dim AllOK As Boolean = True
NameLabel.Text = ""
PasswordLabel.Text = ""
ConfirmLabel.Text = ""
AgeLabel.Text = ""
Status.Text = ""

If Name.Text = "" Then
    NameLabel.Text = "** Please Enter a Username"
    AllOK = False
End If
If Password.Text = "" Then
    PasswordLabel.Text = "** Please Enter a Password"
    AllOK = False
End If
If Confirm.Text = "" Then
    ConfirmLabel.Text = "** Please Confirm Your Password"
    AllOK = False
End If

If Password.Text <> Confirm.Text Then
    PasswordLabel.Text = _
        "** Your Password and Confirmation Don't Match"
    AllOK = False
End If

If Age.Text <> "" And Age.Text < 18 Or Age.Text > 120 Then
    AgeLabel.Text = _
        "** Please Enter an Age Between 18 and 120"
    AllOK = False
End If

If AllOK = True Then
    Status.Text = _
        "Everything Looks Good - Creating New Account"
    Create.Enabled = False
    ' Create new user account
End If

End Sub
</script>
<body>
<h1>Create a New Account</h1>
<form runat="server">

Enter a Username:<br>
<asp:textbox id="Name" runat="server" />
```

```
<asp:label id="NameLabel" runat="server"
forecolor="red" /><br>

Enter a Password:<br>
<asp:textbox id="Password" textmode="password"
runat="server" />
<asp:label id="PasswordLabel" runat="server"
forecolor="red" /><br>

Confirm Password:<br>
<asp:textbox id="Confirm" textmode="password"
runat="server" />
<asp:label id="ConfirmLabel" runat="server"
forecolor="red" /><br>

Enter Your Age:<br>
<asp:textbox id="Age" runat="server" />
<asp:label id="AgeLabel" runat="server"
forecolor="red" /><br><br>

<asp:button text="Create" id="Create"
onclick="CreateButton_Click" runat="server"/><br>
<asp:label id="Status" runat="server" /><br>

</form>
</body>
</html>
```

This page presents a form that enables the user to enter the information necessary to sign up for an account at a Web site. The form looks like Figure 13-1.

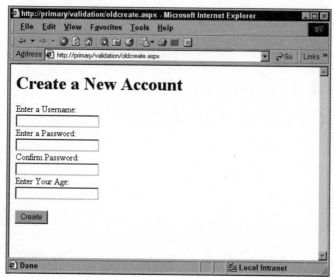

Figure 13-1:
Signing up
for an
account.

Yup, that looks familiar

The example page in the section, "Validation — The Old Way," should look pretty familiar to you. In Classic ASP, you can write your own client-side script, or you can do it on the server side (or both). But you have to do it all by hand with If...Then statements. Pay close attention to the stuff in this chapter and the next one. ASP.NET gives you a whole new way of thinking about validation!

You won't find anything new on this page that you haven't seen before — just some textboxes, some labels, and a bunch of If...Then statements that get executed when the user clicks the button.

Take a closer look at the subroutine. First, it creates a Boolean variable AllOK that is initially set to True. This variable keeps track of whether any errors have been triggered. Then, all the labels are cleared out (in case errors were displayed before that are no longer applicable). Finally, the Name, Password, and Confirm textboxes are checked to see if they are filled in. If not, the corresponding label beside them is filled with appropriate text and AllOK is set to false.

Next, the Password and Confirm textboxes must contain the same text or else another error message is displayed. Finally, the Age is not required so it can be blank. But if it's filled in, the value must be between 18 and 120.

If, after all this validation, no errors have been triggered (AllOK is still true), the user is informed, and the new account can be created.

Rethinking Validation: Validation Server Controls

The preceding section describes a common scenario. Whenever you go to the trouble of collecting information, you need to make sure the information is right. Although you can't be sure it's perfect, you can, at least, help the user by pointing out obvious typos and missed fields.

In fact, this scenario is so common that the Microsoft folks who created ASP.NET gave it extra attention. They wondered whether they could handle this type of validation without so many lines of code. After all, the more code you have to write, the longer it takes and the more chances for errors to creep in.

Their solution involves creating a new kind of server control: a *validation server control*. Validation server controls (or simply *validation controls*) differ from the server controls that I describe in the previous chapters. They don't show up on the page, at least initially. And they are not designed to accept input.

Instead, they bundle together common validation functions in a way that's easy to use and integrate with the rest of the controls on your page.

In the following sections, I introduce you to three of the more important validation controls and show you how they work. Then, I revisit the example from the preceding section and show you how it would look using validation controls instead of code.

Making Sure They Filled It In: RequiredFieldValidator

The simplest of the validation controls is the RequiredFieldValidator. This one simply makes sure the user doesn't leave anything blank that you want filled in.

Using it with a TextBox

You can use the RequiredFieldValidator with various controls. But a couple of examples should give you the general feel for how it works. Here's how it works with a textbox:

```
<%@Page Explicit="True" Language="VB" Debug="True" %>
<html>
<body>
<form runat="server">
What's Your Email Address?<br>
<asp:textbox id="Email" runat="server" /><br>
<asp:requiredfieldvalidator id="EmailRequired"
controltovalidate="Email" runat="server" >
Whoops! You forgot to enter an email address!
</asp:requiredfieldvalidator><br>
<asp:button id="OK" text="OK" runat="server" />
</form>
</body>
</html>
```

In this example, the textbox is followed by a control called `<asp:required fieldvalidator>`. This validation control has several important attributes:

- ✔ `id`: Gives it a name.
- ✔ `controltovalidate`: Identifies the control it validates.
- ✔ `runat`: Identifies it as a server control.

In addition, inside the tag is an error message. This message appears only when the control identified in the `controltovalidate` is empty.

When you first bring up this page, click the OK button before entering anything in the textbox. The error message immediately appears, as shown in Figure 13-2.

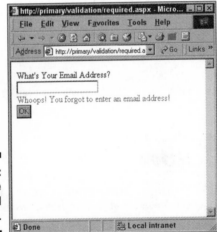

Figure 13-2:
Missing the
e-mail
address.

Now type some text in the textbox and click the button again. The error message goes away.

Using it with a DropDownList

You can also use the `RequiredFieldValidator` with a `DropDownList`:

```
<%@Page Explicit="True" Language="VB" Debug="True" %>
<html>
<body>
<form runat="server">
What Color Do You Prefer?<br>
<asp:dropdownlist id="Color" runat="server" >
    <asp:listitem>Pick A Color</asp:listitem>
```

```
    <asp:listitem>Red</asp:listitem>
    <asp:listitem>Green</asp:listitem>
    <asp:listitem>Blue</asp:listitem>
</asp:dropdownlist><br>
<asp:requiredfieldvalidator id="ColorRequired"
controltovalidate="Color" runat="server"
initialvalue="Pick A Color">
Whoops! You forgot to choose a color!
</asp:requiredfieldvalidator><br>
<asp:button id="OK" text="OK" runat="server" />
</form>
</body>
</html>
```

By default, the first item in a `DropDownList` initially appears in the box. Often, instead of offering a real choice, this item includes instructions for the user. In this case, the user must "Pick A Color." The `RequiredFieldValidator` includes a property called `initialvalue`, which lets the validation control know that this value appears initially in the control and shouldn't be counted as a real selection.

If you retrieve this page, you immediately see `Pick A Color` in the drop-down list. As shown in Figure 13-3, if you click the button, the validation control displays the error because you haven't chosen a real value from the list.

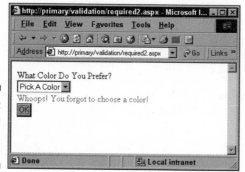

Figure 13-3:
You forgot to
choose a
color!

Making Sure It's on the Mark: CompareValidator

The `CompareValidator` is a relatively simple validation control. It enables you to compare the value in a control to a value that you specify or to the value held in another control.

Comparing with a value

In this example, the validation control requires that the temperature entered is greater than 32:

```
<%@Page Explicit="True" Language="VB" Debug="True" %>
<html>
<body>
<form runat="server">
Enter the temperature:<br>
<asp:textbox id="Temp" runat="server" /><br>
<asp:comparevalidator id="TempCompare"
controltovalidate="Temp" valuetocompare="32"
operator="GreaterThan" type="integer"
runat="server" >
The temperature must be above 32 degrees.
</asp:comparevalidator><br>
<asp:button id="OK" text="OK" runat="server" />
</form>
</body>
</html>
```

The `<asp:comparevalidator>` has some of the same attributes as the `<asp:requiredfieldvalidator>` (see "Making Sure They Filled It In: RequiredFieldValidator," earlier in this chapter). The `id`, `controltovalidate`, and `runat` attributes work just as they do there. However, this example also introduces a few new attributes:

- ✔ `valuetocompare`: As the name implies, provides the value to use when comparing the contents of the control.

- ✔ `operator`: Describes how the comparison should be done. Common values: `Equal`, `NotEqual`, `GreaterThan`, `GreaterThanEqual`, `LessThan`, and `LessThanEqual`. This attribute is *optional,* and if you do not include it, it defaults to `Equal`.

- ✔ `type`: Identifies the type of the data being compared. Common values: `Integer`, `String`, and `Date`.

In this example, the contents of the `Temp` control (which holds an integer) must be greater than the integer value 32. If not, you get an error message, as shown in Figure 13-4.

Comparing with another control

You also can use the `CompareValidator` to compare the contents of this control with the contents of another control, as the following example demonstrates:

```
<%@Page Explicit="True" Language="VB" Debug="True" %>
<html>
<body>
<form runat="server">
How old are you?<br>
<asp:textbox id="YourAge" runat="server" /><br>
How old is your youngest son/daughter?<br>
<asp:textbox id="ChildAge" runat="server" /><br>
<asp:comparevalidator id="AgeCompare"
controltovalidate="ChildAge" controltocompare="YourAge"
operator="LessThan" type="integer"
runat="server" >
Um, your child must be younger than you!
</asp:comparevalidator><br>
<asp:button id="OK" text="OK" runat="server" />
</form>
</body>
</html>
```

If you enter 33 for your age and 55 for your child's age, this page is smart enough to know that those values can't be right, as you see in Figure 13-5.

Figure 13-4:
Getting the temperature right.

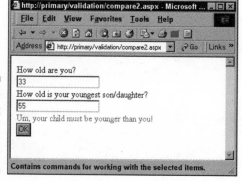

Figure 13-5:
You can't be younger than your child.

The only real difference between this example and the one in the preceding section is that the `valuetocompare` attribute is replaced with the `controltocompare` attribute, and it holds the control's name. Otherwise, `operator`, `type`, and everything else work as they do in the previous example.

Making Sure It's in the Ballpark: RangeValidator

`RangeValidator` goes a step further than the `CompareValidator`. It enables you to check to see if a control holds a value that falls within a specific range. This, too, is a very common type of validation.

Checking the range with two values

Earlier in this chapter, in the section titled "Comparing with a value," I show you how to use the `CompareValidator` to ensure that the user enters a temperature greater than the freezing point for water. Here, I extend that example to check that the water temperature is above freezing and below the boiling point:

```
<%@Page Explicit="True" Language="VB" Debug="True" %>
<html>
<body>
<form runat="server">
Enter the temperature:<br>
<asp:textbox id="Temp" runat="server" /><br>
<asp:rangevalidator id="TempRange"
controltovalidate="Temp"
minimumvalue="33" maximumvalue="219"
type="integer" runat="server" >
The Temperature Must Be Above 32 Degrees and
Below 220 Degrees.
</asp:rangevalidator><br>
<asp:button id="OK" text="OK" runat="server" />
</form>
</body>
</html>
```

Now, instead of a `valuetocompare`, you have a `minimumvalue` and a `maximumvalue`. You'll probably notice those numbers aren't quite what you'd expect them to be. Remember that you are specifying the lowest and highest *acceptable* values. So, to get values *between* 32 and 220, you must specify 33 and 219. If you enter a value that falls outside that range, you get the result shown in Figure 13-6.

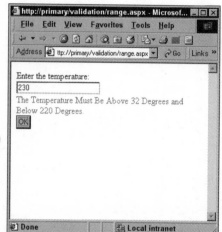

Figure 13-6:
Entering a
temperature
outside the
range.

Checking the range with other controls

Because `CompareValidator` has a `controltocompare` attribute, you might expect to find a `minimumcontroltocompare` and a `maximumcontroltocompare` for the `RangeValidator`. Unfortunately they don't exist.

However, you can check a range of values based on what the user entered in other controls. You just need a little code to help you accomplish it. I demonstrate that technique in Chapter 14.

Validation — The New Way!

Earlier in this chapter, in the section titled "Validation — The Old Way," I use several `If...Then` statements to implement validation for a page designed to accept information to create a new account for a user.

Using some of the more common validation controls, which I describe in previous sections of this chapter, how would you do that page differently?

Give this a shot:

```
<%@Page Explicit="True" Language="VB" Debug="True" %>
<html>
<script runat="server">
Sub CreateButton_Click(Sender As Object, E As EventArgs)
If Page.IsValid = True Then
    Status.Text = _
```

```
        "Everything Looks Good - Creating New Account"
    Create.Enabled = False
    ' Create new user account
End If
End Sub
</script>
<body>
<h1>Create a New Account</h1>
<form runat="server">

Enter a Username:<br>
<asp:textbox id="Name" runat="server" />
<asp:requiredfieldvalidator id="NameRequired"
controltovalidate="Name" runat="server" >
** Please Enter a Username
</asp:requiredfieldvalidator><br>

Enter a Password:<br>
<asp:textbox id="Password" textmode="password"
runat="server" />
<asp:requiredfieldvalidator id="PasswordRequired"
controltovalidate="Password" runat="server" >
** Please Enter a Password
</asp:requiredfieldvalidator><br>

Confirm Password:<br>
<asp:textbox id="Confirm" textmode="password"
runat="server" />
<asp:requiredfieldvalidator id="ConfirmRequired"
controltovalidate="Confirm" runat="server" >
** Please Confirm Your Password
</asp:requiredfieldvalidator>

<asp:comparevalidator id="PasswordCompare"
controltovalidate="Password" controltocompare="Confirm"
type="string" runat="server">
** Your Password and Confirmation Don't Match
</asp:comparevalidator><br>

Enter Your Age:<br>
<asp:textbox id="Age" runat="server" />
<asp:rangevalidator id="AgeRange" controltovalidate="Age"
minimumvalue="18" maximumvalue="120"
type="Integer" runat="server">
** Please Enter an Age Between 18 and 120
</asp:rangevalidator>

<br><br><asp:button text="Create" id="Create"
onclick="CreateButton_Click" runat="server"/><br>
<asp:label id="Status" runat="server" /><br>
</form>
</body>
</html>
```

If you simply click the OK button when the page first comes up, you get lots of error messages, as you see in Figure 13-7.

I use the `RequiredFieldValidator` to ensure that the user enters the username, password, and confirmation. The `CompareValidator` ensures that the password textbox and the confirmation textbox both contain the same value. Notice that I don't specify an operator, so `Equals` is assumed.

Finally, I use a `RangeValidator` to ensure that the `Age` textbox contains a value between (and including) 18 and 120.

Unlike the other small examples in previous sections of this chapter, this one includes a subroutine that gets executed when the user clicks the button on this page.

That subroutine checks something called `Page.IsValid` to see if the page has any errors. This `Page` property replaces the `AllOK` variable from previous examples, but how does it work?

`IsValid` is true if all the validation controls on this page have passed. If any of them fail, `IsValid` is set to false automatically by ASP.NET. This provides a very handy way to be sure that you don't process anything until everything is exactly as you want it!

For a summary of all the validation controls and their commonly used properties, see Tables 14-1 and 14-2 at the end of the next chapter.

Client Versus Server Validation

If you haven't spent some time playing around with the example in the preceding section, take a little time right now to do so.

If you are using a newer version of Internet Explorer as your browser, you'll probably notice very quickly that you don't have to actually click the button in order to make the error messages go away. You can simply enter the right data in the textbox and press Tab or click another control. And you don't see the flicker usually associated with a round-trip to the server. What's going on here?

Well, in the example I describe in the section "Validation — The Old Way," earlier in this chapter, the page has to return to the server to execute the validation code.

But the example in the preceding section uses validation controls instead of server script. These validation controls are very clever. They actually check to see which browser the user has, and they react differently based on the result. For example, if you have an older browser that doesn't support client-side JavaScript, these controls will create server-side ASP.NET code that's very similar to the first example in this chapter.

However, if the user has a newer browser that supports client-side JavaScript, the validation server controls create JavaScript code to do the validation in the browser. That way, you don't waste time sending bad data to the server. You catch it right away and give the user immediate feedback. Then, after it's all set, the data can be sent to the server.

But what if . . .

Theoretically, some clever developers out there could create a form that submits information to *your* server. And if they do, it might not contain the JavaScript that checks to make sure all the data is okay first. What then?

Well, the validation server controls don't actually replace the server validation with client validation when the user has a newer browser. The controls actually do both client *and* server validation. That way, they can be sure that no bad data gets submitted, even if some tricky developers try to send it from their own form.

Chapter 14

Taking Validation to the Next Level

*T*he validation controls that I describe in Chapter 13 enable you to do simple but very common validation operations — making sure the information is filled in, comparing values, and making sure a value is within a specific range.

But suppose you have more extensive validation needs. Perhaps you need to make sure a phone number or product ID is formatted correctly, or maybe you need to look up information in a database to ensure that the user entered a valid employee ID. In such cases, you need a more industrial-strength solution — and ASP.NET delivers!

CustomValidator: The Mod Squad Buys Soda

Whether your validation involves a specific calculation, table-lookup, or database retrieval, if you need to write code to figure out whether a particular value is right or not, use the `CustomValidator`.

A CustomValidator server subroutine

In this page, users visit their online grocer and specify how many cans of cola they want to buy. There's just one catch: The cans come in six-packs.

```
<%@Page Explicit="True" Language="VB" Debug="True" %>
<html>
<script runat="server">
Sub Soda_Validate(Sender As Object, _
    Args As ServerValidateEventArgs)
If (Args.Value Mod 6) = 0 Then
    Args.IsValid = True
Else
    Args.IsValid = False
End If
End Sub
</script>
<body>
<form runat="server">
<h1>Online Grocer</h1>
Number of cans of cola you wish to purchase:<br>
<asp:textbox id="Cola" runat="server" /><br>
<asp:customvalidator id="SodaCustom"
controltovalidate="Cola" onservervalidate="Soda_Validate"
runat="server" >
Soda comes in 6-packs. The number you choose must be
a multiple of 6.
</asp:customvalidator><br>
<asp:button id="OK" text="OK" runat="server" />
</form>
</body>
</html>
```

The resulting page looks like Figure 14-1.

Figure 14-1:
Buying soda
by the six-
pack.

This listing includes several new features. The body of the page includes a textbox and a CustomValidator control. The new attribute is onserver validate. As you might expect, this attribute identifies an ASP.NET subroutine that's executed to validate the Cola textbox.

You find that subroutine in the <script> tag at the top of the page. The subroutine line itself is a bit different from what you've seen before:

```
Sub Soda_Validate(Sender As Object, _
    Args As ServerValidateEventArgs)
```

In other event subroutines, the second argument usually looks like this: E As EventArgs. However, this is not a normal event subroutine. It's a validation event subroutine, so it has a different kind of argument sent to it.

Now look at the body of the subroutine:

```
If (Args.Value Mod 6) = 0 Then
    Args.IsValid = True
Else
    Args.IsValid = False
End If
```

The Args here is the second argument that was sent to this subroutine. It's an object and it has two interesting properties:

- ✔ **Value:** The value that you need to validate.
- ✔ **IsValid:** A Boolean variable that you set to indicate whether the value sent is valid.

For example, if you entered **7** in the textbox, 7 would be in the Value property when this subroutine was called.

But what the heck is Mod? Good question. Mod is an operator in VB.NET. It works a lot like +, -, *, and /. It returns the *modulus* of two numbers. What's a modulus? Well, if you remember way back in elementary school when you did long division, sometimes you'd have a remainder. For example, if you divide 16 by 6, you get 2 with a remainder of 4. A modulus is just that remainder.

So, again, if you entered **7** into the textbox, the first line would take 7 mod 6. The remainder of that is 1. But I'm checking for 0. A 0 remainder means the number can be divided by 6 *evenly.* Numbers like 6, 12, 18, and 24 all produce 0 when you take them mod 6.

And because sodas come in six-packs, that's exactly what you want to do here. If the number is evenly divisible by 6, Args.IsValid is set to True, and the value passes the test. If not, Args.IsValid is set to False, and the text inside the CustomValidator tag (back down in the body of the page) is displayed.

A CustomValidator client subroutine

You may have noticed that the CustomValidator doesn't work exactly like the other validator controls. It has to go to the server to execute your subroutine before it can figure out whether the textbox information is valid. It does that because there's no way to run ASP.NET code in the browser.

However, you can check in the browser, too. Here's the same code from the preceding section, with a client-side VBScript subroutine added to check the value in the browser before the value is sent back to the server:

```
<%@Page Explicit="True" Language="VB" Debug="True" %>
<html>
<script runat="server">
Sub Soda_Validate(Sender As Object, _
    Args As ServerValidateEventArgs)
If (Args.Value Mod 6) = 0 Then
    Args.IsValid = True
Else
    Args.IsValid = False
End If
End Sub
</script>
<script language="vbscript">
Sub Client_Soda_Validate(Sender, Args)
If (Args.Value Mod 6) = 0 Then
    Args.IsValid = True
Else
    Args.IsValid = False
End If
End Sub
</script>
<body>
<form runat="server">
<h1>Online Grocer</h1>
Number of cans of cola you wish to purchase:<br>
<asp:textbox id="Cola" runat="server" /><br>
<asp:customvalidator id="SodaCustom"
controltovalidate="Cola" onservervalidate="Soda_Validate"
clientvalidationfunction="Client_Soda_Validate"
runat="server" >
Soda comes in 6-packs. The number you choose must be
a multiple of 6.
</asp:customvalidator><br>
<asp:button id="OK" text="OK" runat="server" />
</form>
</body>
</html>
```

The only difference in the `CustomValidator` control is the addition of a new attribute: `clientvalidationfunction`.

This is an odd name for two reasons. First, it's inconsistent with the attribute name for the server-side validation subroutine: `onservervalidate`. You might have expected `onclientvalidate`. But, no such luck.

The name `clientvalidationfunction` also is odd because the name that you assign to this attribute may or may not be a function. In fact, if you use VBScript on the client, it's almost always a subroutine, not a function.

And that's the case here. If you look now toward the top of the page, you'll see the usual `<script>` tag, and another one following it. The second `<script>` tag does not include `runat="server"`. So, you can be sure this is client-side script. Also notice the language specified within the script tag: VBScript. The other commonly used language for client scripting is JavaScript.

Inside that second `<script>` tag, you see a subroutine that looks strikingly similar to the ASP.NET subroutine that does the validation on the server. In fact, the only difference is that no data types are specified for the arguments that are passed into the subroutine. VBScript is very similar to VB.NET, but it doesn't use data types — any variable can hold any kind of data. (Although this may seem like an advantage, it's not. The messiness that programming without data types can bring can introduce bugs that are hard to find.)

What happens when you try out this page? Well, the main difference is that if you type in a value like 17 and press the Tab key (without pressing Enter or clicking the button), the validation is done immediately, much like with the other validation controls.

Just as the other validation controls do checking both on the client and on the server, you, too, are better off writing a subroutine for both, as I've done here. That way, users can't sneak data into being accepted by creating their own form to submit the information.

Using VBScript as your client-side language is very handy if you already know VB.NET. It's very similar and you can often use VB.NET subroutines in your VBScript code with only minor modifications (as I've done here). But this approach does pose a problem: Only Internet Explorer understands VBScript. If your applications must run on Netscape browsers as well, you'll have to use JavaScript for your client-side scripting. Both Internet Explorer and Netscape understand JavaScript. The JavaScript syntax is very different from VB.NET, but not too difficult, once you get the hang of it. There are lots of good JavaScript books on the market if you need to learn it. Among them, *JavaScript Weekend Crash Course,* by Steven W. Disbrow, and *JavaScript Bible,* 4th Edition, by Danny Goodman (both published by Hungry Minds, Inc.).

CustomValidator: Lots of potential!

The very simple examples that I show you in the preceding sections don't even begin to scratch the surface of what you can do with the CustomValidator. From complex calculations to table lookups and database retrieval, this control enables you to do anything you could do from code as part of your validation.

Getting the Formatting Right: RegularExpressionValidator

The RegularExpressionValidator enables you to describe the correct format for the information in a textbox. The control compares your description to the information the user enters and then decides whether they match.

RegularExpressionValidator is perfect for validating formatted numbers like phone numbers, Social Security numbers, and complex product codes. In fact, this validation control is very flexible and powerful because it enables you to describe in great detail how the data should look.

That description is done with a little language called *regular expressions*. If you've worked with Unix, Linux, or some PC programming tools, you may be familiar with regular expressions. It has been used in various environments for many years.

The only down-side of this little language is that it is somewhat complex. Its syntax can be very confusing when you first see it.

Unfortunately, the topic of regular expressions is well beyond the scope of this book. In fact, the topic can (and does) fill whole books in its own right!

But I won't leave you out on a limb with this one. The RegularExpression Validator is too handy to ignore. So what I'll do instead is show you an example of how to use it to accept a phone number. Then, I show you some other regular expression strings that you can use to validate other common bits of information. These strings will work just as well for you even if you don't know what they mean, exactly!

```
<%@Page Explicit="True" Language="VB" Debug="True" %>
<html>
<body>
<form runat="server">
Enter your phone number:<br>
```

```
<asp:textbox id="Phone" runat="server" /><br>
<asp:regularexpressionvalidator id="PhoneValidator"
runat="server" controltovalidate="Phone"
validationexpression="^\(?\d{3}\)?(\s|-)\d{3}-\d{4}$" >
Phone number must be in this format: (XXX) XXX-XXXX
</asp:regularexpressionvalidator><br>
<asp:button id="OK" text="OK" runat="server" />
</form>
</body>
</html>
```

This page enables you to enter a phone number. Despite the error message, the number you enter can be in one of two acceptable formats: (111) 222-3333 or 111-222-3333. If you enter something else, you get an error message, as shown in Figure 14-2.

Figure 14-2:
An invalid phone number format.

The important new attribute here, of course, is `validationexpression`. It has this hideous-looking string assigned to it:

```
^\(?\d{3}\)?(\s|-)\d{3}-\d{4}$
```

Basically, this string describes what the phone number text should look like. Just so it's not quite so magical to you, here's a quick rundown of what the different parts of this string do:

Character	*What It Represents*
^	The beginning of the string
\(?	An optional (
\d{3}	Three numeric digits
\)?	An optional)
(\s|-)	Either a space or a dash
\d{3}	Three more numeric digits
-	A dash
\d{4}	Four more numeric digits
$	The end of the string

Even if you understand everything in this list, I'm sorry to say, you are not yet qualified as a regular expression expert. But that's okay, because you don't need to understand regular expressions to use the `Regular ExpressionValidator`. Just plug the right string into the `validation expression` attribute and you're in business.

So what's the right string? Here are a few to get you started:

- A **US phone number** in the form (111) 222-3333 or 111-222-3333:

  ```
  ^\(?\d{3}\)?(\s|-)\d{3}-\d{4}$
  ```
- An **international phone number** like 1-22-3333-4444:

  ```
  ^\d(\d|-){7,20}
  ```
- An **e-mail address** (join the following lines together as one long string):

  ```
  ^([a-zA-Z0-9_\-\.]+)@
  ((\[[0-9]{1,3}\.[0-9]{1,3}\.[0-9]{1,3})|
  ([a-zA-Z0-9\-\.]+))\.(com|net|org|edu|mil)$
  ```
- A **five-digit ZIP code:**

  ```
  ^\d{5}$
  ```
- A **nine-digit ZIP code** in the form of 11111-2222:

  ```
  ^\d{5}-\d{4}$
  ```
- A regular expression that will accept **either five-digit or nine-digit ZIP codes:**

  ```
  ^(\d{5})|(\d{5}\-\d{4})
  ```
- A **Social Security number** in the form 111-22-3333:

  ```
  ^\d{3}-\d{2}-\d{4}$
  ```

If you are interested in learning to create your own regular expressions, I'd recommend a couple of good books: *Sams Teach Yourself Regular Expressions in 24 Hours,* by Alexia Prendergast and Sarah O'Keefe (SAMS), and *Mastering Regular Expressions: Powerful Techniques for Perl and Other Tools,* by Jeffrey E. Friedl and Andy Oram (O'Reiley).

Regular expressions aren't always perfect

Regular expressions may not always do exactly what you expect them to do. For example, the phone number example in this chapter will allow these phone numbers: 111-222-3333 and (111) 222-3333. That example disallows these phone numbers: 1112223333, 111 222 3333, and 11 1 222 33 33.

That's what you'd expect. What you may not expect is that these ill-formed phone numbers

will squeak through: (111-222-3333,111) 222-3333, and (111)-222-3333.

Can you write a better regular expression string that would catch these problems? Probably. But it would be much bigger and much more complex. You make a trade-off between how much time you want to put into creating your regular expressions and how completely fool-proof you want them to be.

Displaying the Results:
ValidationSummary

In this section, I present another validation control. But this one is different — it doesn't actually do any validation. Instead, it provides a common place for displaying all the error messages for all the *other* validation controls on the page.

Because you really need several validation controls on a page to see how ValidationSummary works, I'll modify the example that I present in Chapter 13 in the section, "Validation — The New Way." Instead of displaying the error messages beside the textboxes, this new example simply puts an * beside each textbox that has errors and then summarizes the errors at the bottom of the page:

```
<%@Page Explicit="True" Language="VB" Debug="True" %>
<html>
<head/>
<script runat="server">
Sub CreateButton_Click(Sender As Object, E As EventArgs)
If IsValid = True Then
    Status.Text = _
       "Everything Looks Good - Creating New Account"
    Create.Enabled = False
    ' Create new user account
End If
End Sub
</script>
<body>
<h1>Create a New Account</h1>
<form runat="server">
```

```
Enter a Username:<br>
<asp:textbox id="Name" runat="server" />
<asp:requiredfieldvalidator id="NameRequired"
controltovalidate="Name" runat="server"
errormessage="Please Enter a Username">
*
</asp:requiredfieldvalidator><br>

Enter a Password:<br>
<asp:textbox id="Password" textmode="password"
runat="server" />
<asp:requiredfieldvalidator id="PasswordRequired"
controltovalidate="Password" runat="server"
errormessage="Please Enter a Password">
*
</asp:requiredfieldvalidator><br>

Confirm Password:<br>
<asp:textbox id="Confirm" textmode="password"
runat="server" />
<asp:requiredfieldvalidator id="ConfirmRequired"
controltovalidate="Confirm" runat="server"
errormessage="Please Confirm Your Password">
*
</asp:requiredfieldvalidator>

<asp:comparevalidator id="PasswordCompare"
controltovalidate="Password" controltocompare="Confirm"
type="string" runat="server"
errormessage="Your Password and Confirmation Don't Match">
*
</asp:comparevalidator>
<br>
Enter Your Age:<br>
<asp:textbox id="Age" runat="server" />
<asp:rangevalidator id="AgeRange" controltovalidate="Age"
minimumvalue="18" maximumvalue="120"
type="Integer" runat="server"
errormessage="Please Enter an Age Between 18 and 120">
*
</asp:rangevalidator><br><br>
<asp:button text="Create" id="Create"
onclick="CreateButton_Click" runat="server"/><br>

<asp:label id="Status" runat="server" /><br>

<asp:validationsummary id="Summary"
displaymode="bulletlist" runat="server"
headertext="Validation Errors"/>

</form>
</body>
</html>
```

If you simply bring up the page and immediately click the Create button, your screen will light up with red error messages, as shown in Figure 14-3.

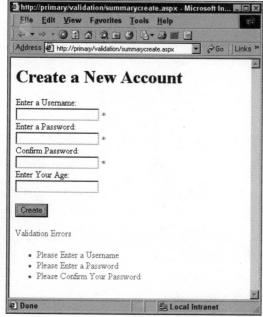

Figure 14-3:
The
Validation
Summary
control in
action using
bulletlist.

This example includes several changes from the one in Chapter 13. The error messages are no longer between the open and close tags of the validation controls. They are now used as the value for the errormessage attribute. Inside the open and close tag, you find only a *.

The ValidationSummary control appears at the bottom. In addition to the id and runat attributes, it has a headertext and a displaymode. The headertext is simple enough — the text appears at the top of the summary of error messages.

The displaymode property can have one of several possible values:

✔ bulletlist: Each error appears as an item in a bulleted list, as shown in Figure 14-3.

✔ list: The errors appear in a simple list with no bullets, as shown in Figure 14-4.

✔ singleparagraph: The header and the errors are all run together as one big paragraph, as shown in Figure 14-5. It doesn't look so good on this page, but if you add a period at the end and different spacing, it can be effective — especially if you're trying to conserve space.

Figure 14-4:
The
Validation
Summary
control
using list.

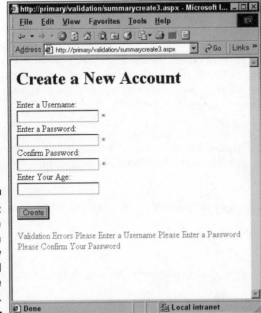

Figure 14-5:
The
Validation
Summary
control
using single
paragraph.

Manipulating Validation Controls from Code

The whole point of creating the validation controls was to reduce the amount of code that you have to write. So, typically, you'll use these controls and set their properties using the tags I show you throughout this chapter.

But validation controls are server controls just like all the other ASP.NET server controls you've explored. So they can be accessed and played with from your server-side ASP.NET code.

For example, in Chapter 13, I explain that, unlike the `CompareValidator`, the `RangeValidator` doesn't have the built-in ability to compare against other controls. You have to set `minimumvalue` and `maximumvalue` to the actual values you want to use for validating the control's contents.

And, although that's true, there is a way, using ASP.NET code, that you can use other controls to check the range. Here's an example:

```
<%@Page Explicit="True" Language="VB" Debug="True" %>
<html>
<script runat="server">
Sub OK_Click(Sender As Object, E As EventArgs)
AgeRange.Type = ValidationDataType.Integer
AgeRange.MinimumValue = ChildAge.Text
AgeRange.MaximumValue = MomAge.Text
AgeRange.Validate
End Sub
</script>
<body>
<form runat="server">
How old are you?<br>
<asp:textbox id="YourAge" runat="server" /><br>
How old is your youngest son/daughter?<br>
<asp:textbox id="ChildAge" runat="server" /><br>
How old is your mother?<br>
<asp:textbox id="MomAge" runat="server" /><br>

<asp:rangevalidator id="AgeRange"
controltovalidate="YourAge"
enableclientscript="false"
runat="server" >
You must be younger than your mother but
older than your son/daughter.
</asp:rangevalidator><br>
```

```
<asp:button id="OK" text="OK" runat="server"
onclick="OK_Click"/>

</form>
</body>
</html>
```

You enter your age, your child's age, and your mother's age. If your age isn't between the other two, you get an error message when you click the OK button, as shown in Figure 14-6.

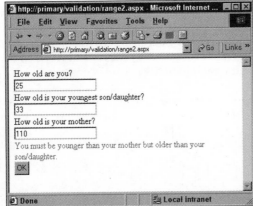

Figure 14-6:
The Range
Validator
at work
comparing
ages.

The RangeValidator in this listing looks a bit different from previous examples. Specifically, the tag doesn't specify a minimumvalue, maximumvalue, or type. Those attributes are specified in code, so there's no point setting them in the tag.

In addition, there's a new attribute: enableclientscript. This attribute is true by default which means that, if the browser supports it, the control will produce the appropriate client-side script to do the validation. (For more details on this process, see Chapter 13 — specifically, the section that contrasts client and server validation.)

Setting this attribute to false enables the page to return to the server before the validation is done. This is important here because server side code sets important validation control properties.

Speaking of which, take a look at the OK_Click subroutine:

```
AgeRange.Type = ValidationDataType.Integer
AgeRange.MinimumValue = ChildAge.Text
AgeRange.MaximumValue = MomAge.Text
AgeRange.Validate
```

AgeRange is the name of the RangeValidator control on this page. The Type property determines the data type of the values compared. When setting this property in the tag, you can simply use the type name. But when doing it in code, you must use an enumeration object, ValidationDataType, and its enumeration properties. In this case, the control compares all the values as integers.

The value entered in the ChildAge textbox becomes the MinimumValue, and the value entered in the MomAge textbox becomes the MaximumValue. Finally, the Validate method is called on the AgeRange control. Essentially, you are saying, "Now that you have all your important properties filled in, do the validation."

This is just one example of how validation controls can be changed and used from your ASP.NET code. Although you'll typically use the validation control tags alone, using code to manipulate their properties and call their methods can sometimes give you an additional level of control or new capabilities.

Summary of Validation Controls and Properties

Table 14-1 summarizes the validation controls that I describe in Chapters 13 and 14.

Table 14-1	Validation Control Summary	
Control	*What It Does*	*Important Properties*
RequiredField Validator	Ensures that the user has entered a value for the control	controltovalidate, initialvalue
Compare Validator	Compares contents of control with a specified value or with the contents of another control	controltovalidate, valuetocompare, controltocompare, operator, type
Range Validator	Ensures that contents of the control fall between two specified values	controltovalidate, minimumvalue, maximumvalue, type
Custom Validator	Enables you to call a server-side and/or client-side subroutine to validate the control	controltovalidate, onservervalidate, clientvalidationfunction

(continued)

Table 14-1 *(continued)*

Control	What It Does	Important Properties
Regular Expression Validator	Compares contents of control against a string which describes how the data should be formatted	`controltovalidate, validationexpression`
Validation Summary	Provides a single spot on the page to list the validation errors from all the validation controls	`displaymode, headertext`

Table 14-2 describes all the properties that you use in these controls and how you set them. I show the name of each property in mixed case, as you would see it in VB.NET code. In this book, when I use these properties in a tag, I put them in all lowercase, as I do with all HTML. Of course, ASP.NET doesn't care about the case in either situation.

The enumerated objects and properties that I mention in the "How to Assign a Value" column of this table are for use when assigning values to these properties in code. (For more information on this topic, see "Manipulating Validation Controls from Code," earlier in this chapter.) When assigning a value to these properties in the tag, simply use the corresponding string value.

Table 14-2   **Common Validation Control Properties**

Name	What It Does	Controls That Use It	How to Assign a Value	Where to Go for More
`ControlToValidate`	Identifies which control to validate	`RequiredFieldValidator,` `CompareValidator,` `RangeValidator,` `CustomValidator,` `RegularExpression-` `Validator`	String — Name of the control	See the section specific to the control that interests you
`EnableClientScript`	Determines whether client-side script is generated to do validation in the browser, if the browser supports it	`RequiredFieldValidator,` `CompareValidator,` `RangeValidator,` `CustomValidator,` `RegularExpression-` `Validator`	Boolean — true or false	"Manipulating Validation Controls from Code," earlier in this chapter
`InitialValue`	Specifies the starting value in a control so that the validation control will know if the current value is different	`RequiredFieldValidator`	String — Starting value contained in the control	"Using it with a DropDownList," in Chapter 13
`ValueToCompare`	Specifies the value that should be compared to the control's contents	`CompareValidator`	String — Value to compare	"Comparing with a value," in Chapter 13
`ControlToCompare`	Specifies the name of the control whose contents should be compared to this control's contents	`CompareValidator`	String — Name of the control	"Comparing with another control," in Chapter 13

(continued)

Table 14-2 (continued)

Name	What It Does	Controls That Use It	How to Assign a Value	Where to Go for More
Operator	The operator that should be used to make the comparison	CompareValidator	Validation-CompareOperator enumerated object values (Equal, NotEqual, GreaterThan, GreaterThan-Equal, LessThan, LessThanEqual). **Default:** Equal	"Comparing with a value," and "Comparing with another control," in Chapter 13
Type	Determines what data type ASP.NET should assume the data is in when comparing it	CompareValidator, RangeValidator	ValidationData-Type enumerated object values (String, Integer, Date, Double, Currency). **Default:** String	"Comparing with a value," "Comparing with another control," and "Checking the range with two values," in Chapter 13
MinimumValue	Contains the lowest acceptable value in a range	RangeValidator	String — Value to compare	"Checking the range with two values," in Chapter 13
OnServerValidate	Identifies the name of the ASP.NET, server-side sub-routine to execute to deter-mine if the data is valid	CustomValidator	String — Name of the subroutine	"A Custom-Validator server subroutine," earlier in this chapter

Name	What It Does	Controls That Use It	How to Assign a Value	Where to Go for More
ClientValidation Function	Identifies the name of the client-side script function or subroutine to execute to determine if the data is valid	CustomValidator	String — Name of the function or subroutine	"A CustomValidator client subroutine," earlier in this chapter
ValidationExpression	Specifies a string that describes the correct format of the data	RegularExpressionValidator	String — A regular expression string	"Getting the Formatting Right: RegularExpression Validator," earlier in this chapter
DisplayMode	Specifies how the list of errors should be formatted	ValidationSummary	Validation SummaryDisplay Mode enumerated object values (BulletList, List, SingleParagraph) **Default:** BulletList	"Displaying the Results: ValidationSummary," earlier in this chapter
HeaderText	Specifies a string of text that appears at the top of the summary of errors	ValidationSummary	String — Text to appear in header	"Displaying the Results: ValidationSummary," earlier in this chapter

Part V
Casting a Wider ASP.NET

The 5th Wave   By Rich Tennant

J & R HYPNOSIS CLINIC
Overcome Technophobia
Contact our Web site
WWW.JRHYPNO.COM

"You know, it dawned on me last night why we aren't getting any hits on our Web site."

In this part . . .

After you have the basics under your belt, you're ready to go a little deeper and wider — and there's plenty to explore! ASP.NET is a very rich technology, and every new feature gives you more power and control over your Web applications.

In this part of the book, you get a better appreciation of VB.NET's data-handling capabilities and you explore the .NET Class Libraries, discovering some neat tricks along the way. You also find out about application-level events and configuration settings that help make large-scale application development easier. All the tools and techniques you need to become a Web guru are within your grasp!

Chapter 15

Variables and Data Types: Preaching to the Converted

Chapter 3 introduces the concept of variables and data types, demonstrating the `Integer`, `Single`, and `String` types. In this chapter, I point out a few other data types you may run across and I explain how to work with them and convert them to and from the types you already know. Trust me, it's much more exciting than it sounds!

Meet the Players

Information comes in so many shapes and sizes, and you have lots of different data types to accommodate them. In the next few sections, I describe different categories of what .NET calls the *elementary data types*.

You probably won't use all of these types in your everyday programming. I've already introduced you to the really common ones. But it's good to know about the rest of them in case you need them or you see them used in code written by other developers.

Whole numbers

Data types that hold whole numbers are called *integral* (meaning *integer-like*). In Chapter 3, I introduce you to `Integer`. It can handle most of your needs for holding whole numbers. But you do have a few other options, just in case. Here's the list of all of them:

- ✔ Byte: Holds values between 0 and 255.
- ✔ Short: Stands for *short integer.* Holds values between –32,678 and 32,767.
- ✔ Integer: Holds values between –2,147,483,648 and 2,147,483,647.
- ✔ Long: Stands for *long integer.* Holds values between –9,223,372,036,854,775,808 and 9,223,372,036,854,775,807.

Unless you have a specific reason, you're usually better off using Integer for everything. Calculations with it are faster than with any other data type that holds numbers.

Numbers with a decimal point

Data types that hold numbers with a decimal point are called *non-integral.* In Chapter 3, I introduce you to Single. Again, Single can handle most of your needs for decimal numbers. But, for completeness, here's the whole list:

- ✔ Single: Holds most decimal numbers you're going to encounter in everyday life.
- ✔ Double: Holds very big and very small (lots of numbers to the right of the decimal point) numbers more accurately than Single. Double is often used in scientific applications.
- ✔ Decimal: Holds even bigger and even smaller numbers even more accurately. In addition, because of the way Single and Double work, they can sometimes make very small rounding mistakes. These mistakes usually aren't a big deal, but when they are, you can use Decimal to make sure those mistakes don't happen. Decimal is usually used in finance and banking applications (where even small mistakes can't be tolerated).

If you're interested in the specific ranges of values held by these different data types, see the online help. Trust me — the numbers are large and ugly enough to scare a math teacher.

Other elementary data types

In Chapters 3 and 4, you become acquainted with String and Boolean. Here's a list of the types that round out the elementary data types:

- ✔ String: Holds a bunch of letters, numbers, and symbols all in a row — as long or short as you like. Can be used to hold names, words, sentences, or paragraphs.

✔ **Char:** Like a string with a length of 1. Holds a single letter, number, or symbol.

✔ **Boolean:** Holds one of two values: True or False.

✔ **Date:** Holds a date or a time or both.

✔ **Object:** Holds *anything!*

You're not likely to use the Char unless you're working with objects or functions written in other languages that require it. If you want more information on String, see Chapter 3. Chapter 3 also includes section in which I present several VB.NET functions that make working with strings easy. For more information on the Boolean data type, see Chapter 4.

I haven't really discussed Date or Object before now, so before I go on, let me tell you a little about them.

How to get a date

The Date data type enables you to create variables that hold a specific date and time. A date variable actually always contains both a date and a time, but if you only need to store a date, you can ignore the time part and vice versa.

You may be wondering why you need a Date data type at all. You can use strings to hold dates, as in this example:

```
<%@ Page Explicit="True" Language="VB" Debug="True" %>
<html>
<body>
<%
Dim ThisDay As String
ThisDay = Today
%>
<p>The date today is <%=ThisDay%>.</p>
</body>
</html>
```

The result looks like this:

```
The date today is 7/19/2001.
```

But suppose you want to compare two dates, as in this example:

```
<%@ Page Explicit="True" Language="VB" Debug="True" %>
<html>
<body>
<%
Dim MyBirthday As String
Dim WifeBirthday As String
MyBirthday = "10/5/1967"
WifeBirthday = "5/6/1967"
```

```
If WifeBirthday < MyBirthday Then
    Response.Write("She was born first.")
Else
    Response.Write("You were born first.")
End If
%>
</body>
</html>
```

In this example, `MyBirthday` is actually five months after my wife's, which means she was born first. But when I try it out, it says

```
You were born first.
```

This doesn't work right because the computer thinks of the two values it compares as strings. So it organizes them alphabetically as you would see in a dictionary. It looks at the first character in both strings — "1" and "5" — and decides that "5" is *not* less than "1" so the `Else` part is executed.

But if you use a `Date` data type, the computer will understand that the values are dates and compare them correctly.

Change the first four lines of the preceding VB.NET code to look like this:

```
Dim MyBirthday As Date
Dim WifeBirthday As Date
MyBirthday = #10/5/1967#
WifeBirthday = #5/6/1967#
```

Notice that when you assign a literal date to a `Date` variable, you put it inside # signs. This looks odd, but you use them just like you use double-quotes around a literal string when assigning it to a string variable.

The result is correct this time:

```
She was born first.
```

You can assign a time and both a date and time to `Date` variables in the same way:

```
LunchTime = #12:30 PM#
PlaneArrives = #12/7/2001 5:53 PM#
```

At the end of Chapter 3, in the section titled, "If You Wanna Date, I Got the Time," I describe several useful date- and time-oriented functions offered by VB.NET. In the examples I use to demonstrate these functions, I use string variables. This works because VB.NET is usually pretty smart at converting between strings and dates when it needs to. But now that you know how the `Date` type works, you're much better off using `Date` variables with these functions. They'll execute faster and you won't run into comparison problems like the one in the preceding example.

You're the Object of my affection

The `Object` data type is the simplest and most primitive type in all of .NET. What does that mean? If you declare a variable of type `Object`, that variable can hold any type of data — string, integer, date/time, whatever. And it can also hold any type of object. You could create an `ArrayList` and put it in there, it could hold a `HashTable` — whatever! This can be very useful for certain situations, but it can also be very dangerous. When a variable is defined as an `Object`, the system doesn't really know anything about it and can't warn you if you try to do something stupid! (Believe me, I've done stupid things often enough to know — I need all the warning I can get!)

Only use `Object` variables when you have a specific need to — that is, you have to work with data and you have no way of knowing what you'll be working with. Even then, try to identify it and put it in a variable of the appropriate type as soon as you can.

Automatic Type Conversion — Bad!

With all these different data types available, you may find yourself working with data of one type when you need it to be in another type.

For example, this page from Chapter 8 tells you how old you'd be if you were a dog:

```
<%@Page Explicit="True" Language="VB" Debug="True" %>
<html>
<script runat="server">
Sub OKButton_Click(Sender As Object, E As EventArgs)
    Dim UserAge, DogAge As Integer
    UserAge = Age.Text
    DogAge = UserAge / 7
    Message.Text="If you were a dog, you'd be " & _
        DogAge & " years old."
End Sub
</script>
<body>
<h1>If You Were A Dog</h1>
<form runat="server">
How old are you?<br>
<asp:textbox id="Age" runat="server"/>
<asp:button text="OK" onclick="OKButton_Click"
runat="server"/><br>
<asp:label id="Message" runat="server"/>
</form>
</body>
</html>
```

When you get information from the Text property of a TextBox, it is always in the form of a string, even if you expect the user to enter a number, as I do here. To get around this problem, I put the string into an Integer variable before I divided it by 7:

```
UserAge = Age.Text
```

VB.NET sees that I am putting a string into an integer variable and automatically does the conversion for me. This is called *implicit conversion*. By default, VB.NET does a lot of automatic or implicit conversions for you. And when you are first trying to figure out how VB.NET works, that's handy. It's just one less thing that you have to think about.

However, as you get a little more experience, start paying attention to these details and clearly specify when you want to convert between data types by using data conversion functions.

For example, here's a better way to code the preceding line:

```
UserAge = CInt(Age.Text)
```

CInt is one of a family of functions that does data type conversion. You can read this function's name as "convert to integer." It takes whatever you send it, converts that data into an integer, and returns the result. This is called *explicit conversion* because you clearly indicate that it is happening by using the function in your code, rather than just letting VB.NET do it automatically.

You should strive to make all the type conversions that happen in your pages explicit. It makes your intentions clearer — to you, to VB.NET, and to any other developers who have to make changes to your pages in the future.

Your Conversion Function Arsenal

But in order to make your conversions explicit, you have to know about all the other conversion functions available.

Standard conversion functions

There's a conversion function for each of the different data types available:

- ✔ **Converting to whole numbers:** CByte, CShort, CInt, and CLng
- ✔ **Converting to decimal point numbers:** CSng, CDbl, and CDec
- ✔ **Converting to** String, Char, Boolean, **or** Date: CStr, CChar, CBool, and CDate

All these functions take virtually anything that you care to send to them and they will do their best to convert it to the data type stated in their name and return the result.

Of course, just as you are not likely to use all the data types available every day, so you're not likely to use all these functions on a regular basis. The most commonly used are probably CInt, CSng, CStr, and CDate.

I present an example using CInt in the preceding section.

CStr is often used to convert a number or a date to a string before it is displayed. For example, in the If You Were A Dog page in the preceding section of this chapter, you should explicitly convert the Integer variable DogAge to a String to concatenate it together with the other strings placed in the Message label:

```
Message.Text="If you were a dog, you'd be " & _
    CStr(DogAge) & " years old."
```

If you retrieve a date from a textbox, convert it to a Date when you use it. Doing so ensures that all comparisons are made correctly. For example, this code compares the value in a textbox with a Date variable called DueDate:

```
If CDate(DateCompleted.Text)  > DueDate Then
    Message.Text = "You're late!"
End If
```

The CType function

The CType function is a generalized version of the functions that I describe in the preceding section. You pass CType two arguments: the value you want to convert and the type to which you want to convert it. Here's an example:

```
UserAge = CType(Age.Text, Integer)
```

Here, CType takes the place of CInt by converting the value in the Age textbox into an Integer. And in the following code, it takes the place of CStr by converting DogAge into a String:

```
Message.Text="If you were a dog, you'd be " & _
    CType(DogAge, String) & " years old."
```

Using one of the conversion functions that I describe in the preceding section is usually simpler than using CType, but you will see CType used from time to time, especially with classes and objects. I explain classes and objects in Chapter 6.

Other conversion functions

Typically when you need to do a conversion, `CInt`, `CStr`, and the others are the easiest to remember and will almost always do the job for you. However, VB.NET provides a few additional functions that you'll see used from time to time:

- ✔ `Val`: Accepts a string and returns a number. The number it returns may be either an integer or a decimal point number.

- ✔ `Int`: Accepts a decimal point number and returns an integer. I introduce this one in Chapter 3.

- ✔ `Str`: Accepts any kind of number and converts it into a string.

Be Strict: Spare the Rod, Spoil the Programmer

As I state earlier in this chapter, always make your conversions *explicit* — that is, use the conversion functions anytime you convert a value from one type to another, rather than just letting VB.NET do it for you automatically.

If you are ready to take your programming to the next level, you can actually enforce this requirement. Simply add the text in bold to your page header:

```
<%@Page Explicit="True" Strict="True" Language="VB"
Debug="True" %>
```

Setting `Strict` to `True` causes VB.NET to stop doing the automatic conversions and start giving you errors any time you fail to use a conversion function when you should.

Why would you ever want to do that? It's like begging VB.NET to nag you with *more* error message!

Actually, some very good reasons exist for setting `Strict` to `True`. By allowing automatic conversions, you can allow subtle bugs to creep into your code that you may have a difficult time finding. By forcing yourself to keep everything explicit, you are more likely to be tipped off if anything happens that you didn't intend. Getting your application running takes a little more time, but you can be more certain that everything is going the way you planned, once it's running.

Chapter 16

Exploring the .NET Framework Class Library

*T*he .NET Framework is more than just a set of languages and an environment for creating Windows and Web applications. It's also a vast library of useful code for your daily work.

In fact, the .NET Framework Class Library implements many of the tedious aspects of common programming tasks and virtually hands them to you on a silver platter to use from any page in your application.

In this chapter, I show you how to use this vast library, and I provide just a glimpse into its many possibilities.

The Great Organizer: Namespaces

In .NET, the word *namespaces* refers to a way of organizing all the objects that Microsoft has created for you to use. With so many objects, you need a very specific organization scheme. Fortunately, the organization scheme itself isn't that complicated.

Namespaces are organized as a hierarchy or tree. Think of them like you think of folders on your hard drive. A folder typically holds files, but a folder also can have subfolders inside it. Those subfolders, in turn, have their own files and subfolders. There's no limit to the number of levels deep this can go.

Likewise, a namespace typically holds objects, but a namespace can also hold other namespaces. Again, there's no limit to the number of levels deep this can go.

Sending E-Mail from Your ASP.NET Page

In this section, I show you how to access objects in a namespace, and I give you a pretty handy technique in the process — sending e-mail from your ASP.NET page:

```
<%@Page Explicit="True" Language="VB" Debug="True" %>
<html>
<body>
<%
Dim EMailTo As String = "brad@edgequest.com"
Dim EMailFrom As String = "bill@edgequest.com"
Dim EMailSubject As String = "Important message!"
Dim EmailBody As String

EmailBody = "Thanks for reading this message. " & _
    "But I must admit, I lied. There's nothing " & _
    "important about this message at all."

System.Web.Mail.SmtpMail.Send(EMailFrom, EMailTo, _
    EMailSubject, EMailBody)
%>
</body>
</html>
```

The `SmtpMail` object is all you need to send e-mail. Its `Send` method accepts four strings: the from-address, the to-address, the subject, and the e-mail body.

But notice that I can't simply call `SmtpMail.Send`. The `SmtpMail` object is in the `Mail` namespace. In turn, the `Mail` namespace is in the `Web` namespace, which is in the `System` namespace. All of this together, as it is in the preceding code, is called the *fully-qualified object name:*

```
System.Web.Mail.SmtpMail.Send(EMailFrom, EMailTo, _
    EMailSubject, EMailBody)
```

It's just like when you want to refer to a file on your hard drive. The path often includes several folder and subfolder names so that you can identify exactly where the file exists on the hard drive.

But there's an easier way to specify a namespace. Add this line at the top of your file, right after the @ Page directive:

```
<%@Import Namespace="System.Web.Mail" %>
```

The @ Import directive is a quick and easy way to say, at the start of your page, "Look, I'm going to be using stuff inside this namespace, so make it immediately available to me everywhere on this page." You can import as many namespaces on a page as you like, but you have to use a separate @ Import directive line for each.

I'll extend the analogy a bit for those of you who are elderly enough to remember the days of DOS. Using the @ Import directive is a little like putting a folder in the Path statement of your Autoexec.bat file. Doing so made all the files in that folder available to you no matter what folder you were in. Whew! Showing my age there.

Now you can change the last line of your code to look like this:

```
SmtpMail.Send(EMailFrom, EMailTo, EMailSubject, EMailBody)
```

In most cases, when you're going to use anything from a namespace, simply importing the namespace at the top of the page is easier than using the fully-qualified object name. However, the choice is yours!

This technique for sending e-mail *only* works if the Web server you are running on has an installed and working version of the Internet Information Server SMTP Service. It does not work with any other e-mail server.

Okay, So Where's the Big Chart?

At this point, you're probably expecting to see a big list or diagram showing you all the available namespaces and the objects they offer. I'm sorry to disappoint, but you won't see it here. Why? Two reasons:

- ✔ There are so many namespaces and so many objects within each namespace that I would need a book twice this size to provide even brief descriptions for them all.

- ✔ Many of the namespaces and objects within them are used by the ASP.NET system itself. All the commands of the Visual Basic .NET language, for example, have their place, as does all the functionality that compiles and runs ASP.NET pages. So, many namespaces wouldn't be of much help or direct use to you in your everyday programming because they're designed to work behind the scenes.

Is that CDONTS?

If you think SmtpMail looks an awful lot like the NewMail component of CDONTS, you're right. This is the .NET equivalent.

Classes? Objects? Automatically instantiated? Static classes? Help, I'm going mad!

Throughout this description of the .NET Framework Class Libraries, I refer to the things inside the namespaces as *objects*. For those purists out there (you know who you are), I must admit that they aren't actually objects — they are *classes* (thus the name *Class Libraries*).

In Chapter 6, I explain that you need to instantiate classes before you can use them. This is often done with the New keyword. After you instantiate a class, it is an object and can be used directly. However, some objects, like the Request and Response objects (which I describe in Chapter 7), are created for you automatically ahead of time so that you always have them available to use.

When you start using the stuff in these namespaces, you'll find classes to use to create your own objects. You'll also use things that look like already-created objects. But a subtle difference exists: The ones that look like already-created objects actually aren't. They are called *static classes*. Static classes are special classes that you can use without the need to ever instantiate them first!

Whether an object is created for you ahead of time or it is, in fact, a static class really ends up making very little difference to you. Either way, you can use them without instantiating them yourself.

To keep things simple, I refer to things you have to instantiate before you can use them as *classes* and things that are ready to use as *objects*.

So what will I do instead? First, I'll tell you where you can go. (Ahem!)

The .NET Framework Microsoft Developer Network (MSDN) documentation provides a pretty complete list of everything that's available. You find the *.NET Framework Class Library* section under *.NET Framework Reference*. That's your exhaustive list. If you'd rather have the information organized by techniques (like *Accessing Data* and *Securing Your Application*), then *Programming with the .NET Framework* might be more to your liking.

The .NET Framework MSDN documentation is much easier to navigate than a diagram or a giant list. But beware — it's not as friendly as this book! And keep your eye out for examples. The documentation has lots of them, and some are even helpful.

In addition to pointing you to the documentation, I spend the next few sections pointing out some highlights and giving you some examples. That'll provide a foundation to build on as you read future books and articles and discover cool stuff exploring on your own.

ASP.NET — It's In There!

The @ Import directive is very handy. But you can actually access many of the .NET Framework libraries from your ASP.NET page without ever using it. Why? Because every ASP.NET page *automatically* includes these namespaces:

- ✔ System
- ✔ System.Configuration
- ✔ System.Collections
- ✔ System.Collections.Specialized
- ✔ System.Text
- ✔ System.Text.RegularExpressions
- ✔ System.Web
- ✔ System.Web.Security
- ✔ System.Web.UI
- ✔ System.Web.UI.WebControls
- ✔ System.Web.UI.HTMLControls
- ✔ System.Web.Caching
- ✔ System.Web.SessionState

These namespaces provide a whole host of capabilities — some of which you already know how to use. The System.Web.UI.WebControls namespace, for example, contains all the server controls I describe in Chapters 8 through 14. And the ArrayList and HashTable I describe in Chapter 7 are made available thanks to System.Collections.

In the next few sections, I show you a few more cool things you can do with .NET Framework objects and classes. Some of them use these already-included namespaces, and some require you to import a namespace before you can use them. I point out which is which as I go along.

You mean they're not built in anymore?

Many of the functions and capabilities in the Math object were built into VBScript in Classic ASP. No longer. But, as you can see, they're not hard to access when you need them.

System Does Higher Math

Here's a simple object you'll find *very* helpful if you ever need to do any serious math:

```
<%@Page Explicit="True" Language="VB" Debug="True" %>
<html>
<body>
<h1>Higher Math</h1>
<%
Dim Num As Integer = 42
Response.Write("Num= " & CStr(Num) & "<br>")
Response.Write("Sin(Num)= " & CStr(Math.Sin(Num)) & "<br>")
Response.Write("Cos(Num)= " & CStr(Math.Cos(Num)) & "<br>")
Response.Write("Log(Num)= " & CStr(Math.Log(Num)) & "<br>")
Response.Write("Tan(Num)= " & CStr(Math.Tan(Num)) & "<br>")
Response.Write("Sqrt(Num)= " & CStr(Math.Sqrt(Num)) & "<br>")
Response.Write("Oh, and by the way, Pi is " & _
    CStr(Math.Pi) & "<br>")
%>
</body>
</html>
```

The Math object is available without an @ Import directive at the top because the System namespace, where Math resides, is imported automatically for all ASP.NET pages (as I mention in the preceding section).

However, if you find yourself using the Math object a lot in a page, you can import that object specifically.

Put this line at the top of the file, just below the @ Page directive:

```
<%@Import Namespace="System.Math" %>
```

Now change the Response.Write lines to look like this:

```
Response.Write("Num= " & CStr(Num) & "<br>")
Response.Write("Sin(Num)= " & CStr(Sin(Num)) & "<br>")
Response.Write("Cos(Num)= " & CStr(Cos(Num)) & "<br>")
Response.Write("Log(Num)= " & CStr(Log(Num)) & "<br>")
Response.Write("Tan(Num)= " & CStr(Tan(Num)) & "<br>")
Response.Write("Sqrt(Num)= " & CStr(Sqrt(Num)) & "<br>")
Response.Write("Oh, and by the way, Pi is " & _
    CStr(Pi) & "<br>")
```

By specifically importing that object, you no longer have to qualify each method with the Math object name. It has been imported into the page, so you can simply refer to the methods almost as if they were built-in VB.NET functions!

System.IO Accesses Files on the Server

The System.IO namespace provides objects that help you access information on the server's hard drive. It enables you to look at the folders and files available as well as copy and move files around. You can even create and write to your own files and then read the information back later.

In the next few sections, I show you how some of the System.IO capabilities work.

For a more complete example, I've included a Guestbook application and a complete description of how it works (see Bonus Chapter 3 on the CD). The application demonstrates how to create a text file, update it with information, retrieve and display the contents of the file on a page, and save off copies of the file and then later restore them.

The power to create and the power to delete

I start off by showing you how to create a file on the hard drive and then delete it:

```
<%@Page Explicit="True" Language="VB" Debug="True" %>
<%@ Import Namespace="System.IO" %>
<html>
<script runat="server">
Dim Path As String = "c:\inetpub\wwwroot\filefun\"

Sub Create_Click(Sender As Object, E As EventArgs)
Dim EmptyFile As TextWriter
EmptyFile = File.CreateText(Path & "empty.txt")
EmptyFile.Close
End Sub

Sub Delete_Click(Sender As Object, E As EventArgs)
File.Delete(Path & "empty.txt")
End Sub
</script>
<body>
<h1>File Fun</h1>
<form runat="server">
<asp:linkbutton id="Create" runat="server"
onclick="Create_Click">
Create File</asp:linkbutton><br>
<asp:linkbutton id="Delete" runat="server"
onclick="Delete_Click">
```

```
Delete File</asp:linkbutton><br>
</form>
</body>
</html>
```

Adjust the path in the `Path` variable as appropriate for your setup.

The body of the page is little more than a couple of link buttons. When you try this page out, be sure to open the folder where this page resides on the server's hard drive. When you click the Create link, a file named `empty.txt` should appear in the folder. After it does, you can click the Delete link, and the file disappears.

You can only try out these examples (and the Guestbook example on the CD-ROM) if you have permissions to create files in the folder where your page is located.

How does it work? Well, you'll notice that the page imports `System.IO` at the top:

```
<%@ Import Namespace="System.IO" %>
```

That makes the `TextWriter` class and the `File` object available (among others). The `File` object has lots of neat methods. Speaking of which, take a look at `Create_Click`:

```
Sub Create_Click(Sender As Object, E As EventArgs)
Dim EmptyFile As TextWriter
EmptyFile = File.CreateText(Path & "empty.txt")
EmptyFile.Close
End Sub
```

`File` has a method called `CreateText`, which, predictably, creates a text file. You send the path and filename you want to use. It returns a `TextWriter`-type object. The `TextWriter` class enables you to create objects that make it easy to put text into a file that you want to store. (For more information on `TextWriter`, see Bonus Chapter 3 and the Guestbook project on the CD.) In this case, I don't really want to store anything; I just want to create the file, so after the file is created, I close it right away and I'm done.

Deleting the file is even easier:

```
Sub Delete_Click(Sender As Object, E As EventArgs)
File.Delete(Path & "empty.txt")
End Sub
```

You send the path and filename to the `Delete` method of the `File` object, and it does the dirty work.

Copying and moving files

Copying and moving files is equally simple.

Add another link button to your page with the text Copy File and set its onclick to call the "Copy_Click" subroutine. Then add this subroutine to the <script> section at the top of your page:

```
Sub Copy_Click(Sender As Object, E As EventArgs)
If File.Exists(Path & "another.txt") = False Then
    File.Copy(Path & "empty.txt", Path & "another.txt")
End If
End Sub
```

Now when you try out the page, check to see if the empty.txt file exists in the folder. If it doesn't, use the Create File link to create it. Then click the Copy File link. A new file should appear in the folder: another.txt.

I use two methods in this subroutine, but both are probably self-explanatory. You pass Exists a path and filename, and it returns True or False, indicating whether the file exists at that location. In this case, I check to make sure that a file called another.txt doesn't already exist before I copy my empty.txt to that name.

The Copy method accepts two arguments: the path and filename of the file you want to copy and the new path and name to be used by the copy. In this case, I'm copying it to the same folder to the new name another.txt.

Now create a fourth link button with the text Move File and set its onclick to call the "Move_Click" subroutine. Add these lines to the <script> section of your page:

```
Sub Move_Click(Sender As Object, E As EventArgs)
If File.Exists(Path & "another.txt") = False Then
    File.Move(Path & "empty.txt", Path & "another.txt")
End If
End Sub
```

Before you try out the page, open the folder you're working in and delete the empty.txt and another.txt files. Then bring up the page. Click the Create File link button. The empty.txt file appears. Now click the Move File link button. The empty.txt file disappears, and the another.txt file appears.

The Move method accepts the same arguments and works just like Copy. The only difference is that it deletes the original after the copy is made.

The System.Web Makes Cookies

The final stop on this .NET Framework Class Libraries sight-seeing tour is System.Web. This namespace contains lots of important stuff. In this section, I show you one in particular — using cookies to keep tabs on your visitors!

What's a cookie?

If you're involved with the Internet, you're bound to hear the word *cookie* from time to time. And when you do, it always jumps out at you because the immediate mental image seems wildly out of place in the midst of a bunch of other techno-babble. During a long, boring, technical lecture, it can cause the mind to go off exploring on its own in a world of warm, gooey chocolate chip, peanut butter, sugar-coated . . . mmm.

But I digress.

No, I mean, what is an Internet cookie?

An Internet cookie is actually a small text file that your browser creates and stores on your hard drive. The browser creates these text files when a particular Web site asks it to. The Web site provides the information that goes into the text file, too.

When you come back to the same site days later, the Web site asks your browser if it has a cookie stored under that Web site's name. The browser finds the one it created last time, gets it off the hard drive, and sends the information back to the Web site.

Make sense? Sure. One question: Why? Well, it turns out cookies have lots of uses. The most common one is to store information about the user and preferences that the user has expressed. For example, suppose you go to a music site. You may tell it that you prefer Alternative to Classical. Or, it may simply notice that you spend more time looking at CDs from R.E.M. and Smash Mouth than you do at those from Mozart and Beethoven. Either way, the site stores that information in your cookie. When you return next week, and the site is running two specials, one on Bach and one on Beck, it knows which one to put front-and-center for you.

Baking your own cookies

Mmmm . . . I can smell them already!

To create a cookie, you need to use a cookie cutter — I mean, a cookie class. The System.Web namespace offers one called HttpCookie. But you don't have to import System.Web to access it. It's imported automatically (see "ASP.NET — It's In There!," earlier in this chapter).

Here's a page that enables the user to enter a name and a musical preference so the page can create a cookie, add the user's information to the cookie, and then send the cookie to the user's browser:

```
<%@Page Explicit="True" Language="VB" Debug="True" %>
<html>
<script runat="server">
Sub Choose_Click(Sender As Object, E As EventArgs)
Dim Cookie As HttpCookie = New HttpCookie("MusicPref")

Cookie.Values.Add("Name",NameText.Text)
Cookie.Values.Add("MusicStyle", _
   StyleRadioList.SelectedItem.Text)
Cookie.Expires = #12/31/2010#

Response.Cookies.Add(Cookie)

Response.Redirect("Default.htm")
End Sub
</script>
<body>
<h1>Preferences</h1>
<form runat="server">
What's your name?<br>
<asp:textbox id="NameText" runat="server" /><br>
<br>
What's your favorite style of music?<br>
<asp:radiobuttonlist id="StyleRadioList" runat="server">
   <asp:listitem selected="true">Alternative</asp:listitem>
   <asp:listitem>Classical</asp:listitem>
</asp:radiobuttonlist>
<i>(Is there anything else?)</i><br><br>
<asp:button id="ChooseButton" text="OK"
runat="server" onclick="Choose_Click"/><br>
</form>
</body>
</html>
```

The body of the page is pretty straightforward — a textbox, a radio button list, and a button. It ends up looking like Figure 16-1.

When the user clicks the button, the Choose_Click subroutine is executed:

```
Sub Choose_Click(Sender As Object, E As EventArgs)
Dim Cookie As HttpCookie = New HttpCookie("MusicPref")

Cookie.Values.Add("Name",NameText.Text)
Cookie.Values.Add("MusicStyle", _
    StyleRadioList.SelectedItem.Text)
Cookie.Expires = #12/31/2010#

Response.Cookies.Add(Cookie)

Response.Redirect("Default.htm")
End Sub
```

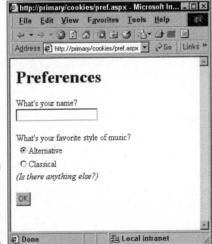

Figure 16-1:
The Music
Preferences
page.

First off, a variable called Cookie is created and an HttpCookie object is instantiated. This particular object enables you to pass a string when you *create* it to identify the name that the browser will use to store the cookie. I called it MusicPref.

After the object is created, you add information to it using the Values property and its Add method.

The cookie holds information in key/value pairs, much like a HashTable (see Chapter 7). The key is the name given to the information, and the value is the information itself. I've stored two pieces of information and given them the names (keys) Name and MusicStyle.

The HttpCookie object has a property called Expires. This property determines the date the cookie should be thrown out. (There's nothing worse than moldy cookies.)

To ensure that the cookie stays on the user's hard drive a good, long while, I set it to a date significantly in the future. (For more on dates and those funny-looking # signs, see Chapter 15.)

Finally, to get this cookie sent back to the user's browser and stored on the user's machine, I must use the Response object. The Response.Cookies property represents any cookies that are to be saved by the user's browser. The Add method enables me to provide an HttpCookie-type object that I've filled in. So I send it my Cookie object. And it is stored!

By the way, the Response.Redirect at the end of this page takes the user to a Default.htm page. I didn't ask you to create this page, but when I originally created this example, I also created a simple Default.htm that provides links to both this page and the one I create in the next section. You may want to do the same to make testing these pages easier.

Getting your cookies and eating them, too

After you store the cookies, they're there later for you to retrieve, as long as they haven't expired. So how do you get them back?

```
<%@Page Explicit="True" Language="VB" Debug="True" %>
<html>
<body>
<h1>Hello, <%=Request.Cookies("MusicPref")("Name")%>!</h1>
We have a special today on music from...<br>
<center>
<table bgcolor="Yellow" border="2" cellpadding="50"><tr><td>
<%
If Request.Cookies("MusicPref")("MusicStyle") = _
    "Classical" Then
%>
<h1>Bach</h1>
<% Else %>
<h1>Beck</h1>
<% End If %>
</td></tr></table>
</center>
<br><a href="default.htm">Home</a><br>
</body>
</html>
```

As shown in Figure 16-2, the page acknowledges the user by name and presents a special it thinks the user might like.

First, notice which object I use to retrieve the cookies. I use Request, not Response. That seems odd because I distinctly remember putting them in Response. What happened? As I explain in Chapter 7, from the Web server's perspective, `Response` is the output object and `Request` is the input object. Each one has a `Cookies` property. When you want to *send* cookies to the user's browser, you use the `Response` object, and when you want to get them back, you use the `Request` object.

But what, exactly, am I doing with the `Cookies` property?

```
<h1>Hello, <%=Request.Cookies("MusicPref")("Name")%>!</h1>
```

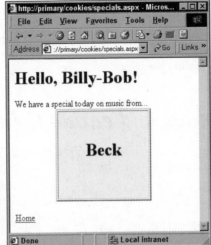

You've seen syntax similar to this for other things. For instance, in Chapter 7, I introduce `Session` variables. You put a value in a `Session` variable like this:

```
Session("UserName") = "Rocketman"
```

I describe something similar earlier in Chapter 7 with the `HashTable`. But in both of those cases, you have only one name inside parentheses. With the `Cookies`, you have two names in parentheses. Why?

The `Cookies` property is actually a *collection*. A collection is a lot like a `HashTable`: It holds multiple objects, and you can refer to them by name. So you can have multiple cookies stored in the `Cookies` collection — each with its own name. But each cookie *also* can hold multiple name/value pairs. I've only stored one cookie: `MusicPref`. In it, I've stored two name/value pairs: `Name` and `MusicStyle`. So the first name in parentheses is the name of the cookie, and the second one is the name of the information you want to get out of that cookie.

Chapter 17

Real-World Web Application Issues

● ●

● ●

As you begin to develop more complex Web applications, they stop being a collection of pages and start to take on a coherent life of their own. But when that happens, you begin to run into questions and problems that you didn't have when you were just creating a few simple pages. To answer these questions and provide mechanisms for creating larger, more flexible Web applications, Microsoft has created a way to identify your jumble of pages as an independent application with its own identity and support. This chapter explains how that works and introduces you to those mechanisms.

What's a Web Application?

Earlier in the book, I describe a Web application as a group of pages that work together to create an experience for the user that is not unlike working with a normal Windows application.

But when you begin to work on larger projects, you need something more concrete than that. Through IIS and its Internet Services Manager, you can identify a specific folder as the root of a Web application. All the files and subfolders within that folder are then considered part of that application.

Clearly, that isn't necessary. You've been creating ASP.NET pages that work together quite well throughout the course of reading this book and trying the examples. What benefits do you gain by identifying your folder as an application?

Actually, I can name several:

- ✔ All the pages that are part of a Web application run in their own process on the Web server. If one Web application locks up, it doesn't bring down all the other Web applications because they are all running as separate processes on the machine.

- ✔ An identified Web application can have its own `global.asax` file. This file always appears in the root folder of a Web application. It provides a place where you can put code that is executed when the application first starts up or when a new user first begins to use an application, for instance. It also enables you to import namespaces for your application globally so you don't need to do it on each and every page.

- ✔ A Web application can also have a `web.config` file. This file also always appears in the root folder of a Web application. It contains all the configuration settings that you want to specify for this application.

- ✔ Web applications each get their own `\bin` folder. This folder always appears just under the root folder for a Web application. It can contain components that you can use to help in your ASP.NET page development. These components may include some provided by Microsoft, others that you purchased from third-party vendors, or components that you created yourself.

I don't have room in this book to get into the details of creating your own components and using them in your applications from the `\bin` folder. However, it is an interesting topic and I encourage you to research it through the documentation and other books and articles.

However, I do want to introduce you to the `global.asax` file and the `web.config` file and give you a glimpse of what they can do for you.

But before I do, let me show you the steps that are involved in identifying a folder as the root folder for a Web application.

Identifying Your Web Application

In order to follow the steps that I describe in this section, you need to have direct access to the Web server and be sitting in front of it. You also need permissions that allow you to create a new Web application in IIS. If you do not have access to your Web server, or you do not have the security privileges to make these changes, contact your system administrator or your Web hosting service to see what options they offer for creating ASP.NET Web applications.

The good news is that after you mark a folder as the root for a Web application, you don't have to bother your system administrator or have much interaction with the server configuration software anymore. Between the global.asax and the web.config, you'll have all the control you need over your application.

To create a new Web application, follow these steps:

1. **Create a new folder under** c:\inetpub\wwwroot **that you want to be the root for your new Web application. Name it anything you like.**

2. **Launch the Internet Services Manager: Choose Start⇨Programs⇨ Administrative Tools⇨Internet Services Manager.**

   The window will look similar to Figure 17-1.

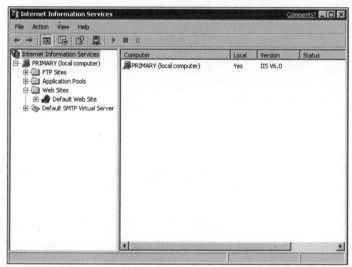

Figure 17-1: The Internet Information Services Manager.

If you've worked with the Internet Information Server (IIS) much, you may be familiar with the Internet Information Services Manager. This application gives you access to the features and configuration settings of IIS.

Along the left side, you'll see a hierarchy of items. Under the top-level Internet Information Services icon is an icon that represents your server. Under that, you'll see one or more entries. Among them should be one titled Default Web Site.

If you don't see Default Web Site, but you do see Web Sites, open that up and Default Web Site should be inside. These differences depend on exactly which operating system you're using.

3. **Open** Default Web Site. **Here you should see a list of all the folders that appear under** c:\inetpub\wwwroot.

4. **Find the folder you created in Step 1. Right-click it and choose Properties from the pop-up menu.**

   You see a Web folder Properties dialog box appear, looking like Figure 17-2.

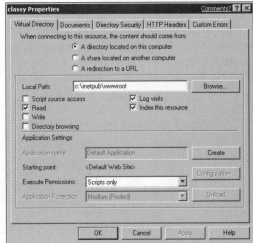

Figure 17-2:
The Web folder's Properties dialog box.

The bottom half of the dialog box is labeled Application Settings. The Application Name textbox is disabled, and beside the textbox is a button with the caption Create.

5. **Click the Create button.**

   The textbox becomes enabled and is automatically filled in with the name of the folder.

6. **Click OK.**

7. **Close Internet Information Services Manager.**

After you complete these steps, you may begin creating your Web application in this folder and its subfolders. You may create a \bin folder under the root and you can create global.asax and web.config files there, too.

The Global.asax File

The global.asax file is like any other page in your application. But this page never gets opened directly. Instead, it contains code that applies to the entire application.

Just like Global.asa?

Yes, as you may expect, the global.asax file is analogous to the global.asa file from Classic ASP. And it does basically the same thing: It offers you a place to put code that responds to Application and Session events. There are more events now — even more than I describe in the next few sections. But some of them are pretty obscure.

You'll find one big difference between the Classic version and its new counterpart: When you made changes to the global.asa file, you had to stop and restart the Web server before those changes would take effect. Now, the system automatically notices and immediately makes use of a newly changed global.asax file. However, the change *does* cause the appli-

Application and Session events

In Chapter 7, I describe the Application and Session objects. These objects enable you to create variables that hold information at the application and session levels, respectively. As I explain in Chapter 7, the application begins when the first person accesses one of the application pages for the first time. The application ends when the last person leaves the application or the server is shut down. It is a truly global scope.

On the other hand, a new session begins every time a new user opens a page in your application. The session continues until that person goes away and the session times out (20 minutes after the last access by that person, by default).

Chapter 7 shows you how to use the Application and Session objects to create application- and session-level variables. But there's more to those objects than simply a place to create variables.

The global.asax file provides a place where you can write code to respond to Application object events and Session object events. Just as the page has a Page_Load event that happens every time the page is retrieved, so the Session object has a Session_Begin event that happens every time a new user begins working with your application. In fact, here are several of the more common events for which you can write code in the global.asax file:

- ✔ Session_OnStart: Happens whenever a new user accesses a page that's part of your application. Can be used to initialize session variables and session-level objects and begin a database connection.

- ✔ Session_OnEnd: Happens when a session times out. Can be used to do any final cleanup and to close a database connection. Also can be used to save any important session variables that have been created while the user has been accessing the site.

✔ Application_OnStart: Happens once — when the first user accesses a page in this application. Can be used to retrieve or initialize information that will be used across all the sessions in the application.

✔ Application_OnEnd: Happens once — when the last person leaves the application or the server is shut down. Can be used to clean up any application-level variables or objects.

✔ Application_OnBeginRequest: Happens every time a page in the application is requested, before the request is serviced.

✔ Application_OnEndRequest: Happens after each request is serviced. This is the last event that can have an effect on the response.

Here's an example of a global.asax file that uses several of these events to initialize and track two application variables that provide interesting statistics that can be displayed from any page in the application:

```
<script runat="server">
Sub Application_OnStart(Sender As Object, E As EventArgs)
Application("TotalSessions") = 0
Application("CurrentSessions") = 0
End Sub

Sub Session_OnStart(Sender As Object, E As EventArgs)
Application.Lock
Application("TotalSessions") = _
   CInt(Application("TotalSessions")) + 1

Application("CurrentSessions") = _
   CInt(Application("CurrentSessions")) + 1
Application.Unlock
End Sub

Sub Session_OnEnd(Sender As Object, E As EventArgs)
Application.Lock
Application("CurrentSessions") = _
   CInt(Application("CurrentSessions")) - 1
Application.Unlock
End Sub
</script>
```

The first thing you should notice about this file is that it doesn't begin with the @ Page directive like ASP.NET pages do. In fact, it has no directive at all at the top. None is necessary. Also, you should never need to include HTML in the global.asax file.

What does it do? TotalSessions tracks the number of sessions for this application over the application's lifetime. CurrentSessions tracks how many people currently have active sessions with this application.

When the application first starts up, both numbers are set to 0. Every time a new session starts, both numbers are increased by one. When a session ends, the CurrentSessions variable is reduced by one.

Use Application.Lock and Application.Unlock whenever you change the value of an Application variable because several sessions could access the same variable at once. If this happens, you can end up with a corrupted value in the variable. Using Lock and Unlock ensures that all the changes happen one after the other, as they should. However, you don't need to use Lock and Unlock in the Application_OnStart or Application_OnEnd events because both will be triggered only once, and you can be sure nothing else will be going on in this application when they are. For more information on Application and Session variables or Lock and Unlock, see Chapter 7.

Global directives: @ Import

In addition to writing code that responds to Application and Session events, you can include directives in the global.asax file. Probably the most important directive you can include is the @ Import directive. In Chapter 16, I discuss using the @ Import directive in your ASP.NET pages. Doing so makes all the objects in a particular namespace available to the page.

Using the @ Import directive in the global.asax file does the same for the *entire application*. For example, if you wanted to make the System.Web.Mail namespace available to every page in your application (without needing to put an @ Import at the top of each page), you'd simply include this line at the top of the global.asax file:

```
<%@Import Namespace="System.Web.Mail" %>
```

The Configuration File

ASP.NET makes configuring your application as easy as editing a text file. No complex Web server configuration applications, no registry settings, and no system administrator privileges required.

The machine.config versus web.config

After you install the .NET Framework on a Web server, all ASP.NET applications draw their configuration information from one file: machine.config. This file is stored deep within the folders of the .NET Framework installation:

```
[Windows]\Microsoft.NET\Framework\[Ver]\Config\machine.config
```

In this path, replace [Windows] with the Web server's primary Windows folder. Replace [ver] with the version number of the .NET Framework.

The machine.config file is a long XML file. (I describe XML in the next section.) Feel free to take a look at it, if you like, but don't make any changes right now.

But when it comes to the specific configuration settings for your ASP.NET application, the machine.config file doesn't have the final say. You can create another file called web.config and put it in the root folder of your application. Your application will use all the configuration settings specified in machine.config *except* for those that are changed in your application's web.config. That is, your web.config file takes precedence and overrides the settings in the machine.config.

You don't have to restate all the configuration information from the machine.config in the web.config. You only include the things you want to change. If you want to change only one setting, your web.config file will be very short — with only one setting.

How does XML work?

The web.config file, like the machine.config file, is formatted using XML. XML is not difficult to understand. It's simply a way of laying out a text file that uses tags, much like HTML does.

You mean I can get off my system administrator's back now?

In Classic ASP, you do all these configuration settings with the Internet Information Services Manager. To make changes, you either become intimately familiar with that program or intimately familiar with your system administrator. (Okay, maybe not *that* familiar . . .)

No more! These files give you all the control you need over your Web application, and after you

finish this chapter, you'll feel comfortable making those changes yourself.

By the way, if you make changes to the settings in the Internet Services Manager, they still affect any Classic ASP applications you have on this server, but they don't have any impact at all on your ASP.NET applications.

Just as in HTML, you can nest tags inside other tags, and some tags have attributes. The following simple HTML file demonstrates both of these concepts:

```
<html>
    <body bgcolor="Yellow">
    </body>
</html>
```

In this code, the `<body>` tag is nested inside the `<html>` tag. Not because the `<body>` tag is indented (that just makes it easier to notice), but because the `<body>` start tag and end tag are both within the `<html>` tag.

In addition, the `<body>` tag has an attribute named `bgcolor`, which has the value `"Yellow"` assigned to it.

XML uses these same rules for layout of information and using tags. However, in XML, you aren't bound to using the tags that are defined for HTML. In fact, different applications can define their *own* set of tags to mean whatever they want them to mean.

And they can define *how* their tags work together. For example, they can say the `<tagA>` always surrounds the entire file, and it can have `<tagB>` and `<tagC>` nested inside it, and `<tagB>` can have three attributes, . . . and so on.

The web.config file

The `web.config` file uses XML and defines its own set of tags and rules about how they are used. In this section, I show you the important tags and rules for the `web.config` file and how to change many of the standard settings for your Web application.

First, everything in a `web.config` file is surrounded by the `<configuration>` tag. You can think of this like you would the `<html>` tag in a Web page:

```
<configuration>
. . .
</configuration>
```

Inside this tag, you can specify numerous things, but I want to focus on two here: `<appSettings>` and `<system.web>`.

```
<configuration>
    <appSettings>

    . . .
    </appSettings>
    <system.web>

    . . .
    </system.web>
</configuration>
```

Although you don't usually have to worry about how you capitalize things in HTML, with the ASP.NET server controls, or in VB.NET code, this file is a big exception! Make sure you capitalize all the tags exactly as you see them here, or they won't work! Typically, the web.config file uses what is called *camel notation*. In that style, if a tag is actually multiple words run together, it starts lowercase, but the first letter of each word after that is capitalized, like this: <exampleOfCamelNotation>. It's called camel notation because it has humps in the middle. (Insert your own joke here.)

I explain <appSettings> in the section "Your own application settings in the web.config file," later in this chapter. For now, you can feel free to leave it out. Most of the settings you want to get to can be accessed through <system.web>.

General settings

You may want to change a couple of general settings:

- ✔ executionTimeout: Determines how long a request — for a page or for a graphic — is allowed to process before the system gives up on it and returns an error. The default for this setting is 90 seconds, but if your pages are doing work that you think may regularly take longer than that to complete, like large database queries, you may want to increase this number.

- ✔ maxRequestLength: Specifies a limit to how many kilobytes of information can be sent *to the server* from your users. Typically, if you're doing nothing more than accepting input from forms and the like, the default of 4096 (4MB) should be more than adequate. However, if you give your users the ability to upload images, MP3 files, or other large files, you may want to increase this limit.

In your web.config file, you change these general settings using a tag named <httpRuntime>. You specify these as attributes of that tag. The following code sets the executionTimeout to 120 seconds and the maxRequestLength to 6,144 Kb, or 6MB:

```
<configuration>
   <system.web>
      <httpRuntime executionTimeout="90"
         maxRequestLength="6144" />
   </system.web>
</configuration>
```

Notice, I've left out the <appSettings> tag — if you aren't using it, you can omit it. In fact, that's true of all the elements I describe in the configuration file. I've specified both attributes in this code but if I wanted to specify only one, I could leave out the other. If I don't want to specify either, I can leave out the <httpRuntime> tag altogether. Remember, if it isn't specified here, the default specified in the machine.config is the value used for the setting.

XML is a lot pickier than HTML about capitalization, as I mentioned. It's also picky about other things. For example, you'll notice that the values assigned to the attributes in the preceding example are in quotes. In HTML, that's usually optional. In XML, it isn't. Attribute values always must be inside quotes. Another important rule to remember is that every opening tag must have a corresponding closing tag. No ifs, ands, or buts! The only way around that is to use the /> at the end of the opening tag, which is the same as including a closing tag right after it.

Page settings

These settings directly affect the pages in your Web application:

- ✔ enableSessionState: Normally, ASP.NET tracks sessions and provides the Session object where you can store session-level variables (see Chapter 7). It also kicks off the Session_OnStart and Session_OnEnd events in the global.asax file (see "Application and Session events," earlier in this chapter). These features can be handy, but if you don't need them, you can save significant resources on the server by turning off this capability. You do this by assigning "false" to this attribute. It's "true" by default.

- ✔ enableViewState: The server controls on a form keep track of their contents from one server round-trip to the next. This is handled by an ASP.NET feature called ViewState. In fact, you can save your own variables in ViewState to be remembered on the next round-trip to the server (as I explain in Chapter 9). You can increase performance a little by turning off this capability. You do that by setting this attribute to "false." It's "true" by default. It's usually a good idea to leave this one alone.

A tag called <pages> provides the page settings. The following example web.config sets the value for both enableSessionState and enableViewState to "false." It also sets the maximum request length to 6,144 Kb (see the preceding section in this chapter):

```
<configuration>
    <system.web>
        <httpRuntime maxRequestLength="6144" />
        <pages enableSessionState="false"
            enableViewState="false" />
    </system.web>
</configuration>
```

Session settings

When you save information in a Session variable, where is it stored, actually? Well, by default, ASP.NET takes that value and stores it in memory along with your running Web application. This works fine in most cases.

But if your Web site begins to receive lots of traffic, you may buy additional Web servers to help keep up with the demand. This is referred to as a *Web farm*. If you ask for a page from a site with a Web farm, Server A may answer your request this time, but later when you request another page, Server B may answer your request. As long as each machine has the identical Web pages, that should work just fine — except for the `Session` variables. If some ASP.NET `Session` variables were created on Server A, how would Server B know about them? It wouldn't. That's a problem.

So Microsoft created two other ways of storing `Session` information. One is called a *Session State server*. This is a program that runs on a single server in the Web farm. Whenever one of the Web servers needs to create a `Session` variable, it does so using the Session State server. Whenever a Web server needs to access a previously created `Session` variable, it goes back to the Session State server. That way, no matter how many servers are in the Web farm, or which one processes your request, they all go to the same place to get your `Session` information.

But what if that Session State server crashes? Then all the `Session` variable information instantly disappears! Microsoft offers another option that addresses this problem, too: SQL Server. With this option, a single machine running SQL Server is used to maintain the `Session` variables — and they are all stored in a SQL Server database. This is perhaps the best way to do it, but also the slowest.

The session settings in the configuration file enable you to choose how you want to keep track of your `Session` variables:

- **mode**: Set to one of these values: `InProc`, `StateServer`, or `SQLServer`. `InProc` is the default; it simply stores the session information in memory with your application. `StateServer` and `SQLServer` are as I describe them earlier in this section.

- **stateConnectionString**: Used only in `StateServer` mode. Provides the address of the machine that will take the role of the State Server.

- **sqlConnectionString**: Used only in `SQLServer` mode. Provides the connection string necessary to connect to the database where the session information will be stored.

- **cookieless**: Specifies whether ASP.NET should use cookies to handle sessions. Usually, sessions are tracked by putting a unique ID in the user's cookie file. When the user comes back, the ID is recognized. If the user has a browser that doesn't support cookies, or the user has turned off cookie support, this method will not work. ASP.NET has an alternate method that it can use, but it requires a little more overhead. This attribute is usually set to "false," meaning that ASP.NET uses cookies to handle sessions. Setting this attribute to "true" causes ASP.NET to use its alternate method. Very few users have browsers that don't support cookies. Unless you have reason to believe that a larger than usual number of your users' browsers won't support them, you're probably better off leaving this setting alone.

✔ timeout: Indicates how long ASP.NET waits between requests from a user before ending a session. A session goes from the time a user first retrieves a page from the site until the user goes away (either to another site or off the Web entirely). How long do you wait for another request before you decide that the user has gone for good and end the session? By default, 20 minutes. You can change that by assigning a different value to this attribute.

The session settings use a tag called `<sessionState>`. The following code sets the session mode to use SQL Server and then provides a connection string to access the database. In addition, it sets `cookieless` to true and `timeout` to 30 minutes:

```
<configuration>
   <system.web>
      <sessionState mode="SQLServer"
         sqlConnectionString=
            "data source=DBServer; uid=usr1; pwd=xyz"
         cookieless="true"
         timeout="30" />
   </system.web>
</configuration>
```

Note that when you need to divide a line in two in the `web.config` file, you don't use the _ as you do in VB.NET. You can divide lines anywhere you like in the configuration file, and it will work fine.

Your own application settings in the web.config file

In addition to setting up ASP.NET to work the way you want it, the `web.config` file has another handy use: It gives you a place to store your own application settings. For example, suppose you want to store the connection string you use to access the database. You can put it in your application's `web.config` file, in the `<appSettings>` section.

The following `web.config` file is the same one used in the preceding section, but I've added the `<appSettings>` tag with connection string information in it:

```
<configuration>
   <appSettings>
      <add key="ConnectStr"
         value="Data Source=ProdServ;uid=usr2;pwd=coco" />
   </appSettings>
   <system.web>
      <sessionState mode="SQLServer"
```

(continued)

```
            sqlConnectionString=
                "Data Source=DBServer; User ID=sa; Password="
            cookieless="true"
            timeout="30" />
    </system.web>
</configuration>
```

You can include as many `<add>` tags inside the `<appSettings>` tag as you like, each with a `key` and a `value` specified.

Now, in your application, you can access the information quickly and easily:

```
Dim ConnectString As String
ConnectString = _
    ConfigurationSettings.AppSettings("ConnectStr")
```

Now all your pages can pull the information from the same source, and if you ever need to change it, you make your changes in only one place: the configuration file.

For more information on connecting to a database, see Chapter 18.

Part VI
Tapping the Database

The 5th Wave — By Rich Tennant

@RICHTENNANT

"I'LL BE WITH YOU AS SOON AS I EXECUTE A FEW MORE COMMANDS."

In this part . . .

What do people look for on the Web? Information! And where can you find the deepest, meatiest information? In databases! But how do you get at the information in those databases? Aren't databases big and complex and don't they require advanced degrees just to understand?

Absolutely not! Databases are actually pretty simple after you get the hang of them. And they provide powerful capabilities for storing, indexing, sorting, and retrieving exactly what you want. In this part of the book, you discover how to retrieve existing data from a database and display it in a pleasant way on your Web page. You also find out how to store your own data.

If you are completely new to databases, you may want to make a quick stop at Bonus Chapter 5 (on the CD) before you dive into this part of the book. Bonus Chapter 5 provides a quick but informative introduction to all the stuff most database books think you already know!

Chapter 18

Accessing a Database
with ADO.NET

A Web page can be flashy. It can even be smart. But without a way to store and retrieve important information, it's just a novelty — not a critical resource. That's why database access and retrieval rank among the hotter topics in Web development today. The Web enables you to take important database information and make it available any time, anywhere.

In this chapter, you discover the key technology that .NET uses to access databases: ADO.NET. ADO.NET is a set of objects that makes accessing virtually any database pretty darn easy. And you should be thankful! Because, trust me, ADO.NET does a whole lot of work behind the scenes to make a very complex process relatively simple.

If you are new to databases, take a quick detour through Bonus Chapter 5, "A Crash Course in Database Basics," on the CD. It's not long, and it gives you the essentials you need to make the most out of this chapter and the next.

Classy Classifieds

The examples I use in this chapter and Chapter 19 are simplified versions of the pages from the Classy Classifieds application that I've included with this book.

Classy Classifieds is an ASP.NET application that organizes classified ads into different categories and enables users to browse them. It even enables users to place their own ads for others to see.

The pages you create here are *not* the Classy Classifieds pages that appear in the final application. They are simplified versions that focus only on database access, retrieval, and update. Although both versions of this application use the same techniques for accessing the database, the organization of the code is very different.

If you want to explore the final Classy Classifieds application, see Bonus Chapter 2 on the CD. That chapter has a complete, page-by-page description of how the final application works.

You can find the complete pages created for this chapter and the next on the CD in these folders: \Author\Chapter18 and \Author\Chapter19. The final Classy Classifieds application is on the CD in this folder: \Author\Classy.

If you have some idea what Classy Classifieds does, the pages you create in this chapter and the next one will make more sense. So you may want to make a quick side trip and read Chapter 21. It provides a short tour of the application from a user's perspective. Don't worry, I'll be here when you get back.

Meet the ADO.NET objects

Before you jump knee-deep into code, I want to introduce you to the more important ADO.NET objects and show you what they do and how they work together to get information from a database into your page.

It almost looks familiar . . .

To Classic ASP developers, ADO.NET looks familiar, yet different. In reality, it's quite different from ADO. The biggest difference is that ADO.NET is *disconnected*.

When you create a Recordset in Classic ASP, it maintains a connection with the associated table. This uses lots of resources and isn't well-suited for Web development.

When I say ASP.NET is *disconnected,* I mean you retrieve the data and then you can close the connection because you don't need it anymore. You still get all the rich capabilities that the Classic ASP Recordset offers (and much more!) but without the continuous connection.

The other big difference is that there is no Recordset anymore. Instead, ADO.NET uses a DataSet. But a DataSet isn't the same as an ADO Recordset. Instead of holding the result from a single query, a DataSet can hold the results from multiple queries as if they were in-memory tables. You can then access and manipulate each table individually or maintain relationships between the tables and work with them together. It's a big step up and a great help when dealing data from lots of tables at once.

Be sure and read over the next couple of chapters carefully. Resist the urge to skim — a whole lot has changed.

Table 18-1 offers a quick overview of those objects.

Table 18-1		Important ADO.NET Objects
Object	*Class Name*	*What It Does*
Connection	OleDbConnection	Contains the information necessary to establish a link to the database.
Command	OleDbCommand	Holds a command that you want to send to the database. Contains a Connection property that points to a Connection object.
DataAdapter	OleDbDataAdapter	Issues commands to the database and retrieves data into a DataSet. Contains a SelectCommand property that points to a Command object.
DataSet	DataSet	Provides an in-memory representation of part of your database. Can hold multiple tables and their relationships to each other.

Figure 18-1 shows how these different objects fit together. It may not make too much sense right now, but hold a finger in this page and flip back to it as I describe each of these objects in the next few sections.

Figure 18-1:
The DataAdapter contains a pointer to a Command object. The Command contains a pointer to a Connection object.

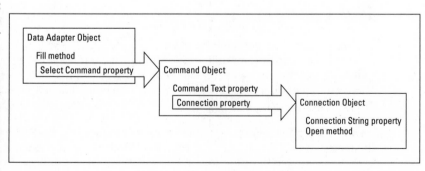

For a more complete summary of these and other database objects covered in this and the next chapter, see the table at the end of Chapter 19.

Using SQL Server

If you're using SQL Server as your database, you can use the standard ADO.NET objects I describe in this chapter, *or* you can use an alternate namespace with an alternate set of objects that were designed and optimized specifically for use with SQL Server. To use these objects, replace the second `Import` line with this one:

```
<%@ Import
    Namespace="System.Data.SqlC
    lient" %>
```

Fortunately, the SQL Server objects work exactly like the standard ADO.NET objects I describe in this chapter and the next. The only difference is their class names. The class names for many of the standard ADO.NET objects begin with `OleDb`. Whenever you see that, simply replace the `OleDb` with `Sql`. So, the SQL Server class names for the objects I describe in this chapter are: `SqlConnect`, `SqlCommand`, and `SqlDataAdapter`. The DataSet class name remains `DataSet`.

Exotic objects, imported from ADO.NET

Before you can make use of the ADO.NET objects, you must make them available to your code. You must import two namespaces: `System.Data` and `System.Data.OleDb`. (For information on namespaces and `@ Import`, see Chapter 16.) Be sure to include these two lines at the top of any page that works with the database:

```
<%@ Import Namespace="System.Data" %>
<%@ Import Namespace="System.Data.OleDb" %>
```

The Connection object

The `Connection` object handles all the details of getting you connected to the database. The information you need to provide to the `Connection` object differs depending on the DBMS with which you're working. For a simple Microsoft Access database, you really only need to tell it that you're using Access and then give it the path and filename of the database itself.

If you're using SQL Server, you need to provide a server name (the name of the machine on the network that runs the DBMS), a database name, and a user name and password to log on. Depending on your configuration, you may need to provide other things, as well.

If you're using Oracle, DB2, or another DBMS, check your DBMS documentation for details on what information it requires in order to connect.

Making a Connection object

Before you create a `Connection` object, you create a variable using the `OleDbConnection` class:

```
Dim Connect As OleDbConnection
```

This statement creates a variable that can hold a `Connection` object. To actually create the `Connection` object, you must use the `New` keyword:

```
Connect = New OleDbConnection
```

This statement creates a new `Connection` object and assigns it to the variable you just created. Or, you can combine all this into one line:

```
Dim Connect As OleDbConnection = New OleDbConnection
```

You create all the ADO.NET objects in this way. For more information on classes and creating objects with the `New` keyword, see Chapter 6.

Filling in the Connection object

After you create a `Connection` object, what do you do with it? Well, you use a `Connection` object to get your page connected to a database. And, as I mention earlier in this chapter, to do that, you need some information.

The first piece of information that you'll always need is called the *provider*. The provider tells the `Connection` object which DBMS you'll be working with. However, you have to use a special name to refer to the DBMS. Here are the provider names for several common DBMSs:

DBMS	*Provider Name*
Microsoft Access	Microsoft.Jet.OLEDB.4.0
SQL Server	SQLOLEDB
Oracle	MSDAORA

TECHNICAL STUFF

Who comes up with these names?

What does OleDb mean? Db is probably database, right? But Ole? Is it Spanish?

The term *OLE* has been around Microsoft for a long time. It used to mean "Object Linking and Embedding." Along with the term COM (which stands for Component Object Model, if you must know), it now refers to Microsoft's technologies that enable different applications or components to talk to each other. OLE DB is a technology that works behind the scenes, enabling your pages to talk to DBMSs from various vendors in pretty much the same way. You no longer need to know the nit-picky details of SQL Server and how it differs from Oracle or DB2. All you have to think about are tables, rows, and columns.

If you have a different DBMS, check its documentation or contact the company that provides it to find out what "OLE DB .NET Data Provider name" you should use.

What other information do you need? Well, if you're using an Access database, you need the filename and the path for the database to which you want to connect. But if you're using SQL Server, you need the server name, database name, username, and password.

In either case, you combine all this information together into a *connection string*. Here's what a connection string for an Access database might look like:

```
ConnectString = "Provider=Microsoft.Jet.OLEDB.4.0;" & _
    "Data Source=c:\inetpub\wwwroot\classy\classydb.mdb"
```

The string contains several values assigned to the appropriate names, each separated from each other with a semi-colon (;). For Microsoft Access, the provider is assigned to `Provider`, and the filename of the database is assigned to `Data Source`.

Here's a SQL Server connection string:

```
ConnectString = "Provider=SQLOLEDB;UID=sa;PWD=pass;" & _
    Data Source=myServer;Initial Catalog=Northwind;"
```

Here, `Data Source` refers to the server where the DBMS is running, and `Initial Catalog` refers to the database you want to access on that server. `UID` and `PWD` refer to the user ID and password used to log on.

After you have your connection string, simply assign it to the appropriate property on the `Connection` object:

```
Connect.ConnectionString = ConnectString
```

Note that this does *not* actually connect you to the database. It simply gives the `Connection` object all the information it needs in order to connect. I show you how to make the connection in the section "Making the connection," later in this chapter.

Stop! My head is spinning!

All these terms can get confusing! Read carefully, and re-read if necessary. Take a look at the diagram in Figure 18-1 back at the beginning of the chapter. You've got a few more terms and concepts to go, but don't worry! I give you a real page that you can type in and try out yourself very soon! That will bring it all together for you.

After you get your connection string right, you don't usually have to think a whole lot about which DBMS you're using. All the ADO.NET objects work the same way, regardless.

The Command object

The Command object enables you to create commands to be sent the database to retrieve data and do other things.

As the following example shows, you can create a new Command object the same way you create a Connection object:

```
Dim GetAdsCommand As OleDbCommand = New OleDbCommand
```

The Command object holds two important things: the command you want to execute and the Connection object that contains the information needed to connect to the database. You provide this information to the Command object using the CommandText and Connection properties:

```
GetAdsCommand.CommandText = "Select * From Ads"
GetAdsCommand.Connection = Connect
```

In this example, Connect is simply the Connection object that you created in the preceding section of this chapter. The string assigned to CommandText is written in SQL. It retrieves all the information from the Ads table in the database. In Bonus Chapter 5, on the CD, I describe the SQL Select statement and how it works. If you are unfamiliar with it, or you want to brush up, you might want to quickly read that section before you go on.

To make your life a little easier, the Command object enables you to save a couple of steps and simply give it the SQL command and the Connection object when you create it:

```
Dim GetAdsCommand As OleDbCommand = _
    New OleDbCommand("Select * From Ads", Connect)
```

The DataAdapter object

The DataAdapter is the object that makes it all happen! The objects that I show you how to create in previous sections of this chapter simply store the appropriate information. They don't actually do anything until you hook them up with the DataAdapter object. Now it's time to do something.

Plugging in the Command object

After you have the `Command` object, you can create a `DataAdapter` and put the `Command` object in it:

```
Dim Adapter As OleDbDataAdapter = New OleDbDataAdapter
. . .
Adapter.SelectCommand = GetAdsCommand
```

Or, if you want to combine all these steps together in a different way, you could do this:

```
Dim Connect As OleDbConnection = New OleDbConnection
Dim Adapter As OleDbDataAdapter = New OleDbDataAdapter
. . .
```

```
ConnectString = "Provider=Microsoft.Jet.OLEDB.4.0;" & _
    "Data Source=c:\inetpub\wwwroot\classy\classydb.mdb"
Connect.ConnectionString = ConnectString
Adapter.SelectCommand = _
    new OleDbCommand("Select * From Ads", Connect)
```

In this code, you don't create a separate variable to hold the `Command` object. You simply create the object in the same line where you assign it to the `DataAdapter`. ASP.NET is very flexible about allowing you to save steps like this.

Making the connection

Finally, you can make the connection to the database. The `Command` object is stored in the `SelectCommand` property of the `DataAdapter`. The `Connection` object is stored in `Command` object. So, here's how you call the `Open` method of the `Connection` object:

```
Adapter.SelectCommand.Connection.Open
```

This is where the database connection is established. If this statement doesn't work, you probably have a mistake in the connection string that's assigned to the `Connection` object.

The DataSet object

The `DataSet` object is a place where you can put all the information you retrieve from the database. The data in a `DataSet` is stored in tables, just as it is in the database. And you can maintain the relationships between the tables in a `DataSet`, just as they exist in the database.

Think of a DataSet as an in-memory copy of parts of your database.

Creating a DataSet

You create a DataSet just like all the other objects:

```
Dim ClassyDS As DataSet = New DataSet
```

One important thing to notice: no OleDb prefix. Because DataSet isn't actually involved in connecting and then going out and getting the information, it doesn't make use of database communication or OLE DB. It's simply a place in memory where retrieved data can live.

Retrieving information from the database

In a previous section, I show you how to use the DataAdapter object to connect to the database. You can also use the DataAdapter to retrieve information from the database and fill the DataSet. You do all that with the DataAdapter's Fill method:

```
Adapter.Fill(ClassyDS,"Ads")
```

When you call the DataAdapter's Fill method, you pass the DataSet you want to fill and the name you want to give the table *inside* the DataSet. It's okay to give it the same name in the DataSet as the table you took it from in the database, as I've done here.

What does Fill do? It executes the command in the Adapter's SelectCommand property and then takes the result and makes an in-memory table inside the ClassyDS DataSet called Ads.

Data Bound (And Gagged)

The process takes the coordination of several different ADO.NET objects, but now you know everything you need to get a connection to the database and data retrieved into memory, ready to be displayed on your page. But how do you go about displaying that data?

You could simply go in and get the data from the DataSet, one piece at a time, and plunk the data into server controls on your page. That process works fine and it might be the best way to go in some cases. But ADO.NET provides a simpler approach to presenting database information: *data binding*.

Data binding simply means associating a certain control with data in the DataSet. Then, when the control appears on the page, it contains the associated data, automatically. One of the easier-to-use data-bound controls is the DataGrid.

The DataGrid: Your Data's Bound to Show Up!

The `DataGrid` server control is basically a big Web page table, with rows and columns, that displays information. And it's surprisingly easy to use:

```
<asp:datagrid id="AdsGrid" runat="server" />
```

Of course, it has more properties that you can specify if you want to customize the way it looks. A *whole* lot more, actually. But if you just want to show the results of your database query, this tag provides the control to do it.

But you still need to bind the control to the data:

```
AdsGrid.DataSource = ClassyDS.Tables("Ads")
AdsGrid.DataBind
```

The `DataGrid` (which I've named `AdsGrid` here) has a property called `DataSource`. Simply associate it with one of the tables in your `DataSet`, as I've done here. That creates the link. Then, you call the `DataBind` method of the `DataGrid` to actually transfer the information from the `DataSet` to the `DataGrid` on the page.

Actually, if you have more than one data-bound control on your page, just call the `DataBind` method on the page:

```
Page.DataBind
```

Of course, the page itself isn't bound to anything, but this method causes all the data-bound controls on the page to call *their* `DataBind` method, so you don't have to remember to call each of them individually.

In fact, even if you have only one data-bound control on the page, just go ahead and use `Page.DataBind` anyway. That way, if you add more data-bound controls in the future, you don't have to remember to call their `DataBind` method separately.

All Right! Let's Do It!

I hate to load you up with information without giving you a chance to try it out. So in the next few sections, I show you how to take all that you've discovered so far this chapter and put it together into a working page that retrieves data and displays it on the page.

Getting the database

First, you need a database. I've provided one on the CD in the back of this book in the `\Author\Chapter18` folder. It's called `classydb.mdb`. If you know anything about Microsoft Access, feel free to double-click it and take a look in Access. There's no magic. In fact, this database holds only one table, called **Ads.** It has these columns:

- ✔ **AdNum:** The primary key of the table. Access calls it an `AutoNumber`, which means that when you create a new record, Access automatically generates a unique value for this field. This is a *surrogate key,* which means the field doesn't hold any important data itself and won't be entered or viewed by the users. It just uniquely identifies each row. (See Bonus Chapter 5, on the CD, for more on primary keys and surrogate keys.)

- ✔ **Title:** The name of the item, like "Michael Jordan Rookie Playing Card."

- ✔ **Category:** A string holding the name of the category with which this item is associated. The table has five categories: Vehicles, Computers and Software, Real Estate, Collectibles, and General Merchandise.

- ✔ **Description:** The actual classified ad itself. This information is held in a *memo* field — a type of field that's designed to hold a *lot* of text. Bits are cheap! So we don't charge by the word.

- ✔ **Price:** The amount the user wants to get for the item.

- ✔ **Phone:** The user's phone number, including area code.

- ✔ **Email:** The user's e-mail address.

- ✔ **State:** The state the user lives in (for geographical searches).

- ✔ **Posted:** The date the ad was posted.

- ✔ **Password:** User-created secret word, entered when the ad is created. Passwords enable users to identify themselves later to edit or delete their ads.

The database included on the CD-ROM has quite a few rows — several ads for each category.

Create a folder under your `wwwroot` and call it `simplyclassy` (do not name it `classy`, because you will want to use a folder with that name for the final application). Copy the `classydb.mdb` file to that folder.

There's no place like home (click, click, click)

You need to create two pages: `default.aspx` and `category.aspx`. The first is the Home page for Classy Classifieds. It provides a link for each category.

But no matter which link users click, they are sent to `category.aspx`. The Category page is sent the name of the category the user wants to see. It uses this information to retrieve the data from the database and display the list.

The `default.aspx` page is pretty simple:

```
<%@ Page Explicit="True" Language="VB" Debug="True" %>
<%@ Import Namespace="System.Data" %>
<%@ Import Namespace="System.Data.OleDb" %>
<html>
<body vlink="red">
<h1>Classy Classifieds</h1>
<p>Welcome to Classy Classifieds. We make it easy to turn
your stuff into cash and to get other people's stuff
cheap.</p>
<asp:label runat="server" font-size="18 pt"
font-name="Arial" font-bold="true"
text="The Categories:" /><br><br>
<table width=100% cellpadding="10">
<tr><td>
<asp:hyperlink id="VehiclesLink" runat="server"
navigateurl="category.aspx?Category=VEHICLES"
font-name="Arial" font-size="16 pt">
Vehicles</asp:hyperlink>
</td><td>
<asp:hyperlink id="ComputersLink" runat="server"
navigateurl="category.aspx?Category=COMPUTERS"
font-name="Arial" font-size="16 pt">
Computers and Software</asp:hyperlink>
</td></tr><tr><td>
<asp:hyperlink id="RealEstateLink" runat="server"
navigateurl="category.aspx?Category=REALESTATE"
font-name="Arial" font-size="16 pt">
Real Estate</asp:hyperlink>
</td><td>
<asp:hyperlink id="CollectiblesLink" runat="server"
navigateurl="category.aspx?Category=COLLECTIBLES"
font-name="Arial" font-size="16 pt">
Collectibles</asp:hyperlink>
</td></tr><tr><td>
<asp:hyperlink id="GeneralLink" runat="server"
navigateurl="category.aspx?Category=GENERAL"
font-name="Arial" font-size="16 pt">
General Merchandise</asp:hyperlink>
</td></tr>
</table>
</body>
</html>
```

This page simply provides the user with several links, one for each category, as you can see in Figure 18-2.

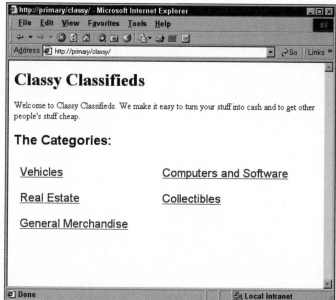

Figure 18-2:
Classy
Classifieds
Home page.

The links, created with HyperLink server controls, all point to the same page: category.aspx. But the Category page needs to know which category the user wants to see. So that information is sent after the question mark on the URL line. For more on passing information from one page to another using this technique, see Chapter 7.

The Category page

The Category page displays a list of ads that are in a particular category, enabling users to browse:

```
<%@ Page Explicit="True" Language="VB" Debug="True" %>
<%@ Import Namespace="System.Data" %>
<%@ Import Namespace="System.Data.OleDb" %>
<html>
<script runat="server">
Sub Page_Load(Sender As Object, E As EventArgs)
If Not IsPostBack Then
    Dim Connect As OleDbConnection = New OleDbConnection
    Dim Adapter As OleDbDataAdapter = New OleDbDataAdapter
    Dim ClassyDS As DataSet = New DataSet
    Dim ConnectString, SelectStatement As String
    Dim Category As String
```

```
        Category = Trim(Request.QueryString("Category"))

        If Category <> "" Then
            Header.Text = "Category Listing: " & Category
            SelectStatement = _
                "Select * From Ads Where Category='" & _
                Category & "'"
        Else
            Header.Text = "Ad Listing"
            SelectStatement = "Select * From Ads"
        End If

        ConnectString = "Provider=Microsoft.Jet.OLEDB.4.0;" & _
            "Data Source=c:\inetpub\wwwroot\classy\classydb.mdb"

        Connect.ConnectionString = ConnectString
        Adapter.SelectCommand = _
            new OleDbCommand(SelectStatement, Connect)
        Adapter.SelectCommand.Connection.Open
        Adapter.Fill(ClassyDS,"Ads")
        AdsGrid.DataSource = ClassyDS.Tables("Ads")
        Page.DataBind
    End If
End Sub
</script>
<body vlink=red>
<asp:label id="Header" runat="server"
font-size="18 pt" font-bold="true"/><br><br>
<asp:datagrid id="AdsGrid" runat="server" />
<br><center>
<asp:hyperlink id="HomeLink" runat="server"
navigateurl="default.aspx" font-bold="true"
font-name="Arial" font-size="12 pt">
[ Home ]</asp:hyperlink>
</center>
</form>
</body>
</html>
```

The result is impressive, if not actually beautiful, as you can see in Figure 18-3.

The body of this page is pretty simple. A label provides the header for the page, the DataGrid doesn't have any special properties specified, and a HyperLink control at the bottom of the page provides a quick path home.

The interesting stuff in this page is definitely in the Page_Load event. First, I declare a bunch of variables I'll need. In the process, I go ahead and create a Connection object, a DataAdapter object, and a DataSet object so they're ready to use:

```
Dim Connect As OleDbConnection = New OleDbConnection
Dim Adapter As OleDbDataAdapter = New OleDbDataAdapter
Dim ClassyDS As DataSet = New DataSet
Dim ConnectString, SelectStatement As String
Dim Category As String
```

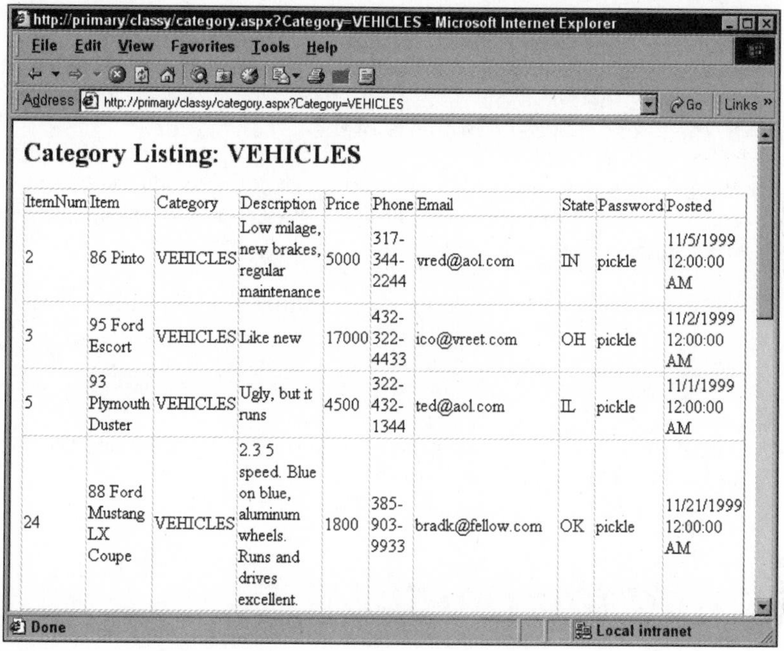

Category Listing: VEHICLES

ItemNum	Item	Category	Description	Price	Phone	Email	State	Password	Posted
2	86 Pinto	VEHICLES	Low milage, new brakes, regular maintenance	5000	317-344-2244	vred@aol.com	IN	pickle	11/5/1999 12:00:00 AM
3	95 Ford Escort	VEHICLES	Like new	17000	432-322-4433	ico@vreet.com	OH	pickle	11/2/1999 12:00:00 AM
5	93 Plymouth Duster	VEHICLES	Ugly, but it runs	4500	322-432-1344	ted@aol.com	IL	pickle	11/1/1999 12:00:00 AM
24	88 Ford Mustang LX Coupe	VEHICLES	2.3 5 speed. Blue on blue, aluminum wheels. Runs and drives excellent.	1800	385-903-9933	bradk@fellow.com	OK	pickle	11/21/1999 12:00:00 AM

Figure 18-3: Classy Classifieds Category page.

Next, I get the `Category` that was sent on the URL line. If a `Category` was sent, I set the header label to identify the category and create a Select statement string that retrieves the ads in that category. If no category was sent, I change the header to `Ad Listing` and then create a Select statement that will simply retrieve *all* the ads:

```
Category = Trim(Request.QueryString("Category"))
If Category <> "" Then
   Header.Text = "Category Listing: " & Category
   SelectStatement = _
      "Select * From Ads Where Category='" & Category & "'"
Else
   Header.Text = "Ad Listing"
   SelectStatement = "Select * From Ads"
End If
```

Now you get to the meat of the page. I create the connection string to access the Microsoft Access database. (Be sure to change the path if it's different on your machine.) The connection string is then set in the `Connection` object:

```
ConnectString = "Provider=Microsoft.Jet.OLEDB.4.0;" & _
    "Data Source=c:\inetpub\wwwroot\classy\classydb.mdb"

Connect.ConnectionString = ConnectString
Adapter.SelectCommand = _
    new OleDbCommand(SelectStatement, Connect)
Adapter.SelectCommand.Connection.Open
Adapter.Fill(ClassyDS,"Ads")
```

As you can see, I create a new `Command` object using the Select statement
string and the `Connection` object. I immediately assign that `Command` object
to the `SelectCommand` property of the `DataAdapter`.

Next, I open the connection, and the `ClassyDS` DataSet is filled with the data
returned from the database. The data is placed in an in-memory table inside
the DataSet called `Ads`.

Now that the data is in memory, you simply bind it to the `DataGrid`:

```
AdsGrid.DataSource = ClassyDS.Tables("Ads")
Page.DataBind
```

The data is associated with the grid, and `DataBind` causes the data to appear
in the control.

Revisiting the DataGrid

In the preceding section of this chapter, you get a chance to actually retrieve
some data and display it in a grid. This example is a perfect test page to begin
playing around with some of the options the `DataGrid` provides.

In this page, users see everything at once — very confusing. It'd be better if
just a few of the columns were visible. Then, if they wanted to see more
detail, users could click a link in a specific row to go to another page with
details of that ad.

If the `DataGrid` were a lesser control, that would be a lot to ask for. But the
`DataGrid` turns out to be more than up to the task — it has power and flexibility to spare!

Narrowing the list of columns

Replace the `DataGrid` tag in the `categories.aspx` page with this, more
extended tag:

```
<asp:datagrid id="AdsGrid" runat="server"
autogeneratecolumns="false"
border="1" backcolor="yellow" width="100%"
bordercolor="Black" cellspacing="0" cellpadding="5">

<columns>

<asp:boundcolumn
headertext="Title"
datafield="Title">
</asp:boundcolumn>

<asp:boundcolumn
headertext="Price"
datafield="Price">
</asp:boundcolumn>

<asp:boundcolumn
headertext="State"
datafield="State">
</asp:boundcolumn>

</columns>
</asp:datagrid>
```

The results are quite different, as you can see in Figure 18-4.

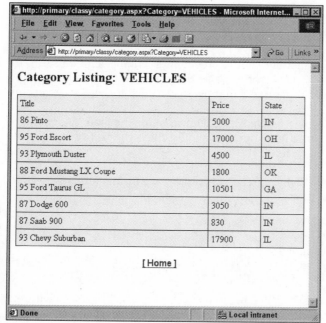

Figure 18-4:
The Category page with fewer columns.

First, take a look at the opening `<asp:datagrid>` tag itself. I've added several attributes that are probably pretty self explanatory. The `border`, `backcolor`, `width`, `bordercolor`, `cellspacing`, and `cellpadding` all correspond to similar attributes you can specify for an HTML table.

But the opening `<asp:datagrid>` tag also includes one unusual attribute: `autogeneratecolumns`. By default, the `DataGrid` takes all the database table columns you bind to it and creates table columns on the page to display them. If you want to specify which columns to display and which not to display, you need to set this property to false.

So how do you specify which columns to include and which to leave out? With the `<columns>` tag, which is nested within the `DataGrid` begin and end tags.

Notice that `<columns>` does not have the `asp:` prefix. Why? Who knows! Sometimes when you put tags within server control tags like this, you're supposed to use the `asp:` prefix, and sometimes you're not. You just have to pay close attention to the online help.

Inside the `<columns>` tag are several `<asp:boundcolumn>` tags. (Here you *do* use the `asp:` prefix!) In fact, there's one for each column that you want to appear in the table. I've chosen to keep it simple and show only the title, price, and state. Inside the `<asp:boundcolumn>` tag, you use `headertext` to specify the header to use for the column, and `datafield` to provide the name of the data column in the table to display.

Adding the link

The page as modified in the preceding section is a lot closer to the final look and feel for the categories page. But you need to add one more important thing: a link on each row that users can click to see the details for that row.

So should you create a new column just for the link? You could, but it's probably more intuitive if the user simply clicks the ad title itself to see its detail. How do you do that?

Replace the first `<asp:boundcolumn>` tag inside `<columns>` (the one for Title) with this:

```
<asp:hyperlinkcolumn
headertext="Title"
datanavigateurlfield="AdNum"
datanavigateurlformatstring="detail.aspx?AdNum={0}"
datatextfield="Title"/>
```

Now each title appears as a link, as you can see in Figure 18-5.

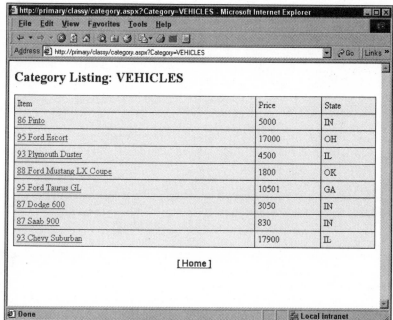

Figure 18-5:
The
Category
page with
links.

Instead of a bound column, you've specified a hyperlink column. You give it the headertext just as you did for the bound column. And the column you want to display goes in the datatextfield (not the datafield, as on the bound column).

But there are two additional attributes: datanavigateurlformatstring and datanavigateurlfield. The datanaviageurlformatstring provides the URL of the page that will be linked to. But there's a catch — it has a wildcard in it: {0}. That wildcard is filled in with the value specified in the datnaviga- teurlfield — in this case, AdNum.

Here's an example. If the Title is "87 Saab 900" and the AdNum is 27, this column would display "87 Saab 900" as a hyperlink. If the user clicked the hyperlink, this page would be displayed:

```
detail.aspx?AdNum=27
```

This is quite powerful. Now the detail.aspx page can use Request. QueryString to get the AdNum of the ad to display, just as the categories page used it to get the category to display. (Of course, you'll get an error if you click any of these links, because you haven't created a detail.aspx page yet.)

One last detail

The page now lists only a few columns, and each title is a hyperlink that will go to a page to display the details. What's left? Well, in looking at the result, I thought that it would look better if the column headers were bolded. Difficult? Nope.

Add the following line just before the `<columns>` tag:

```
<headerstyle font-bold="true" />
```

Just like the `<columns>` tag, the `<headerstyle>` goes between the `<asp:datagrid>` open and close tags and, also like `<columns>`, it is not pre-fixed with `asp:`. Go figure.

Of course, you can change more than just the boldness of the header with this tag. Just add in the appropriate attributes to change the `font-name`, `font-size`, `forecolor`, `backcolor`, and so on.

And you can include additional tags inside `<asp:datagrid>` (but outside `<columns>`) to do things like change the style of the footer and the style of the individual rows in the list. You can even change the style of *alternating* rows so that every other one has, for example, a green background to repro-duce that fetching green-bar paper look!

Chapter 19

Updating the Database

● ●

In This Chapter

▶ Editing a row

▶ Adding a new row

▶ Deleting an existing row

● ●

*I*n the preceding chapter, you find out about getting connected to the database, retrieving data, and binding the data to a DataGrid to display it on a page.

In this chapter, you create pages that enable users to edit the information, add new rows, and delete rows that are no longer needed. With this basic knowledge, you can begin tackling your own database projects.

More Examples from Classy Classifieds

In Chapter 18, I show you how to create a simplified version of two important pages in the Classy Classifieds application — the Home page and the Category page. In this chapter, you create a simplified version of the Edit Ad page, the Place Ad page, and the Delete Ad page. These pages aren't directly connected to either of the pages in the preceding chapter or to each other, so you need to test each one by itself.

These simplified pages are significantly different from the final Classy Classifieds pages included on the CD-ROM. They do essentially the same job, but I've scaled them back so you can focus specifically on their database tasks. See Bonus Chapter 2 on the CD for a complete, page-by-page description of how the final application works.

You can find the complete pages created for this chapter and the previous one on the CD in these folders: \Author\Chapter18 and \Author\Chapter19. The final Classy Classifieds application is on the CD in this folder: \Author\Classy.

Editing a Row

The process of connecting to a database and retrieving the information into a `DataSet` is the same no matter what you want to do with the information — look at it, edit it, add new rows, or delete existing rows.

In this section, I show you how to access the individual database columns, get the information, and put it into textboxes. Then, after the users make their changes, you can put the changed information back into the database.

Presenting: EditAd.aspx

I start off by showing you the entire page. You can type this in (or steal it off the CD-ROM) and try it out. After you play around with it, I'll take you through the pieces to show you how it works.

```
<%@ Page Explicit="True" Language="VB" Debug="True" %>
<%@ Import Namespace="System.Data" %>
<%@ Import Namespace="System.Data.OleDb" %>
<html>
<script runat="server">
Dim ConnectString, SelectStatement As String
Dim Connect As OleDbConnection = New OleDbConnection
Dim Adapter As OleDbDataAdapter = New OleDbDataAdapter
Dim ClassyCB As OleDbCommandBuilder
Dim ClassyDS As DataSet = New DataSet
Dim Row As DataRow
Dim AdNumSent As Integer
Dim CatListIndex As Integer

Sub Page_Load(Sender As Object, E As EventArgs)
If Not IsPostBack Then
   AdNumSent = Request.QueryString("AdNum")
   GetAd(AdNumSent)
   Row = ClassyDS.Tables("Ads").Rows(0)

   TitleText.Text = Row.Item("Title")
   DescriptionText.Text = Row.Item("Description")
   For CatListIndex=0 To CategoryDropDown.Items.Count -1
      If CategoryDropDown.Items(CatListIndex).Value =
            Row.Item("Category") Then
         CategoryDropDown.Items(CatListIndex).Selected = True
      End If
   Next
   PriceText.Text = Row.Item("Price")
   PhoneText.Text = Row.Item("Phone")
   EmailText.Text = Row.Item("Email")
   StateText.Text = Row.Item("State")
End If
```

```
End Sub

Sub Submit_Click(Sender As Object, E As EventArgs)
AdNumSent = Request.QueryString("AdNum")
GetAd(AdNumSent)
Row = ClassyDS.Tables("Ads").Rows(0)
Row.Item("Title") = TitleText.Text
Row.Item("Description") = DescriptionText.Text
Row.Item("Category") = CategoryDropDown.SelectedItem.Value
Row.Item("Price") = PriceText.Text
Row.Item("Phone") = PhoneText.Text
Row.Item("Email") = EmailText.Text
Row.Item("State") = StateText.Text

Adapter.Update(ClassyDS, "Ads")

If ClassyDS.HasErrors Then
   Message.Text = "There was an error placing your ad. " & _
      ClassyDS.Tables("Ads").Rows(0).RowError
Else
   Message.Text = "Your classified ad changes have been made"
   TitleText.Enabled=False
   DescriptionText.Enabled=False
   CategoryDropDown.Enabled=False
   PriceText.Enabled=False
   PhoneText.Enabled=False
   EmailText.Enabled=False
   StateText.Enabled=False
   Submit.Enabled=False
End If
End Sub

Sub GetAd(AdNumSent As Integer)
SelectStatement = "Select * From Ads Where AdNum=" & _
   AdNumSent
ConnectString = "Provider=Microsoft.Jet.OLEDB.4.0;" & _
   "Data Source=c:\inetpub\wwwroot\classy\classydb.mdb"
Connect.ConnectionString = ConnectString
Adapter.SelectCommand = _
   new OleDbCommand(SelectStatement, Connect)
ClassyCB = New OleDbCommandBuilder(Adapter)
Adapter.Fill(ClassyDS,"Ads")
End Sub
</script>
<body vlink=red>
<form runat="server">
<asp:label id="Header" runat="server"
font-name="arial" font-size="22" font-bold="true"
text="Edit Ad"/>
<p>Edit any of the information you like. Make sure each
textbox has a valid value before you click the Make Changes
button.</p>

<table><tr><td>Title:</td><td>
```

```
<asp:textbox id="TitleText" runat="server" columns="50"
text="Edit Ad"/>

</td></tr><td valign=top>Description:</td><td>
<asp:textbox id="DescriptionText" runat="server"
textmode="multiline" rows="3" columns="40" />

</td></tr><tr><td>Category:</td><td>
<asp:dropdownlist id="CategoryDropDown" runat="server" >
  <asp:listitem >* Pick a Category *</asp:listitem>
  <asp:listitem value="VEHICLES">Vehicles</asp:listitem>
  <asp:listitem value="COMPUTERS">Computers</asp:listitem>
  <asp:listitem value="REALESTATE">Real Estate</asp:listitem>
  <asp:listitem value="COLLECTIBLES">Collectibles
    </asp:listitem>
  <asp:listitem value="GENERAL">General Merchandise
    </asp:listitem>
</asp:dropdownlist>

</td></tr><tr><td>Price:</td><td>
<asp:textbox id="PriceText" runat="server" columns="10" />
</td></tr><tr><td>Phone</td><td>
<asp:textbox id="PhoneText" runat="server" columns="15" />
</td></tr><tr><td>Email:</td><td>
<asp:textbox id="EmailText" runat="server" columns="50" />
</td></tr><tr><td>State:</td><td>
<asp:textbox id="StateText" runat="server" columns="2"/>
</td></tr><tr><td>

<asp:button id="Submit" runat="server" text="Make Changes"
onclick="Submit_Click"/>

</td><td align="center">
<asp:label id="Message" runat="server" font-italic="true"
font-size="16 pt" />
</td></tr></table>
<br><center>
<asp:hyperlink id="HomeLink" runat="server"
navigateurl="default.aspx" font-bold="true"
font-name="Arial" font-size="12 pt">
[ Home ]</asp:hyperlink>
</center>
</form>
</body>
</html>
```

When you try out this page, you must send it a valid ad number. In the database
I've included on the CD-ROM, valid ad numbers range from 10 to 30. Of course,
other numbers are valid, too, but those are easy to remember. So if you want to
edit the ad with the number 17, you'll use a URL that looks like this:

```
http://localhost/classy/editad.aspx?AdNum=17
```

Of course, if you're not working on the server itself, replace localhost with the server name. And if you're working on a site on a hosting service, replace localhost with your IP address or your domain name.

When you do, you should see a page that looks something like Figure 19-1.

Figure 19-1:
Classy
Classifieds
Edit Ad
page.

This page provides textboxes for editing all but two of the columns: Password and Posted. Password simply cannot be changed after the classified ad is first placed. The Posted date is automatically filled in using the system date when the ad is posted, so that can't be changed, either.

But users can make changes to any of the information they see. Try changing some of the information and clicking the Make Changes button. Then briefly go to another Web page and then type the URL for this page again (including the AdNum). Click Refresh to make sure you get a fresh copy of the page. You should see the information as you modified it.

What a body!

Take a look at the body of the page. A label provides a header at the top of the page and is followed by some instructions for the user. Then a table organizes the textboxes into a layout that makes clear what each control holds.

The Category drop-down list has a couple of twists. The first item in the list isn't actually a valid selection. It just tells users that they need to pick a category. If the user selects this top item and tries to save the page, problems will result. In the final version of this page, I use validation controls (see Chapters 13 and 14) to make sure that doesn't happen.

The drop-down list also includes a `value` for each valid option. This `value` is the information that will actually be stored in the `Category` column of the `Ads` table.

Retrieving the row

As with the example in Chapter 18, your first step is to connect to the database and retrieve information.

To make things simple, I've bundled the code to do all this into a subroutine called `GetAd`. It accepts an integer — the ad number for the row you want to retrieve. I call this subroutine first thing in the `Page_Load` event:

```
Sub Submit_Click(Sender As Object, E As EventArgs)
AdNumSent = Request.QueryString("AdNum")
GetAd(AdNumSent)
. . .
```

The code in the `GetAd` subroutine itself should be pretty familiar to you by now:

```
Sub GetAd(AdNumSent As Integer)
SelectStatement = "Select * From Ads Where AdNum=" & _
    AdNumSent
ConnectString = "Provider=Microsoft.Jet.OLEDB.4.0;" & _
    "Data Source=c:\inetpub\wwwroot\classy\classydb.mdb"
Connect.ConnectionString = ConnectString
Adapter.SelectCommand = _
    new OleDbCommand(SelectStatement, Connect)
ClassyCB = New OleDbCommandBuilder(Adapter)
Adapter.Fill(ClassyDS,"Ads")
End Sub
```

Two differences exist between this code and the code used in examples in the preceding chapter. First, the Select statement is different — I modified it to get a specific row by using the table's primary key — `AdNum`.

Second, a new kind of object is created: `OleDbCommandBuilder`. I discuss this object a little later in this chapter (in the section titled "The CommandBuilder object"). It doesn't affect the retrieval of information, which is what you're interested in right now.

Filling in the textboxes

After you get the row you need in memory, the next step is to fill in the textboxes with the information so the user can see what it looks like.

If you want to get at the information in the Title column and put it into the TitleText textbox, you could do this:

```
TitleText.Text = _
    ClassyDS.Tables("Ads").Rows(0).Item("Title")
```

Essentially, this line says, "Inside the ClassyDS DataSet, there is a table named Ads. Go to that table and then go to row number 0, the very first row in that table. In that row, there's a column called Title. Now take that value and put it in the TitleText textbox." Whew!

Fortunately, you can use a shortcut instead of typing all this code every time you need to fill in a textbox. Create a variable of type DataRow, assign the row to that variable, and then use that variable to access the individual columns. To see an example of this, look at the Page_Load event, just after the GetAd subroutine is called:

```
Dim Row As DataRow
. . .
GetAd(AdNumSent)
Row = ClassyDS.Tables("Ads").Rows(0)

TitleText.Text = Row.Item("Title")
DescriptionText.Text = Row.Item("Description")
```

Those last two lines just pop the column values from the retrieved row into the appropriate textboxes.

The For...Next loop that follows sets the drop-down list to the appropriate value. It's not as simple as you might expect because what I store in the database isn't the Text of the SelectedItem. It's the Value of the SelectedItem. So I have to take what I get from the database, walk through each item, find the value that matches, and then select that item:

```
For CatListIndex=0 To CategoryDropDown.Items.Count -1
    If CategoryDropDown.Items(CatListIndex).Value = _
        Row.Item("Category") Then
        CategoryDropDown.Items(CatListIndex).Selected = True
    End If
Next
```

The rest of the Page_Load subroutine simply fills in the other textboxes with the appropriate values from the DataSet row:

```
PriceText.Text = Row.Item("Price")
PhoneText.Text = Row.Item("Phone")
EmailText.Text = Row.Item("Email")
StateText.Text = Row.Item("State")
```

Applying the user's changes to the database

After you retrieve the information and place it in the textboxes, the user can fiddle with it as much as necessary. When the user makes all the desired changes and clicks the button, the Submit_Click subroutine gets triggered.

Triggering Submit_Click

Just as in the Page_Load event, Submit_Click starts off by getting the AdNum using QueryString and then passes it to the GetAd subroutine:

```
Sub Submit_Click(Sender As Object, E As EventArgs)
AdNumSent = Request.QueryString("AdNum")
GetAd(AdNumSent)
. . .
```

Why is the GetAd subroutine called again? When the page is first loaded, you call GetAd to retrieve the row and display it in the textboxes. But Submit_Click is triggered when the user clicks the button. This is a second round-trip to the server, and the server doesn't hold on to the objects and database information you retrieved from one round-trip to the next. So, once again, you have to get the ad number and retrieve the row.

Using the CommandBuilder object

The GetAd subroutine includes one line that I mention earlier in this chapter and promised to explain later. And now is the time . . .

```
ClassyCB = New OleDbCommandBuilder(Adapter)
```

This is the CommandBuilder object. To explain what it does, I need to back up for a moment to review and expand a bit on the DataAdapter.

The DataAdapter holds a Command object in its SelectCommand property. That command is the SQL Select statement used to retrieve the data from the database. But SelectCommand isn't the only command property the DataAdapter has. It also has an UpdateCommand, an InsertCommand, and a DeleteCommand. These properties give the DataAdapter the commands it should use to update the database with changes that are made in the DataSet. The DataAdapter cannot update the database unless these properties are filled in.

You could create your own `Command` objects using SQL statements and assign them to these properties. And often that's beneficial. But if you have a simple single-table Select statement like this one, you can use a shortcut: the `CommandBuilder` object.

The `CommandBuilder` object takes the `DataAdapter` you send when you create it, looks at the `SelectCommand` you've assigned, and creates corresponding update, insert, and delete commands and puts them in the right `DataAdapter` properties. Very handy.

Now that these other properties are filled in, you're ready to update the database with any changes the user made.

Updating the DataSet and sending the changes to the database

After calling `GetAd`, the `Submit_Click` subroutine applies the changes the user made in the textboxes to the `DataSet`. To accomplish that, you simply do the opposite of what you did to get the data into the textboxes:

```
Row = ClassyDS.Tables("Ads").Rows(0)
Row.Item("Title") = TitleText.Text
Row.Item("Description") = DescriptionText.Text
Row.Item("Category") = CategoryDropDown.SelectedItem.Value
Row.Item("Price") = PriceText.Text
Row.Item("Phone") = PhoneText.Text
Row.Item("Email") = EmailText.Text
Row.Item("State") = StateText.Text
Row.Item("State") = StateText.Text
```

The `DataSet` is just an in-memory representation of the database. Changing it doesn't change the database. In order to do that, you have to call the `Update` method of the `DataAdapter`, passing the changed `DataSet` and the name of the table in the `DataSet` from which you want to update the database:

```
Adapter.Update(ClassyDS, "Ads")
```

`Update` takes a look at the `Ads` table inside the `ClassyDS` DataSet and figures out what has changed. In this case, the table has only one row, but the `Update` command can handle any number of rows. After it figures out the table has only one row and that it has been changed, `Update` gets the command stored in the DataAdapter's `UpdateCommand` property (which, in this case, was generated by the `CommandBuilder` object), and uses it to make the necessary changes in the database.

No runs, no hits, no errors!

The last `If...Then` checks to see if the `DataSet` contains any errors:

```
If ClassyDS.HasErrors Then
    Message.Text = "There was an error placing your ad. " & _
        ClassyDS.Tables("Ads").Rows(0).RowError
Else
    Message.Text = "Your classified ad changes have been made"
    TitleText.Enabled=False
    DescriptionText.Enabled=False
    CategoryDropDown.Enabled=False
    PriceText.Enabled=False
    PhoneText.Enabled=False
    EmailText.Enabled=False
    StateText.Enabled=False
    Submit.Enabled=False
End If
```

Always check for errors whenever you do any work with the database. Lots of things could potentially go wrong.

The DataSet's HasErrors property will be true if one or more errors have happened. Then, each row in the DataSet has its own RowError property. If that row has an error, RowError describes it. In this case, because the table has only one row, you know right where to look if an error occurs.

If you were working with multiple rows in a DataSet, you'd want to loop through them all, checking each for problems.

Where's DataBinding when you need it?

If you've worked with other languages or development environments that use data binding, you may be surprised to see that you have to do all the heavy lifting of moving data around in ASP.NET when you want to update information — especially when I seem to imply in the preceding chapter that ASP.NET supports data binding.

Well, in ASP.NET, data binding is mostly about automatically filling in controls with information retrieved from the database. It isn't so much focused on getting the data back out of the controls and into the DataSet after the data has been changed. You usually have to do that part yourself.

I could use data binding with the textboxes in this application to have them automatically filled in when the data is retrieved into the DataSet. However, when you're only showing the columns for one row, doing the data binding doesn't take any less work than simply copying the information, column-by-column, into the textboxes — so, that's what I did. However, as I show you in Chapter 18, when working with a control that presents multiple rows of information at once (like a DataGrid, a listbox, or even a collection of checkboxes), ASP.NET data binding can definitely save you a lot of work.

In addition, mechanisms provided with the DataGrid and the DataList controls do allow user editing of individual rows and data-binding support to help make it relatively painless.

If there are no errors, the user is notified that everything went as planned and then all the controls are disabled. The user can see the data but not make further changes.

After completing all the editing work, the user can click the Home link.

Adding a New Row

The process for adding a new row is very similar to the process for editing a row. I've created a separate Place Ad page for this section, but in the final Classy Classifieds application, I've combined the Edit Ad and Place Ad pages into one.

Presenting: PlaceAd.aspx

`PlaceAd.aspx` is similar to `EditAd.aspx` and because the listing is so long, I've omitted part of the body of the page. You can steal this portion from `EditAd.aspx` when you create your own page. (Or, you can just steal `PlaceAd.aspx` from the CD, instead!)

I've also highlighted things that are new or changed with bold text. Note that this listing has no `Page_Load` event subroutine. (See "What's changed?" later in this chapter to find out why.)

```
<%@ Page Explicit="True" Language="VB" Debug="True" %>
<%@ Import Namespace="System.Data" %>
<%@ Import Namespace="System.Data.OleDb" %>
<html>
<script runat="server">
Dim ConnectString, SelectStatement As String
Dim Connect As OleDbConnection = New OleDbConnection
Dim Adapter As OleDbDataAdapter = New OleDbDataAdapter
Dim ClassyCB As OleDbCommandBuilder
Dim ClassyDS As DataSet = New DataSet
Dim Row As DataRow
Dim AdNumSent As Integer
Dim CatListIndex As Integer

Sub Submit_Click(Sender As Object, E As EventArgs)
AdNumSent = Request.QueryString("AdNum")
GetAd(0)
Row = ClassyDS.Tables("Ads").NewRow
Row.Item("Title") = TitleText.Text
Row.Item("Description") = DescriptionText.Text
Row.Item("Category") = CategoryDropDown.SelectedItem.Value
```

```
Row.Item("Price") = PriceText.Text
Row.Item("Phone") = PhoneText.Text
Row.Item("Email") = EmailText.Text
Row.Item("State") = StateText.Text
Row.Item("Password") = PasswordText.Text
Row.Item("Posted") = Today

ClassyDS.Tables("Ads").Rows.Add(Row)

Adapter.Update(ClassyDS, "Ads")

If ClassyDS.HasErrors Then
   Message.Text = "There was an error placing your ad. " & _
      ClassyDS.Tables("Ads").Rows(0).RowError
Else
   Message.Text = "Your classified ad has been placed"
   TitleText.Enabled=False
   DescriptionText.Enabled=False
   CategoryDropDown.Enabled=False
   PriceText.Enabled=False
   PhoneText.Enabled=False
   EmailText.Enabled=False
   StateText.Enabled=False
   PasswordText.Enabled=False
   Submit.Enabled=False
End If
End Sub

Sub GetAd(AdNumSent As Integer)
SelectStatement = "Select * From Ads Where AdNum=" &
            AdNumSent
ConnectString = "Provider=Microsoft.Jet.OLEDB.4.0;" & _
   "Data Source=c:\inetpub\wwwroot\classy\classydb.mdb"
Connect.ConnectionString = ConnectString
Adapter.SelectCommand = _
   new OleDbCommand(SelectStatement, Connect)
ClassyCB = New OleDbCommandBuilder(Adapter)
Adapter.Fill(ClassyDS,"Ads")
End Sub
</script>
<body vlink=red>
<form runat="server">
<asp:label id="Header" runat="server"
text="Place an Ad" font-name="arial"
font-size="22" font-bold="true"/>
<p>Please fill in <i>all</i> of these textboxes below. Be
careful when entering a Password and be sure to remember what
you type. You may be required to enter the password later to
identify yourself if you need to edit or delete this ad.</p>
<p>When you are finished, click the Place Ad button.</p>

<table>
<tr><td>Title:</td><td>
```

```
<asp:textbox id="TitleText" runat="server" columns="50"/>
</td></tr>

' This is where the Description, Category, Price
' Phone and Email controls go. See EditAd.aspx

. . .

</td></tr><tr><td>State:</td><td>
<asp:textbox id="StateText" runat="server"
columns="2"/>

</td></tr><tr><td>Password:</td><td>
<asp:textbox id="PasswordText" runat="server"
columns="15" textmode="password"/>

</td></tr><tr><td>
<asp:button id="Submit" runat="server"
text="Place Ad" onclick="Submit_Click"/>

</td><td align="center">
<asp:label id="Message" runat="server"
font-italic="true" font-size="16 pt" />
</td></tr>
</table>

<br><center>
<asp:hyperlink id="HomeLink" runat="server"
navigateurl="default.aspx" font-bold="true"
font-name="Arial" font-size="12 pt">
[ Home ]</asp:hyperlink>
</center>
</form>
</body>
</html>
```

This page doesn't require any special instructions for using it. It doesn't expect to receive any information on the URL as EditAd.aspx did. Just bring it up the way you would any ASP.NET page. It should look a lot like Figure 19-2.

Enter information for a classified ad and click the Place Ad button. The row is added to the database.

What's changed?

I've made a few important changes. First, I've added a new textbox at the bottom of the page for the Password. Although users can't modify this column after the row has been created, they do need to enter it initially.

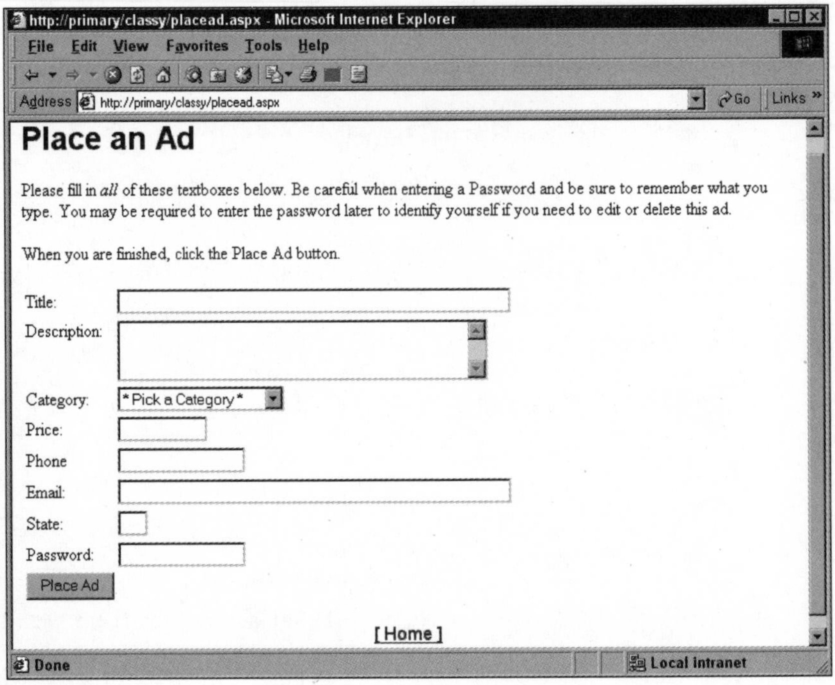

Figure 19-2:
Classy
Classifieds
Place Ad
page.

Second, there's no Page_Load event here. You don't need it because there's nothing to retrieve when the users first arrive. They come to this page so they can enter a new row, so they expect to enter their information into empty textboxes.

Why do a GetAd(0)?

You may be wondering why I go to all the trouble of doing all the stuff in GetAd when I'm not even really retrieving anything. I send a 0 to the GetAd routine. Because Microsoft Access's AutoNumber capability always starts numbering with 1, you'll never have an ad number 0. So why go through the motions of retrieving it? After all, what I'm trying to do is add a *new* row.

This is true. But the mechanism for adding rows is the DataSet. And to be able to add a row in the DataSet, you need to have an in-memory copy of the table there. It doesn't need to have anything in it, but you need a complete description of the table and all its columns.

By creating a Command object with the Select statement that retrieves from that table (even if it doesn't retrieve anything), and then putting that

Command object in the DataAdapter and calling the Fill method, you cause ADO.NET to retrieve all the information about that table and its columns and create a corresponding in-memory table in the DataSet.

Now you're ready to add a new row to the table in the DataSet.

And once again, notice that the CommandBuilder object is used here to generate the other commands for the DataAdapter, so you don't have to fill them in. (See "The CommandBuilder object," earlier this chapter, for more information on that.) The important DataAdapter command for this page is the InsertCommand.

Adding the row

To add a row into a DataSet, you complete three steps:

1. **Create a new row object.**
2. **Fill that object with data for each column.**
3. **Add the row object into the DataSet as a new row for the given table.**

You accomplish the first step with this line:

```
Row = ClassyDS.Tables("Ads").NewRow
```

This line creates a new row object which can hold data for each column of the Ads table. This new object is stored in the Row variable. Don't be confused — this line does *not* create a blank row in the DataSet table. It still has no rows after this line is executed. This line simply creates a new row object and puts that object in the Row variable.

The following lines accomplish the second objective — filling the object with data:

```
Row.Item("Title") = TitleText.Text
Row.Item("Description") = DescriptionText.Text
Row.Item("Category") = CategoryDropDown.SelectedItem.Value
Row.Item("Price") = PriceText.Text
Row.Item("Phone") = PhoneText.Text
Row.Item("Email") = EmailText.Text
Row.Item("State") = StateText.Text
Row.Item("Password") = PasswordText.Text
Row.Item("Posted") = Today
```

This is very much like the Edit Ad page. The only differences are that the Password is included and the Posted column is filled with today's date.

Finally, the row object is added to the DataSet table:

```
ClassyDS.Tables("Ads").Rows.Add(Row)
```

This line does, in fact, add the row to the DataSet table. But that only happens after the row is created and filled in. This line does *not* add the row to the database.

Reflecting the changes from the DataSet to the database is done in exactly the same way it is in the Edit Ad page:

```
Adapter.Update(ClassyDS, "Ads")
```

Again, the Update method causes the DataAdapter to look through the DataSet and find out what it needs to do. In this case, it finds one newly added row, which causes the DataAdapter to look for its InsertCommand (filled in by the CommandBuilder) and execute it with the newly entered information. This causes the new row to be added to the table in the database.

Deleting a Row

You've added a row and you've edited a row. The only thing left is deleting a row. And actually, it's quite easy. I named this file DelAd.aspx:

```
<%@ Page Explicit="True" Language="VB" Debug="True" %>
<%@ Import Namespace="System.Data" %>
<%@ Import Namespace="System.Data.OleDb" %>
<html>
<script runat="server">
Dim ConnectString, SelectStatement As String
Dim Connect As OleDbConnection = New OleDbConnection
Dim Adapter As OleDbDataAdapter = New OleDbDataAdapter
Dim ClassyCB As OleDbCommandBuilder
Dim ClassyDS As DataSet = New DataSet
Dim AdNumSent As Integer

Sub Page_Load(Sender As Object, E As EventArgs)
If Not IsPostBack Then
    AdNumSent = Request.QueryString("AdNum")
    GetAd(AdNumSent)
    TitleLabel.Text = _
        ClassyDS.Tables("Ads").Rows(0).Item("Title")
End If
End Sub


Sub Submit_Click(Sender As Object, E As EventArgs)
```

```
AdNumSent = Request.QueryString("AdNum")

GetAd(AdNumSent)

ClassyDS.Tables("Ads").Rows(0).Delete

Adapter.Update(ClassyDS, "Ads")

If ClassyDS.HasErrors Then
   Message.Text = "There was an error deleting the ad. " & _
      ClassyDS.Tables("Ads").Rows(0).RowError
Else
   Message.Text = "The classified ad has been deleted"
   Submit.Enabled=False
End If
End Sub

Sub GetAd(AdNumSent As Integer)
SelectStatement = "Select * From Ads Where AdNum=" &
          AdNumSent
ConnectString = "Provider=Microsoft.Jet.OLEDB.4.0;" & _
   "Data Source=c:\inetpub\wwwroot\classy\classydb.mdb"
Connect.ConnectionString = ConnectString
Adapter.SelectCommand = _
   new OleDbCommand(SelectStatement, Connect)
ClassyCB = New OleDbCommandBuilder(Adapter)
Adapter.Fill(ClassyDS,"Ads")

End Sub
</script>
<body vlink=red>
<form runat="server">
<asp:label id="Header" runat="server"
font-name="arial" font-size="22"
font-bold="true" text="Delete Ad"/>
<p>Please verify that you want to delete the ad below by
clicking the Delete button. If you don't want to delete this
ad, simply click Home.</p>
Title: <asp:label id="TitleLabel" runat="server" /><br><br>
<asp:button id="Submit" runat="server" text="Delete"
onclick="Submit_Click"/><br>
<asp:label id="Message" runat="server"
font-italic="true"
font-size="16 pt" />
<br><center>
<asp:hyperlink id="HomeLink" runat="server"
navigateurl="default.aspx" font-bold="true"
font-name="Arial" font-size="12 pt">
[ Home ]</asp:hyperlink>
</center>
</form>
</body>
</html>
```

This page receives an AdNum, just as the Edit Ad page does. When you send it a valid number, you see a page that looks like Figure 19-3.

Figure 19-3:
Classy
Classifieds
Delete Ad
page.

Just click the button, and the row is history.

Just like the Edit Ad page, this page uses GetAd twice — once in Page_Load to get the Title of the ad and once again in the Submit_Click to identify the row you want to delete.

These lines do the deletion:

```
GetAd(AdNumSent)
ClassyDS.Tables("Ads").Rows(0).Delete
Adapter.Update(ClassyDS, "Ads")
```

GetAd retrieves the single row to be deleted into the DataSet table. Because there's only one row, you can be sure it's Row(0), so the Delete method of that row is called to delete the row from the DataSet.

The Update, as usual, looks through the DataSet, finds the indication that a row should be deleted, and uses the DataSet's DeleteCommand (again, filled in automatically by CommandBuilder). That command then removes the row from the table in the database. Apart from standard error checking, you're done!

ADO.NET Quick-Reference

To summarize the topics you explore in this chapter and the preceding one, and to provide quick-reference for you when you need to look things up in the future, I created Table 19-1 to provide all the ADO.NET object information covered at a glance.

Table 19-1		ADO.NET Objects	
Object	*Class Name*	*What It Does*	*Common Properties and Methods*
Connection	OleDb Connection	Holds the information needed to connect to the database.	**Property:** Connection String. **Method:** Open
Command	OleDb Command	**Contains a SQL command and the connection to use when sending it.**	**Properties:** Command Text, Connection
Data Adapter	OleDb DataAdapter	**Contains the commands necessary to handle retrieving and updating information from the database. Acts as the go-between or the database and the** DataSet.	**Properties:** Select Command, Update Command, Insert Command, Delete Command. **Method:** Fill
DataSet	DataSet	**Contains one or more in-memory tables of information that have been retrieved from the database.**	**Property:** Tables
Command Builder	OleDb Command Builder	**Based on a simple** SelectCommand **in a** DataAdapter, **the** CommandBuilder **creates a corresponding** UpdateCommand, InsertCommand, **and** DeleteCommand.	Only works with single-table Select statements.

Part VII

Really Cool ASP.NET Applications

The 5th Wave   By Rich Tennant

"I have to say I'm really impressed with the interactivity on this car wash Web site."

In this part . . .

*I*n order to demonstrate many of the techniques that I describe in this book, I've created two real-world applications: The Café Chat Room and Classy Classifieds.

The Café is a place for your users to relax, unwind, and share their feelings about whatever they have on their minds. A real-time chat room actually isn't all that complicated. A few tricky bits keep it interesting, but you'll be surprised at how quickly you'll be adding this one to your own site!

Classy Classifieds implements a full-blown classified ads application that enables users to search ads by category to find just the item they want. Or, they can place their own ad for others to see.

The chapters in this part provide a quick look at the applications and show you how to work with them from a user's perspective. If you want to dig deeper and understand the code that makes these pages tick, check out Bonus Chapter 1, "Inside the Café Chat Room," and Bonus Chapter 2, "Inside Classy Classifieds," both on the CD.

Chapter 20

A Quick Look at the Café Chat Room

Chat rooms are to the Internet generation what diners were to previous generations — places to socialize, meet new people, and talk with old friends about everything from world affairs and politics to music and pop culture. Chat rooms enable people from all over the world to meet in the same place to discuss topics that interest them with people they've never met before.

When you enter a chat room, you use a nickname. These nicknames provide anonymity, which, in turn, tends to make people feel free to loosen up and have a good time, without worrying about how they look or sound. Ironically, nicknames, and the anonymity that goes along with them, don't stop people from getting to know each other and developing long-term relationships. In fact, hearing about a newlywed couple who met online is not at all unusual these days.

In this chapter, I demonstrate the Café Chat Room, an ASP.NET application I've created to include in this book. After you get the basics down, I encourage you to take this application and adapt it for your own use. You can use it as a meeting place to discuss topics of interest or as a forum to introduce an expert who can "speak" and answer visitors' questions live. Any browser that supports frames can access this chat room, and users don't need to download or install anything.

This chapter really just explains how to use the Chat Room application. If you want the nitty-gritty, how-it-works chapter, see Bonus Chapter 1, "Inside the Café Chat Room," on the CD. That chapter explores the source code for each page and shows how all the pages work together.

The Café Entrance

Before you can use the Café Chat Room, you must sign in by entering a name that you'll use as your nickname when you're in the room. The page is pretty simple, as you can see in Figure 20-1.

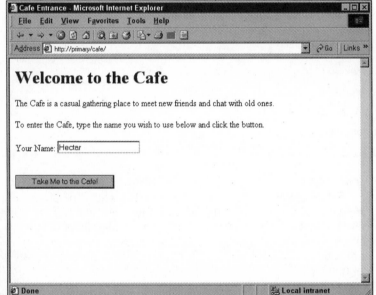

Figure 20-1:
Signing in to
the Café
Chat Room.

The Chat Room's Primary Page

The Café Chat Room's primary page looks like Figure 20-2.

As you can see, this page is divided into three frames: one along the top, one down the right-hand side, and the final one fills the rest of the browser window. In the frame at the top, users type what they want to say and then click a button to send the message to the server. The frame along the right provides a continually updated list of all the people in the chat room. Finally, the biggest part of the page is dedicated to displaying the conversation in the room.

Who's here? Entering and leaving

When you first enter the Café, you're presence is announced with a message:

```
Hectar Enters The Room
```

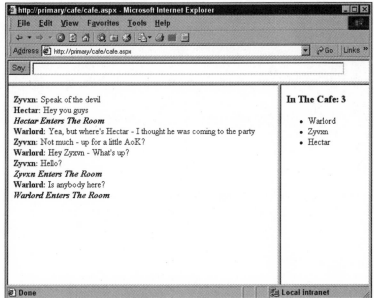

Figure 20-2:
Café Chat
Room
Primary
Page.

Likewise, if you stay long enough, you'll see messages when others leave the room:

```
Zyvxn Leaves The Room
```

You can confirm this information by checking the frame along the right, which lists all the people currently in the room. However, the conversation and the list of current visitors aren't updated at the same time, so they can occasionally appear out-of-sync for a few seconds.

Making conversation

To communicate with the others in the room, you simply type a line of text into the long textbox at the top and then click the button to send your text to the server. You may notice that your message sometimes takes a second or two before it actually appears in the conversation window below. That's normal. (To find out why and how to minimize the delay, see Bonus Chapter 1, "Inside the Café Chat Room," on the CD-ROM.)

Another unusual feature is that new messages appear at the top of the conversation frame, causing all the previous messages to scroll down. This works fine for an active chat, but if you want to read back through the conversation, you have to start at the bottom and work your way up to read them in chronological order.

You can easily add a little pizzazz to your text by typing any valid HTML in the textbox at the top of the page. Whatever you type is simply displayed as-is in the conversation page, so you can use the bold, italic, and font tags to your heart's content.

However, for the same reason, you should avoid typing things like this:

```
He is funny <g>
```

If you do, it's likely to come out like this:

```
He is funny
```

By typing **<g>**, you probably intend to indicate that you are grinning. But the browser interprets <g> as an unknown tag and simply ignores it.

Chapter 21

A Quick Look at Classy Classifieds

· ·

In This Chapter

▶ Browsing, searching, and viewing ads

▶ Placing new ads and editing existing ads

▶ Deleting old ads

· ·

Where can your users go to find that used car, vacation home, or priceless collectible? Your Web site, of course! With Classy Classifieds, your users can browse through ads listed by category, geography, or price to find exactly what they want. And when they run out of cash, they can place their own ads for others to browse.

In this chapter, I just introduce you to Classy Classifieds. I show you what the various pages do and how users navigate them. I provide figures to show off my impeccable taste in Web-page design (impeccable, that is, if you really like yellow). But to get the full impact, you should install the complete application from the CD-ROM and walk through the pages as I describe them. That way, you can experiment with the application to get a better feel for how it works.

 This chapter describes how the final Classy Classifieds application works. The pages created in Chapters 18 and 19 are simplified versions of Classy Classified pages and look different from the ones pictured here. For more information, see those chapters.

 This chapter really just explains how to use Classy Classifieds. If you want the nitty-gritty, how-it-works chapter, see Bonus Chapter 2, "Inside Classy Classifieds," on the CD. That chapter explores the source code for each page and shows how all the pages work together.

Your Classy Home

The Classy Classifieds Home page (Default.aspx) is a launching point that enables you to access all the application's key features with just a click or two. You can see it in Figure 21-1.

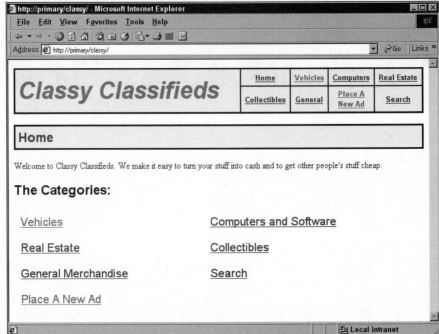

Figure 21-1:
Classy
Classifieds
Home page.

At the top of the page is the Classy Classifieds application banner. This banner appears at the top of every page to clearly identify the application. It also links to all the popular destination spots in this application.

Below the application banner is a page banner that contains the comforting word Home. The page banner appears on every page, albeit with a different name for each page. I implemented these banners with a user control. Find more on that topic in Bonus Chapter 2.

From the Home page, users can view ads in any of the five categories: Vehicles, Computers and Software, Real Estate, Collectibles, and General Merchandise. Or, if they're looking for something more specific, they can use the Search capability to find ads for products based on the product's name, description, or price. Finally, if users have junk — ahem, I mean fine merchandise they'd like to offer to others, they can click the Place A New Ad link to do just that.

Pick Your Category

If you click one of the five categories on the Home page (or the banner atop *any* page), you promptly arrive at the Category page (Category.aspx). For example, if you click General Merchandise, you're likely to see a Category page that looks like Figure 21-2.

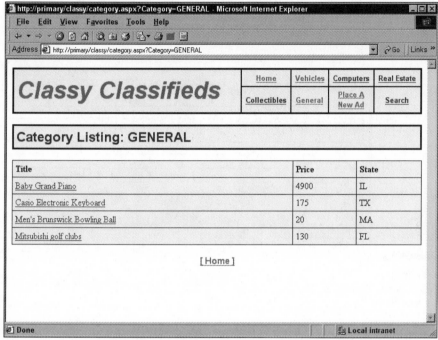

Figure 21-2:
Classy
Classifieds
Category
page.

If you look up at the Address line in the browser, you'll see that this page receives a Category. It's passed by the page that linked to it. (See Chapter 7 for more information on how this works.)

This page takes the category sent and lists all the ads in that category. Only the ad's title, price, and state appear. The title for each ad is a link users can click to go to the Detail page.

Or, they can scroll to the bottom of the page and click the Home link.

Devilish Details

The Detail page (Detail.aspx) receives an ad number. It retrieves the ad with that number and displays all the columns, as shown in Figure 21-3.

To purchase the item in the ad, the user can contact the seller by clicking the e-mail address (which shows up as an e-mail link) or by calling on the phone.

Two links at the bottom of the page enable the person who originally placed this ad to edit or delete it. Clicking either of these links sends the user to the Confirm page to verify the user's password.

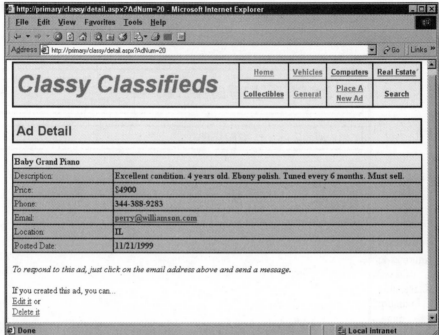

Figure 21-3:
Classy
Classifieds
Detail page.

Is It Really You?!?

Confirm (`Confirm.aspx`) is used to verify that the person who is asking to edit or delete a particular ad is the same person who originally placed the ad. This page asks the user to enter the password that was provided when the ad was first placed, as you see in Figure 21-4.

The page receives two pieces of information on the Address line: `AdNum` and `Operation`. `AdNum` is the ad number of the ad to be edited or deleted, and `Operation` indicates which operation is to be performed: edit or delete — indicated by the values `EDIT` and `DEL`, respectively.

If users enter the wrong password, they may try again or click the Home link.

If users enter the correct password, they are sent on to the appropriate page, based on the value sent for `Operation` — Edit Ad if it is `EDIT`, or Delete Ad if it is `DEL`.

By the way, all the ads in the database I've provided have the same password: `pickle`.

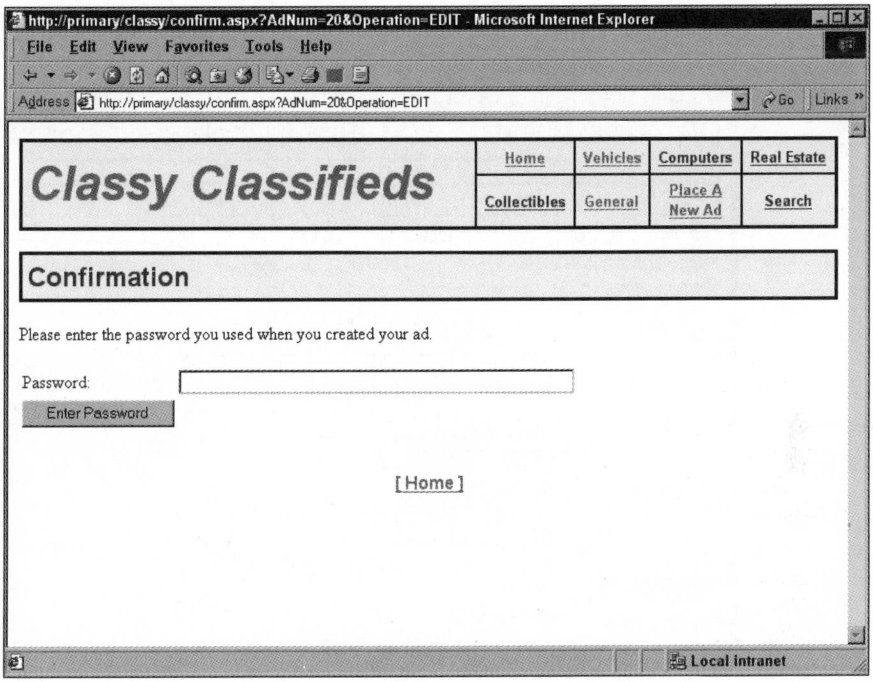

Figure 21-4:
Classy
Classifieds
Confirm
page.

Just a Quick Edit — It Won't Hurt . . .

You can arrive at the Edit Ad (EditAd.aspx) page in one of two ways. You can arrive here to edit an ad from the Confirm page, as I describe in the preceding section. If you do, the page will look similar to Figure 21-5.

On the other hand, you could arrive here directly from the Home page by clicking the Place A New Ad link. If you do, the page looks a bit different, as you see in Figure 21-6.

How does the page know which way to act? That depends on what it receives on the Address line. If it receives an ad number, it assumes that you want to edit an ad. If it doesn't receive anything, it assumes you want to place a new ad.

When editing an ad, the page first goes out to the database, finds the ad with the number sent, and fills in the textboxes on the page with the row's current values. It enables the user to edit those values and when the user clicks the button, the changes are sent to the database.

When placing an ad, the page comes up with nothing in the textboxes. Enter all the information (including the password) and click the button. The information is used to create a new row in the database.

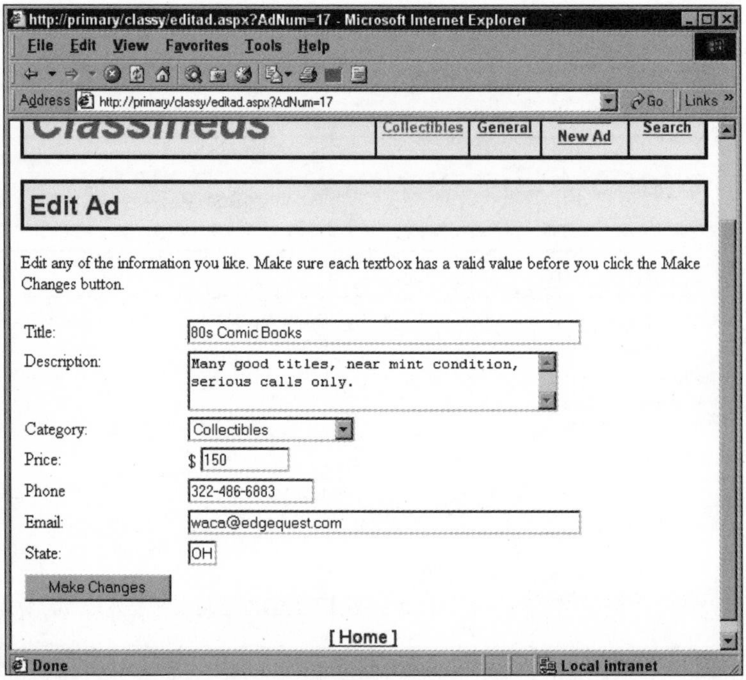

Figure 21-5:
Classy
Classifieds
Edit Ad
page, for
editing
an ad.

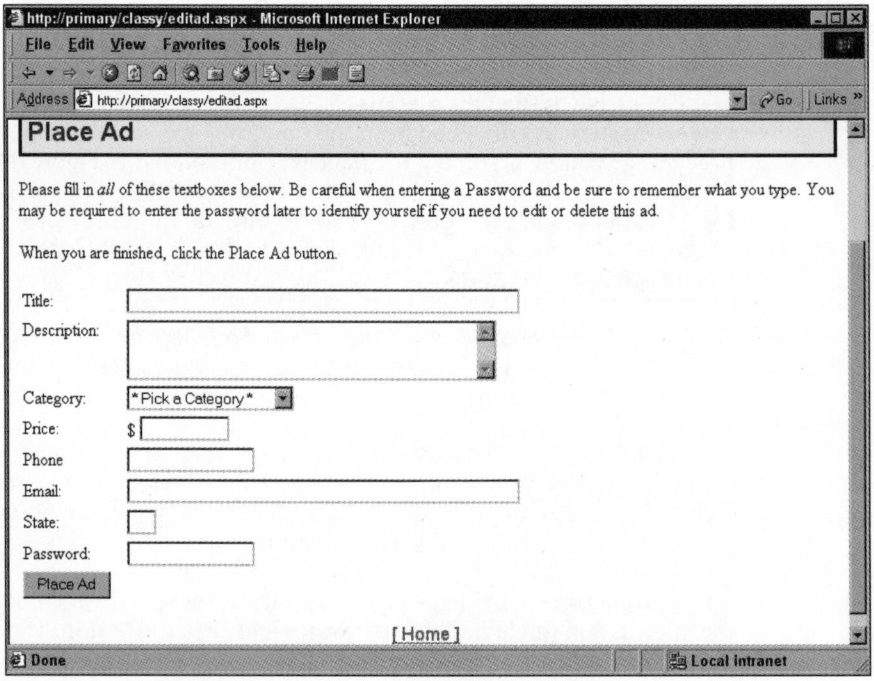

Figure 21-6:
Classy
Classifieds
Edit Ad
page, for
placing
an ad.

Either way, you can click the Home link when you're done with this page.

Delete! Delete — Darn Spot!

The Delete Ad page (`DelAd.aspx`) first verifies that you do, in fact, want to delete this row. As shown in Figure 21-7, it displays the row (much as the Detail page does) and then asks you to type the word DELETE into a textbox to verify that this is what you want to do. This additional step may be a bit extreme, but it does ensure that you'll have fewer accidental deletes!

If you enter anything besides DELETE and clicks the button, nothing happens — and you're informed that clicking the Home link cancels the Delete Ad process.

If you do type **DELETE** and click the button, the ad is deleted from the database.

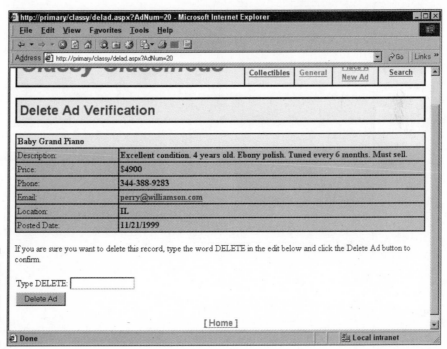

Figure 21-7:
Classy
Classifieds
Delete Ad
page.

Now Where Did I Put That Ad?

Finally, the Search page (Search.aspx) enables the user to enter a title, description, category, state, price range, or any combination of these to locate ads that match, as you can see in Figure 21-8.

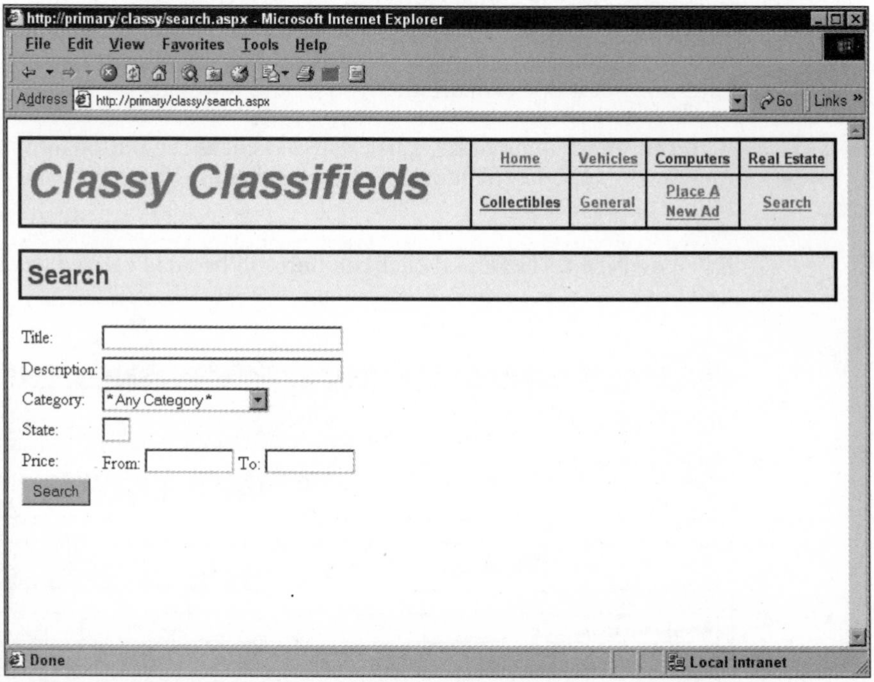

Figure 21-8:
Classy
Classifieds
Search
page.

When the user enters the criteria and clicks the button, a table appears below the button, listing the ads that match. The table looks a lot like the one on the category page. The user can then click an ad's title to see the detail for that ad.

Part VIII
The Part of Tens

The 5th Wave® By Rich Tennant

"Great goulash, Stan. That reminds me, are you still scripting your own Web page?"

In this part . . .

Where do you go for help when you have a problem with an ASP.NET page you are creating? What if you just want to learn more about a particular topic? What does it take to be an ASP.NET guru? I answer all these questions and more in The Part of Tens.

Chapter 22

The Ten Best Places to Get Answers

*Y*ou have a killer idea for a new Web application. You've designed your masterpiece and you've already started developing it. Then you hit a snag — a *big* one. You can't really go on until you get an answer to the problem that has tripped you up. Where do you turn? What do you do?

This chapter gives you ten answers to those questions. Only one of these answers has to work to get you back on track. Good luck!

RTFM: Read the Flippin' Manual!

You may be surprised by all the information they've put in those books and help files that came with your Web server and the .NET Framework. So *use* them!

Check the online help first. Searching for the help you need is easier and usually much faster than flipping through the index of a huge manual.

Check the IIS online help and manuals for Web server configuration issues and scalability questions. The online help that comes with the .NET Framework offers a wealth of information on ASP.NET, server controls, Visual

Basic .NET, and lots more. In addition, the .NET Framework comes with an ASP.NET Quick Start tutorial, lots of examples, and answers to many common questions.

Books

In this book, you get a good introduction to ASP.NET development topics as well as answers to the questions you need to get started with ASP.NET. But this is just the beginning! After you take the leap into ASP.NET development, you're bound to run into more complex topics that you need to understand better. So check out these great intermediate/advanced ASP.NET books:

- *ASP.NET Database Programming Weekend Crash Course,* by Jason Butler and Tony Caudill
- *ADO.NET and XML: ASP.NET On The Edge, Unlimited Edition,* by Greg Beamer and Govind Kanshi
- *ASP.NET Programming,* by Richard Mansfield
- *ASP.NET Bible,* by Anju Sani, Rick Lassan, and Peter Macintyre

If you run into Web development problems that aren't specifically ASP.NET-related, these books may help:

- *HTML 4 For Dummies,* by Ed Tittel, et al.
- *JavaScript For Dummies,* 3rd Edition, by Emily A. Vander Veer
- *Visual Basic .NET For Dummies,* by Wallace Wang
- *Visual Basic .NET Database Programming For Dummies,* by Richard Mansfield

Technical Journals

Looking for source code and articles squarely focused on Microsoft Web development technologies, delivered every month? *ActiveWeb Developer* is a technical journal published by Pinnacle Publishing. Edited by yours-truly, *ActiveWeb Developer* picks up where this book leaves off and jumps into real-world development with both feet. Another Pinnacle journal, called *.NET Developer,* focuses on all aspects of development with .NET. You can find more information about both journals at

www.pinnaclepublishing.com

Newsgroups and ListServs

Newsgroups are like bulletin boards where you can post a message and come back in a day or two to find replies and help from others around the world. They are a great peer-support option. To access newsgroups, you must have a newsgroup reader. The one that comes with Microsoft Internet Explorer is called Outlook Express. Microsoft hosts numerous newsgroups on its server:

```
news://msnews.microsoft.com
```

Point your news reader to that server and then subscribe to these newsgroups:

- microsoft.public.dotnet.framework
- microsoft.public.dotnet.framework.adonet
- microsoft.public.dotnet.framework.aspnet
- microsoft.public.dotnet.framework.aspnet.mobile
- microsoft.public.dotnet.framework.aspnet.webservices
- microsoft.public.dotnet.framework.documentation
- microsoft.public.dotnet.framework.odbcnet
- microsoft.public.dotnet.framework.performance
- microsoft.public.dotnet.framework.setup
- microsoft.public.dotnet.languages.vb
- microsoft.public.dotnet.languages.vb.upgrade
- microsoft.public.dotnet.scripting
- microsoft.public.msdn.drgui.drguidotnet.discussion
- microsoft.public.vsnet.documentation
- microsoft.public.vsnet.general
- microsoft.public.vsnet.ide
- microsoft.public.vsnet.setup
- microsoft.public.vsnet.servicepacks

You also can use a Web-based interface to Microsoft's newsgroups. You can find all the developer-oriented newsgroups here:

```
communities.microsoft.com/newsgroups/
    default.asp?icp=msdn&slcid=us
```

A List Server (or ListServ) is similar to a newsgroup, but you don't use a special reader to access it. Instead, you post a message by sending it via e-mail to a central server that compiles it together with all the other postings and then sends them back out again to everyone who is a member of the List Server. Some ListServs are set up so you immediately receive a message whenever it is posted. Others compile the messages so you receive one long e-mail message that contains all the posted messages for that day. Although List Servers are a little more primitive and a little more cumbersome to use, they are still very popular and a great way of getting and sharing information on a topic.

Even if you don't want to subscribe to a ListServ, you can still visit its Web site, browse recent postings, and even search the postings for a specific topic.

Interested in finding ListServs? You can find a whole slew of ASP.NET-oriented ListServs listed at this Web page:

```
www.asplists.com/asplists/aspngevery.asp
```

DevelopMentor also hosts several .NET ListServs:

```
discuss.develop.com/
```

Web Sites

You can find tutorials, source code, answers to common questions, discussion groups, and all kinds of other stuff from ASP.NET Web sites. And there are *lots* of them! So many, in fact, that I dedicate a whole other Part of Tens chapter to them. Flip over to Chapter 23 for the Ten Coolest Web Sites for ASP.NET Developers.

Microsoft Web Technical Support

Microsoft provides online access to the same documents and source material that the telephone technical support people use. Chances are, if you're persistent, you can get as much help using this Web site as you would by calling the telephone support line. And the Web site is free! Just go to

```
search.support.microsoft.com/
```

First, select the appropriate product for your question from a drop-down list. The list includes `Active Server Pages`, **as well as** `ActiveX Data Objects (ADO)`, `Internet Explorer`, `Internet Information Server`, `Visual`

Studio, and many, many more. Next, decide how you want to search — by keyword, article ID, free text query, or whatever. Finally, type in your question or keywords in the textbox. The Web site presents you with a list of articles that it thinks match your question. If you aren't getting any hits or you're getting hits for the wrong kind of thing, try rewording the question or using different terms.

Microsoft Telephone Support

Telephone support has a bad reputation — and for good reasons. For most people, trying to reach tech support means busy signals or long periods of time spent listening to unpleasant music while waiting for someone to help. And even when you do get through to real, live humans, they often don't know as much about the product as you do! So the best they can do is search their database and read to you what they found. This can be frustrating. But it's doubly frustrating if they turn around and charge you $200 for the privilege!

Having said all that, I must admit that my experience with Microsoft technical support has been much better than average. But it certainly isn't free. For issues associated with NT, IIS, or Web application development, you can expect a per-incident charge in the $100 to $225 range.

I recommend that you thoroughly check into other options before choosing this one. But if you are interested, here's a good place to start:

```
support.microsoft.com/directory/directory/phonepro.asp
```

You also can buy a complete support package for your company:

```
support.microsoft.com/directory/overview.asp
```

ASP.NET Geeks

Programming geeks are hard to miss. You often see them in their native habitat — surrounded by computers, computer parts, and books and manuals stacked to the ceiling. If you have an ASP.NET programming geek near you, I strongly suggest that you strike up a relationship with this person. Your time will be well spent, because ASP.NET geeks often can be your best resource for quick answers and explanations. If your resident geeks need a little encouragement to share their prized information, you'll find that high-caffeine beverages, pizza, and munchies work best. But no matter how you add it up, it's cheaper than a telephone call to tech support.

User Groups

If you don't have your own geek handy, you have to go where they hang out: user groups. A *user group* is a place where computer people who are interested in a particular technology can come together and share their knowledge. You may or may not find an ASP.NET-specific user group in your area, but you may find groups dedicated to Windows .NET/2000 or to Web development.

For a list of user groups dedicated to .NET, check out this page:

```
www.gotdotnet.com/resourcecenter/
    resource_center.aspx?classification=.NET%20User%20Groups
```

Conferences

Conferences are great places for getting answers to your questions and learning more about specific topics. And don't skip the social activities! I've found that the value you get at a good conference comes as much in the people you meet and the discussions you have as it does from the formal conference sessions.

Each conference that I list in this section is presented at least once a year and some of them more often than that. Go to the Web sites listed to find out when the next conference is coming around and where it will be held.

Microsoft Tech-Ed

Where else can you hear Bill Gates himself speak, get special-release software, get in-depth technical information on a broad range of technologies, and hit the legendary Tech Ed party and Jam session all in one week?

```
www.msdn.microsoft.com/events/teched
```

Microsoft Professional Developers Conference (PDC)

If you're looking for more serious, hard-core development information, tools, and techniques, hit the PDC. Get your information direct from the horse's mouth!

```
www.msdn.microsoft.com/events/pdc/
```

VBits and VSLive!

VBits focuses on Visual Basic. Although not specific to ASP.NET, it has plenty to keep your interest. If you use Visual Studio for your Web application or desktop development, check out VSLive! Often, these two conferences, sponsored by the same company, are held at the same place and same time so you can attend both at once:

```
www.vbits.net
www.vslive.com
```

ASP.NET Connections

If you want a conference 100-percent dedicated to ASP.NET technology, you can't go wrong with ASP.NET Connections:

```
www.asp-connections.com/
```

Others

You can keep up with upcoming ASP.NET events at one location:

```
www.asp.net/events.aspx
```

Other developer-oriented conferences are listed here:

```
www.msdn.microsoft.com/events/
```

Chapter 23

The Ten Coolest Web Sites for ASP.NET Developers

In This Chapter

▶ Finding original ASP articles, tips, and tricks

▶ Downloading free server components

▶ Getting up-to-date Web news

*T*he Web is a great place to browse, but it isn't exactly the best place to go when you're looking for something specific — unless you already know where to look. Between wading through the random results you get from search engines and the recommended links on sites that you find, you can eventually tell the fool's gold from the real stuff. But that effort takes precious time you may not have.

I've included this chapter to save some of that time for you. I've already done all the footwork and come up with the best sites on the Web. Isn't it odd that I found exactly ten?

Microsoft's ASP.NET

Microsoft has created a site to provide support, information, and links to other ASP.NET sites. The address is really easy to remember:

```
www.asp.net
```

Microsoft's GotDotNet.com

Although not ASP.NET-specific, this Microsoft-supported site provides a wealth of news, information, links, and user-contributed source code examples. It's definitely worth a look!

```
www.gotdotnet.com
```

The EdgeQuest Web Site

This is my Web site. It has informative articles, examples, free downloads, links, and a complete site dedicated to this book. Check it out!

```
www.edgequest.com
```

123ASPX.com Directory

This site doesn't contain much in the way of its own content. Instead, it acts as a portal to lots and lots of information from other sites. Its links are divided into Yahoo!-style categories and subcategories, or you can simply search for exactly what you want:

```
www.123aspx.com/
```

ASPNG.com

ASPNG.com has lots of articles, tutorials, and links. But the real attraction is the amazing variety of ListServ discussion groups. This is the place to subscribe and get interactive with the ASP.NET community:

```
www.aspng.com
```

ASPNextGen.com

Here's a well-organized site that provides news, tutorials, source code, and an *Ask the CodeJunkies* section, where you can ask questions and see them posted with very complete answers:

```
www.ASPNextGen.com
```

DotNetWire.com

This is the place for news, product releases, information on new postings from other sites, and lots more. Here's your one-stop destination for keeping up on what's hot:

```
www.dotnetwire.com
```

ASPFree.com

If you're looking for free ASP.NET source code for solving real-world problems, make this site your first stop:

```
www.aspfree.com
```

AngryCoder.com

An eZine with attitude, this is a fun and informative place to visit regularly:

```
www.angrycoder.com
```

IBuySpy.com

IBuySpy.com is a very clever site that purports to sell fictional spy equipment of all shapes and sizes. It is, in fact, a full-blown Business-to-Consumer (B2C) e-commerce site. It was developed in close association with Microsoft to demonstrate the best way to go about creating real-world e-commerce applications using ASP.NET and other Microsoft Web technologies. All the source code is free for the downloading.

And now, in addition to the store, an IBuySpy Portal, IBuySpy News, and other new projects are being developed to demonstrate real-world techniques for a wide variety of application scenarios. Don't miss this site:

```
www.ibuyspy.com
```

Appendix

About the CD

*T*he CD in the back of this book is a valuable resource. It not only saves your typing fingers when it comes to book examples, it also provides you with real-world applications that demonstrate the concepts in this book, as well as a whole Bonus Part with five chapters to extend, explain, and supplement the content in the book. In this appendix, you discover all that's there and how to use it.

System Requirements

This section lists the requirements for a Windows 2000 machine running Internet Information Server and the .NET Framework. This is the minimum setup needed to create an ASP.NET Web server for use either locally, on an intranet, or on the Internet:

✔ A PC with a 133 MHz or higher Pentium-compatible CPU

✔ Windows .NET Server, Windows XP Professional, Windows 2000 Server/Professional, or Windows NT 4.0 (with Service Pack 6a or higher)

✔ Internet Information Server (comes with all these operating systems)

✔ The .NET Framework (see Chapter 1 for information on getting the .NET Framework for free from Microsoft)

✔ At least 128MB of total RAM installed on your computer; for best performance, we recommend 256MB

✔ A CD-ROM drive

✔ A VGA or higher-resolution monitor

However, you don't need a machine with these requirements in order to use this book or explore ASP.NET. You may have an intranet server at work running ASP.NET. Or you may subscribe to an ASP.NET hosting service. In either case, you can use virtually any machine you like to access the ASP.NET Web server, send your files to it, and test them in your browser. (For more information on the hosting service option, see Chapter 1.)

You cannot run ASP.NET on a Windows 95/98/ME machine with Personal Web Server.

Using the CD

To install items from the CD to your hard drive, follow these steps:

1. **Insert the CD into your computer's CD-ROM drive.**

2. **Click Start⊅Run.**

3. **In the dialog box that appears, type** d:\start.htm.

   Replace *d* with the proper drive letter for your CD-ROM if it uses a different letter. (If you don't know the letter, double-click My Computer on your desktop and see what letter is listed for your CD-ROM drive.)

   Your browser opens, and the license agreement is displayed.

4. **Read through the license agreement, nod your head, and click the Agree button if you want to use the CD.**

   After you click Agree, you're taken to the Main menu, where you can browse through the contents of the CD.

5. **To navigate within the interface, click a topic of interest to take you to an explanation of the files on the CD and how to use or install them.**

6. **To install software from the CD, simply click the software name.**

   You'll see two options: to run or open the file from the current location or to save the file to your hard drive. Choose to run or open the file from its current location, and the installation procedure continues. When you finish using the interface, close your browser as usual.

Note: These HTML pages include an "easy install" option. If your browser supports installations from within it, go ahead and click the links of the program names you see. You'll see two options: Run the File from the Current Location and Save the File to Your Hard Drive. Choose to Run the File from the Current Location, and the installation procedure will continue. A Security Warning dialog box appears. Click Yes to continue the installation.

To run some of the programs on the CD, you may need to keep the disc inside your CD-ROM drive. This is a good thing. Otherwise, a very large chunk of the program would be installed to your hard drive, consuming valuable hard drive space and possibly keeping you from installing other software.

What You'll Find on the CD

The following sections are arranged by category and provide a summary of the software and other goodies you'll find on the CD. If you need help with installing the items provided on the CD, refer back to the installation instructions in the preceding section.

Shareware programs are fully functional, trial versions of copyrighted programs. If you like particular programs, register with their authors for a nominal fee and receive licenses, enhanced versions, and technical support. Freeware programs are copyrighted games, applications, and utilities that are free for personal use. Unlike shareware, these programs do not require a fee or provide technical support. GNU software is governed by its own license, which is included inside the folder of the GNU product. See the GNU license for more details.

Trial, demo, or evaluation versions are usually limited either by time or functionality (such as being unable to save projects). Some trial versions are very sensitive to system date changes. If you alter your computer's date, the programs will "time out" and will no longer be functional.

Here's what you'll find on the CD.

Bonus Part: Napoleon (Get It?) — On the CD

The CD includes several important bonus chapters. They provide detailed, blow-by-blow descriptions on how each page of the Café Chat Room and Classy Classifieds applications works. You also get a Guestbook application and a detailed description of how that application is constructed. In all, you get more than 80 pages of information showing you all the tricks you need to make ASP.NET sing.

The CD also includes a chapter specifically for Classic ASP developers. This bonus chapter provides a fast-paced overview of all the key changes Classic ASP developers need to consider. Finally, you get a chapter covering all the fundamental concepts for databases and DBMSs. It's a great pace to stop before you tackle Chapters 18, 19, and beyond.

Source code from the book

This CD includes three major examples: The Café, Classy Classifieds, and The Guestbook — each of which is described in the following sections. In addition, the CD provides source code from numerous smaller examples from individual chapters — primarily to help you avoid carpal tunnel syndrome.

The Café

The Café is a complete, real-time chat room. Users sign in and choose a nickname to identify themselves in the room. From there, they enter the primary window, where they can type messages and see messages typed by others. There's even a list down the right-hand side of the window of all the users currently in the Café.

For an overview of the Café application and how to use it, see Chapter 20. For a detailed examination of the code used to create this application, see Bonus Chapter 1 on the CD. The \Author\Cafe folder contains all the source code.

Classy Classifieds

Classy Classifieds provides a complete solution for offering classified ads on your site. Users can also browse the ads by category or search for specific ads. Then they can respond to an ad via e-mail. Users also can place their own ads and then update or delete their ad, as necessary.

For an overview of Classy Classifieds and a description of how to use it, see Chapter 21. For a detailed examination of the code used to create this application, see Bonus Chapter 2 on the CD. For all the source code, see the \Author\Classy folder on the CD.

The Guestbook

The Guestbook provides a place where your visitors can check in with you and tell you a little about themselves. The application stores this information in a text file and also enables you to view a list of all the entries. Maintenance functions like saving off a list, deleting a list, and restoring a list from a saved file are also provided.

For an overview of some of the techniques used in this application, see Chapter 16. For a detailed examination of the code used to create this application, see Bonus Chapter 3 on the CD. For complete source code, see the \Author\Guestbook folder on the CD.

Smaller examples

The rest of the source code included on the CD is organized into folders that are named according to the chapter number in which the example appears in the book: Author\Chapter01, Author\Chapter02, and so on.

Demos, Shareware, and Freeware

"Free downloads!" Whenever I see a link on a Web page with that headline, I can't help myself — I always have to check it out. What could be more fun than free downloads? In that spirit, I've collected a bunch of ASP.NET-related software components, languages, tools, and editors or development environments and provided them here for you on the CD. Have fun exploring!

- ✔ **Eiffel:** _Trial._ Eiffel language plug-in for the .NET Framework. For more, see `eiffel.com`.

- ✔ **XPressSideBar Free Edition:** _Freeware._ ActiveX and .NET component. For more, see `devexpress.com`.

- ✔ **Combit List and Label:** _Trial._ User interface components. For more, see `www.combit.net`.

- ✔ **Sax Basic Engine:** _45-day Trial._ ActiveX components. For more, see `www.saxsoft.com`.

- ✔ **August Wind ASPExpress:** _Shareware._ ASP.NET-compatible editor. For more, see `aspexpress.com`.

- ✔ **Tashcom ASPEdit 2001:** _Demo._ ASP.NET-compatible editor. For more, see: `www.tashcom.co.uk`.

- ✔ **Helios TextPad:** _Shareware._ Editor for ASP.NET. For more, see `www.textpad.com`.

- ✔ **C Point Antechinus C# Editor:** _Demo._ Editor for the C# language. For more, see `www.c-point.com`.

- ✔ **WebGecko ASPCache and Active Page Generator:** _Trial._ Caching and page generation software for ASP. For more, see `www.webgecko.com`.

- ✔ **Xceed .NET Compression Library:** _Trial._ Library of components for compressing files. For more, see `www.xceedsoft.com/dotnet`.

- ✔ **Adobe Acrobat Reader:** Page viewer for PDF (Portable Document Format) files. Use it to read the five bonus chapters on the CD. For more, see `www.adobe.com`.

Troubleshooting

I tried my best to compile programs that work on most computers with the minimum system requirements. Alas, your computer may differ, and some programs may not work properly for some reason.

The two likeliest problems are that you don't have enough memory (RAM) for the programs you want to use, or you have other programs running that are affecting installation or running of a program. If you get an error message such as Not enough memory or Setup cannot continue, try one or more of the following suggestions and then try using the software again:

- ✔ **Turn off any antivirus software running on your computer.** Installation programs sometimes mimic virus activity and may make your computer incorrectly believe that it's being infected by a virus.

- ✔ **Close all running programs.** The more programs you have running, the less memory is available to other programs. Installation programs typically update files and programs; so if you keep other programs running, installation may not work properly. This may include closing the CD interface and running a product's installation program from Windows Explorer.

- ✔ **Reference the ReadMe:** Please refer to the ReadMe file located at the root of the CD-ROM for the latest product information at the time of publication.

- ✔ **Have your local computer store add more RAM to your computer.** This is, admittedly, a drastic and somewhat expensive step. However, adding more memory can really help the speed of your computer and enable more programs to run at the same time.

If you still have trouble installing the items from the CD, please call the Hungry Minds, Inc. Customer Service phone number at 800-762-2974 (outside the U.S.: 317-572-3994) or send e-mail to techsupdum@hungryminds.com.

Index

• B •

• Q •

• R •

Hungry Minds, Inc.
End-User License Agreement

READ THIS. You should carefully read these terms and conditions before opening the software packet(s) included with this book ("Book"). This is a license agreement ("Agreement") between you and Hungry Minds, Inc. ("HMI"). By opening the accompanying software packet(s), you acknowledge that you have read and accept the following terms and conditions. If you do not agree and do not want to be bound by such terms and conditions, promptly return the Book and the unopened software packet(s) to the place you obtained them for a full refund.

1. **License Grant.** HMI grants to you (either an individual or entity) a nonexclusive license to use one copy of the enclosed software program(s) (collectively, the "Software") solely for your own personal or business purposes on a single computer (whether a standard computer or a workstation component of a multi-user network). The Software is in use on a computer when it is loaded into temporary memory (RAM) or installed into permanent memory (hard disk, CD-ROM, or other storage device). HMI reserves all rights not expressly granted herein.

2. **Ownership.** HMI is the owner of all right, title, and interest, including copyright, in and to the compilation of the Software recorded on the disk(s) or CD-ROM ("Software Media"). Copyright to the individual programs recorded on the Software Media is owned by the author or other authorized copyright owner of each program. Ownership of the Software and all proprietary rights relating thereto remain with HMI and its licensers.

3. **Restrictions on Use and Transfer.**

   (a) You may only (i) make one copy of the Software for backup or archival purposes, or (ii) transfer the Software to a single hard disk, provided that you keep the original for backup or archival purposes. You may not (i) rent or lease the Software, (ii) copy or reproduce the Software through a LAN or other network system or through any computer subscriber system or bulletin-board system, or (iii) modify, adapt, or create derivative works based on the Software.

   (b) You may not reverse engineer, decompile, or disassemble the Software. You may transfer the Software and user documentation on a permanent basis, provided that the transferee agrees to accept the terms and conditions of this Agreement and you retain no copies. If the Software is an update or has been updated, any transfer must include the most recent update and all prior versions.

4. **Restrictions on Use of Individual Programs.** You must follow the individual requirements and restrictions detailed for each individual program in the "About the CD" appendix of this Book. These limitations are also contained in the individual license agreements recorded on the Software Media. These limitations may include a requirement that after using the program for a specified period of time, the user must pay a registration fee or discontinue use. By opening the Software packet(s), you will be agreeing to abide by the licenses and restrictions for these individual programs that are detailed in the "About the CD" appendix and on the Software Media. None of the material on this Software Media or listed in this Book may ever be redistributed, in original or modified form, for commercial purposes.

5. **Limited Warranty.**

   (a) HMI warrants that the Software and Software Media are free from defects in materials and workmanship under normal use for a period of sixty (60) days from the date of purchase of this Book. If HMI receives notification within the warranty period of defects in materials or workmanship, HMI will replace the defective Software Media.

   (b) **HMI AND THE AUTHOR OF THE BOOK DISCLAIM ALL OTHER WARRANTIES, EXPRESS OR IMPLIED, INCLUDING WITHOUT LIMITATION IMPLIED WARRANTIES OF MERCHANTABILITY AND FITNESS FOR A PARTICULAR PURPOSE, WITH RESPECT TO THE SOFTWARE, THE PROGRAMS, THE SOURCE CODE CONTAINED THEREIN, AND/OR THE TECHNIQUES DESCRIBED IN THIS BOOK. HMI DOES NOT WARRANT THAT THE FUNCTIONS CONTAINED IN THE SOFTWARE WILL MEET YOUR REQUIRE-MENTS OR THAT THE OPERATION OF THE SOFTWARE WILL BE ERROR FREE.**

   (c) This limited warranty gives you specific legal rights, and you may have other rights that vary from jurisdiction to jurisdiction.

6. **Remedies.**

   (a) HMI's entire liability and your exclusive remedy for defects in materials and workmanship shall be limited to replacement of the Software Media, which may be returned to HMI with a copy of your receipt at the following address: Software Media Fulfillment Department, Attn.: *ASP.NET For Dummies*, Hungry Minds, Inc., 10475 Crosspoint Blvd., Indianapolis, IN 46256, or call 1-800-762-2974. Please allow four to six weeks for delivery. This Limited Warranty is void if failure of the Software Media has resulted from accident, abuse, or mis-application. Any replacement Software Media will be warranted for the remainder of the original warranty period or thirty (30) days, whichever is longer.

   (b) In no event shall HMI or the author be liable for any damages whatsoever (including without limitation damages for loss of business profits, business interruption, loss of business information, or any other pecuniary loss) arising from the use of or inability to use the Book or the Software, even if HMI has been advised of the possibility of such damages.

   (c) Because some jurisdictions do not allow the exclusion or limitation of liability for consequential or incidental damages, the above limitation or exclusion may not apply to you.

7. **U.S. Government Restricted Rights.** Use, duplication, or disclosure of the Software for or on behalf of the United States of America, its agencies and/or instrumentalities (the "U.S. Government") is subject to restrictions as stated in paragraph (c)(1)(ii) of the Rights in Technical Data and Computer Software clause of DFARS 252.227-7013, or subparagraphs (c) (1) and (2) of the Commercial Computer Software - Restricted Rights clause at FAR 52.227-19, and in similar clauses in the NASA FAR supplement, as applicable.

8. **General.** This Agreement constitutes the entire understanding of the parties and revokes and supersedes all prior agreements, oral or written, between them and may not be modified or amended except in a writing signed by both parties hereto that specifically refers to this Agreement. This Agreement shall take precedence over any other documents that may be in conflict herewith. If any one or more provisions contained in this Agreement are held by any court or tribunal to be invalid, illegal, or otherwise unenforceable, each and every other provision shall remain in full force and effect.

Installation Instructions

To install items from the CD to your hard drive, follow these steps:

1. **Insert the CD into your computer's CD-ROM drive.**
2. **Click Start⇨Run.**
3. **In the dialog box that appears, type** d:\start.htm.

   Replace *d* with the proper drive letter if your CD-ROM uses a different letter.

4. **Read through the license agreement that's displayed in your browser and then click the Agree button if you want to use the CD.**

   Your browser displays the Main menu, from which you can browse through the contents of the CD.

5. **To navigate within the interface, click a topic of interest to take you to an explanation of the files on the CD and how to use or install them.**
6. **To install software from the CD, simply click the software name.**

   You'll see two options: to run or open the file from the current location or to save the file to your hard drive. Choose to run or open the file from its current location, and the installation procedure continues. When you finish using the interface, close your browser as usual.

Note: These HTML pages include an "easy install" option. If your browser supports installations from within it, go ahead and click the links of the program names you see. You'll see two options: Run the File from the Current Location and Save the File to Your Hard Drive. Choose to Run the File from the Current Location, and the installation procedure will continue. A Security Warning dialog box appears. Click Yes to continue the installation.

To run some programs on the CD, you may need to keep the disc inside your CD-ROM drive. For more information about the CD's contents, see the "About the CD" appendix.

Notes